Relationship Coaching

MW00790659

Relationship Coaching provides a comprehensive guide to coaching to achieve relationship success and enrichment in three main areas: to help single people form and secure stable relationships, to assist couples seeking to enhance their relationships, and to support parents looking to improve their relationships with their children.

Yossi Ives is an experienced relationship coach, and Elaine Cox is an expert on developmental coaching approaches. They explain how the fundamental elements of coaching are customised and adapted to meet the needs of relationship enhancement. The book introduces specific coaching theories, processes and techniques through the use of practical case studies, which provide insight into a range of applications and contexts and it introduces new ways of approaching marriage and singles coaching.

Relationship Coaching combines an accessible, practical guide with a strong theoretical underpinning. It will be an essential guide for coaches, counsellors and students, as well as other professional helpers, including social workers and ministers.

Yossi Ives is a relationship coach who co-runs a European singles organisation. He holds a PhD in Coaching and is the co-author, with Elaine Cox, of *Goal-Focused Coaching* (Routledge, 2012). He is also founder and CEO of Tag International Development and the Tag Institute for Social Development.

Elaine Cox is principal lecturer and leader of programmes within the International Centre for Coaching and Leadership development at Oxford Brookes University. She is an experienced researcher, author and editor and also directs the Doctor of Coaching and Mentoring Programme.

Relationship Coaching

The theory and practice of coaching with singles, couples and parents

Yossi Ives and Elaine Cox

 Routledge
Taylor & Francis Group

LONDON AND NEW YORK

First published 2015
by Routledge
27 Church Road, Hove, East Sussex, BN3 2FA

and by Routledge
711 Third Avenue, New York, NY 10017

Routledge is an imprint of the Taylor & Francis Group, an informa business

British Library Cataloguing in Publication Data
A catalogue record for this book is available from the British Library

Library of Congress Cataloging in Publication Data
Relationship coaching : the theory and practice of coaching with singles, couples and parents / Yossi Ives and Elaine Cox.
pages cm
1. Personal coaching. 2. Interpersonal relations. 3. Interpersonal conflict.
I. Cox, Elaine. II. Title.
BF637.P361846 2015
158.3—dc23
2014021746

ISBN: 978-0-415-73794-4 (hbk)
ISBN: 978-0-415-73795-1 (pbk)
ISBN: 978-1-315-74093-5 (ebk)

Typeset in Times
by Cenveo Publisher Services

Dedications

From Yossi
For Team Ives: Rivkie, Chaya, Miriam, Meir, Ahuva, Dov, Dina and Rosie

And for Ricardo: Thanks for being a true friend

From Elaine
For Chris, of course,
and our five children, Elliott, Sophia, Jeremy, Maria and Christian

Contents

Figures and Tables

Figures

Tables

Foreword

Nick Turner, Former Director of the Relate Institute and Head of Clinical Services at Relate

This is an important book that presents in an integrated way how to apply a coaching methodology, as opposed to a counselling or psychotherapeutic methodology, to supporting people as they explore their fundamental human need for connection by seeking, developing, and maintaining relationships with others. The quest to find and sustain healthful and satisfying relationships is hard-wired in us all; yet, as we know, this quest is often unfulfilled and can lead to considerable hurt and suffering. Much attention is paid in the therapeutic world to how damaged relationships might be repaired, but less attention is paid to helping people adopt a more helpful approach to achieving a more satisfactory life-affirming outcome to their quest. This book rectifies that imbalance, providing a model that fosters human flourishing, supporting people in their pursuit of relationship fulfilment and success.

Relationship distress now receives widespread attention. According to the latest Relationships Foundation *Cost of Family Failure Index* (March 2014), the full social cost of relationship breakdown in the United Kingdom is in the region of £46 billion. Relationship breakdown affects health, wealth, and well-being, costing each current UK taxpayer more than £1,500 a year. Clearly, relationship breakdown is of enormous significance to the life of the nation; yet, sadly, the scale of the provision of services to address and remedy the causes of relationship breakdown is grossly out of proportion with these social costs. The current government spends £30 million supporting the work of the organisations in the relationship support sector, which, while reflecting their commitment to supporting not only the parent–child relationship but also the parents' own relationship, falls far short of the full cost of relationship breakdown to the nation. The work of a number of these organisations was the subject of a recent study[1] commissioned by the Department for Education that evaluated the services they provided. The study reported, amongst other things, that 'attending couple counselling was found to result in positive changes in individuals' relationship quality, well-being and communication'. Moreover, the study also found that, for Relate as an example, the overall benefit–cost ratio of expenditure in Relate was 11.4 – in other words, every £1 spent on service delivery yields £11.40 of benefit.

While there is a long and rich tradition of support services for couples experiencing relationship distress (including that provided by, for example, Relate), there does not appear to be a culture in the United Kingdom for people to see that their relationship is something to be invested in and nurtured. We are familiar with the notion of 'emotional intelligence', but we do not yet have the same familiarity with what might be described as 'relationship intelligence'. Educational programmes in schools have in the past perhaps placed too strong an accent on sex education and social responsibility at the expense of promoting the skills and attitudes that are needed to enable intimate relationships to prosper. In the absence of this culture, relationships do not receive the attention or investment they deserve. As a relationship counsellor for many years, I have found, for example, that clients often baulk at the prospect of having to pay for relationship therapy to help them through a crisis when they might not think twice, for much the same cost, of replacing their fridge. With much the same attitude of 'ignore it until it goes wrong' that is applied to kitchen appliances, the relationship support services that are available are probably regarded by the public as a kind of last chance saloon, a remedy more akin to an operating theatre rather than a gym.

Most of the relationship support services that are available are located in a counselling and psychotherapeutic tradition, although there are some that are also aimed at preparing people once they have decided to embark on a relationship. The counselling and psychotherapy services often carry a stigma of failure and possibly of shame. This important book, however, sets out a refreshingly different approach to relationship support that, being drawn from the coaching tradition, is stigma-free and positively oriented. Relationship coaching is not yet as prominent an intervention for people in relationships as is counselling and psychotherapy, and, as the authors say, relationship coaching itself has not attracted significant attention in the coaching literature so far. This book, therefore, will be a helpful contribution to the evolving field of relationship support, and in particular to the development of a new relationship coaching professional skill set that will have appeal to practitioners working with people for whom relationship counselling may seem shaming and a sign of failure.

Relationship counsellors will be familiar with the relationship territory that this book describes. What this book does, however, is offer new maps to guide practitioners in helping them and their clients navigate this territory with a more pragmatic goal-focused compass that prioritises work with behaviours and cognition, as opposed to work on affect and deeper-rooted psychological processes. Whereas therapy often has as its central activity addressing unfinished business, such as addressing traumas from previous relationships, the authors demonstrate how relationship coaching concentrates on dealing with the current or future relationships. The authors are careful to note that differences exist between these two ways of working, but present a sophisticated blend of theory and skills to support their coaching approach to relationship work.

In the early chapters of the book, the authors locate relationship coaching against a backdrop of the wider context of coaching, with its emphasis on the importance of prioritising personal growth and development as well as the value of clarifying and achieving goals. The approach that the authors take is one that promotes investigation and construction of a different vision for the future rather than an undue focus on the past and its associated problems. Their approach is pragmatic, helping people to recognise how their thinking may be contributing to their difficulties in the here and now and offering tools to equip them to change their behaviours in order to achieve greater fulfilment in their relationships in the future. Because this is a book about *relationship* coaching, their approach addresses how this work is done from a couple and relational perspective as opposed to an individual perspective. Indeed, the authors demonstrate how it might be the case that by adopting an approach that gives undue attention to the individual, as opposed to the couple, the relationship may suffer as a consequence.

In the central chapters of the book, the authors bring together three main relationship contexts: coaching with single people seeking to form relationships, coaching with couples who want to enhance their relationships, and coaching for parents desiring to create better relationships with their children and teenagers. In each of these contexts, the authors present a coaching overview focusing on ways of helping people address their relational needs. In the chapter on the singles context, attention is given to helping people to recognise what obstacles they may have erected that get in the way of forming successful relationships. A number of case studies illustrate the various ways that people do this and the practical steps that can be taken and goals generated and acted upon that can assist in changing attitudes and behaviour. In the chapter on the couples context, examples are given of cases where coaching can provide space for couples to reflect on the pressures they are under and to focus on forming a joint vision of how they want their relationship to develop. Finally, in the chapter on the parenting context, ideas are given about how parents can plan parenting strategies, consider and determine their priorities, and ensure their parenting values and parenting practices are aligned.

In the concluding chapters, attention is paid to the ethical, professional, and contextual issues that are pertinent for relationship counselling. Here, there is discussion of the need for coaches to receive appropriate training, develop their own ethical and professional ways of working that align with their own value system equally as much as with any professional codes of practice, and, importantly, for ongoing supervision. There is also a welcome reference to the need for ethical contracting and boundary setting at the start of a coaching assignment, where the essential rules of engagement are set out so that the coach and the client(s) can explore their assumptions of relationship coaching.

This book is a valuable resource both for coaches wishing to consider applying their skills with a new client group and for relationship counsellors who wish to develop brief, collaborative, and pragmatic ways to work with their clients while applying a coaching methodology.

Note

1 Department for Education, *Relationship Support Interventions Evaluation*, January 2014.

Chapter 1

Introduction

> The sad thing is that the people who would most benefit from coaching may not know of the existence or the availability of coaching.
>
> Whitmore 2009

Whitmore's observation applies most aptly to relationship coaching. Many people experience difficulties in forming relationships or in keeping, managing, or enhancing their relationships and would benefit from relationship coaching. However, they are often unaware that such coaching exists or how it could help them. Even amongst coaches, there is a lack of understanding about the application of coaching to relationship issues. Therefore, this book combines a theoretical and practical guide to relationship coaching to deepen the perception of how relationship coaching works and to increase awareness of how it can help clients improve their key human relationships.

The desire for close personal relationships is regarded as a basic human motive and need (Baumeister and Leary 1995; Deci and Ryan 2002) and is a key factor in quality of life. Baumeister and Leary (1995: 497) stated that 'human beings have a pervasive drive to form and maintain at least a minimum quantity of lasting, positive, and significant interpersonal relationships'. Not surprisingly then, success or failure with regard to such relationships significantly affects life satisfaction (Myers and Deiner 1995), psychological well-being (Schwarzer and Leppin 1992), and physical health (Kaplan and Manuck 1994). Romantic relationships are the cause of great joys, such as a deep sense of connection and fulfilment (Hatfield and Rapson 2002); however, when they go wrong, they are also the source of some of life's greatest difficulties, including depression and homicide (Cupach and Spitzberg 2011). As an aspirational discipline fostering human flourishing, coaching is naturally suited to support people in their pursuit of relationship fulfilment and success.

Coaching has been usefully described as a human development process that entails 'structured, focused interaction and the use of appropriate strategies, tools and techniques to promote desirable and sustainable change for the benefit of the client and potentially for other stakeholders' (Bachkirova et al. 2014: 1). In this book, we illustrate how such a framework for helping people can be used in three main relationship contexts: coaching for single people seeking to form relationships, coaching for couples who want to enhance their relationships, and coaching for parents desiring to create better relationships with their children and teenagers. Often, people make the transition from being single to being part of a couple to being a parent in a short span of time, so we address this key development arc, during which many people need support.

Brennan and Wildflower (2014: 438) explained that the role of the coach is 'to facilitate the client's learning to find his/her own answers'. They pointed out that there could be times when coaches need to strategise or brainstorm with clients or offer ideas, but these ideas should not be proposed as solutions. Rather, they should always only be offered as possibilities.

> If the client's expectation is that the coach will have the solution to their concern, perhaps the client does not understand the coaching relationship. If coaches feel they need to offer advice to give value to the client, they may need to step back to examine the relationship with the client and their own understanding of coaching.
>
> (Brennan and Wildflower 2014: 438)

In goal-focused and developmental approaches to coaching, coaching is nondirective in the way that Brennan and Wildflower described. Similarly, in relationship coaching, advice-giving should be offered selectively and with caution. It is not the role of the coach to advise the client on his or her goal, but it is appropriate to share ideas around development and learning and propose new perspectives for the client's consideration.

We have discussed elsewhere (Ives 2008, 2011; Ives and Cox 2012) that approaches to coaching can be usefully categorised into three broad paradigms: goal-focused, developmental, and therapeutic. This book proposes that relationship coaching is, in fact, a fusion of goal-focused and developmental coaching, with the need for an understanding of therapeutic concerns. Relationship coaching focuses on a combination of the client's self-management skills, together with the development of different attitudes and perceptions, while acknowledging the interplay of certain psychodynamic factors. Given that people will come to relationship coaching with a clear aim in mind, such as a lasting and rewarding relationship (with a new partner, an existing partner, or with their children), relationship coaching needs to harness the strengths of the different types of coaching – especially goal-focused coaching, with its emphasis on achieving tasks and developmental coaching, which uses reflection and critical analysis to foster shifts in perspective. In this book, these elements of goal-focused and developmental coaching are incorporated into an effective relationship coaching methodology.

The relationship coaching paradigm

Most support for people in their relationships has, until recently, been undertaken by counsellors or therapists. People tend to go to a counsellor or to a marriage guidance specialist when their relationship with their child or with their partner is in trouble. Less frequently, people may seek therapeutic assistance if they are struggling to form or secure a lasting relationship. The counsellor will then work from a single theoretical approach or a variety of approaches that have their genesis in psychological theory. For example, a counsellor may favour the person-centred approach (Rogers 1959) or a humanistic position (Maslow 1998), or may deploy family therapy (Nichols and Schwartz 1995) or adopt a psychodynamic approach (Jacobs 2004). Eclectic counsellors and integral therapists will select any number of approaches tailored to their clients' needs, especially because there is currently little to suggest that one approach is significantly more effective than another. In fact, some researchers (e.g. de Haan et al. 2013) claim that the quality of the relationship between the counsellor and the client is more important than the approach the therapist uses, and that it is the trust built during the counsellor–client relationship that is central to progress being made.

Amongst the choices counsellors make is to use a coaching approach. Indeed, within counselling, as Nelson-Jones (2006: 20) pointed out, the rise of cognitive behavioural approaches has given rise to 'an increasing emphasis on psychological education or coaching'. However, Nelson-Jones' definition of coaching is somewhat different to our own. He put the emphasis on people learning to 'improve and maintain their mind skills and communication/action skills', whereas we believe that in relationship coaching there has to be a change in mindset as well. In relationships, people often have to transform their outlook and even change their feelings, which requires a developmental approach. So, relationship coaching is about more than skills development and more than goal attainment. It often includes a change in the 'way of being' for the client.

Bachkirova (2007, 2011) has discussed how the difference between coaching and counselling is often one of purpose and initial motivation, highlighting a fundamental paradigmatic variance between the two approaches. According to this definition, counselling and therapy focus primarily on 'eliminating psychological problems and dysfunctions', whereas coaching has an overriding focus on 'enhancing life, improving performance' (Bachkirova 2007: 357). For this reason, we detect a difference between coaching and therapy in their approach to client 'assessment' and 'treatment'. Coaching, as most commentators will attest, is necessarily free of assessment or judgement and this, they claim, is what distinguishes it from counselling or therapy. We like the way John Rowan (2014: 150) explained coaching:

> The role of the coach is that of a companion along the way. There is no assumption of expertise, or leadership, or superiority in any way. It is more like a wise companion on a journey, who does not argue about the way, does

not criticize any mistakes, encourages the weary, witnesses the struggles, offers a presence that is nourishing and warm.

Within such a definition, psychological theories, with their sometimes inherent assessment focus, may not at first glance seem appropriate. However, coaches' psychological knowledge contributes vital insight and adds significantly to their capacity to help clients understand and manage their relationship situations. Indeed, in recent years, the practice of integrative coach-therapy, where the aim is to integrate coaching and therapy for the benefit of clients, has increased (Passmore 2007; Popovic and Jinks 2014; Lee 2014).

Such integrative interventions are driven by the coach's understanding and skill and the client's needs, irrespective of which disciplinary knowledge is being tapped. Thus, coaching – as we conceive it – belongs to a pragmatic paradigm rather than a medical paradigm (Cox 2013). As Grant and Cavanagh (2014: 298) explained, it involves the client 'examining and evaluating his or her life' and then making systematic life-enhancing changes with the support of the coach. In this paradigm, the coach is the client's equal. There is no superior knowledge or 'treatment plan': the coach is just present for the client and focuses on the client's articulated agenda.

For us, then, coaching is different from some types of therapy that adopt a more scientific/objectivist approach and determine appropriate techniques or 'treatment' via formal assessment of the client. In coaching, assessment is merely a tool that enables the client and the coach to understand the context of the coaching, including the client's values and aims. The use of assessment in relationship coaching is therefore based on a pragmatic paradigm, in which the objective is for the coach to facilitate exploration of the lived experience of the client in order to improve his or her life in some way. Of course, many person-centred counsellors also resist assessment. They are influenced by Carl Rogers' belief that people have a 'directional flow' (Kirschenbaum and Henderson 1989), and so clients are trusted to make progress without being guided or influenced. For these counsellors, assessment could be seen as making some sort of diagnosis, which could contaminate this natural progression.

The results of the pragmatic use of assessments are used as a guide for the client and to ensure that targeted outcomes are appropriate and realistic to his or her overarching goal. With its focus on enhancing life, coaching involves generating ideas and developing strategies. In this process, it is from the objectives set by the client that 'strategies are developed, methods are selected and this is followed by the chosen interventions and actions' (Bachkirova 2007: 361). Thus, while coaching interventions can be enriched by the use of carefully chosen therapeutic methods, as Bachkirova noted, strategies are only selected through a process of open communication and sharing between the coach and the client, and they are strictly focused on achieving the goal set by the latter.

Bachkirova (2007: 360) also explained that, to use developmental coaching, the coach will need to understand the theories that underpin adult development and the processes involved in facilitating such development, including the dynamics of the coaching relationship itself. She makes the case for coaching practitioners to have an understanding of psychological theories so that they can 'notice and interpret developmental phenomena and blocks to development'. However, a distinctive feature of relationship coaching is that where theories are used to facilitate development, the coach will always share such knowledge very openly with the client. The knowledge and understanding of psychological and developmental theories is important for coaches because, in supporting the achievement of the coaching task, all knowledge is 'grist to the mill', but such knowledge does not dictate the way in which the coaching proceeds and it does not generate a 'cure'. In Chapters 2–4, we discuss the main theories that underpin relationship coaching.

In relationship contexts, Nelson Jones talked about three levels of well-being of clients: those requiring remedial help, those who have a fairly normal relationship, and those who are seeking growth. Using these levels will help to clarify the function of relationship coaching, as described in the following.

- *Remedial:* Until recently, most people only sought outside intervention when they were experiencing a relationship crisis. For people needing help to remedy a significant problem in their relationships, counselling may indeed be the most appropriate intervention. It would benefit them to explore in detail the root causes of the problem and so begin to explore where a solution might be found. There may be underlying psychological issues for one or the other partner that impact the relationship and that are serious enough to require some psychological intervention. However, in some instances, coaching could also be useful, especially to help someone to get around a specific challenge that blocks their progress towards securing a lasting relationship.
- *Normal:* Until something prompts them, people in this category typically do not consider that they need to change anything or that the struggles that they are experiencing merit any form of intervention. A majority of single people, couples, and parents might suppose that everything is 'normal' for them, even if they are experiencing considerable difficulties. Perhaps they recognise that something is not working out in one or more areas of their relationship, but their frustration does not amount to them feeling they are in crisis. They may initially view coaching as unnecessary, because in their mind there is nothing majorly wrong with how their relationship is functioning: they accept routine annoyances and a measure of dissatisfaction. These people generally do not need counselling because there is no profound problem to be understood or overcome, but they could benefit from coaching to help them address the issues they face in their relationships.
- *Growth:* Beyond the status quo created by the 'normal' relationship is another level of happiness, which entails increasing people's sense of well-being and enjoyment within a relationship. Here, coaching can be leveraged to enhance and develop a relationship to achieve its full potential or to improve a person's ability to form or secure a lasting relationship.

Relationship coaching: a fusion of approaches

Throughout this book, we demonstrate how relationship coaching is a fusion of different types of coaching, particularly goal-focused coaching and developmental coaching, which we see as vital approaches to use in combination to support people in relationship contexts. We suggest that relationship coaching should incorporate goal-focused coaching's emphasis on establishing a clear goal and creating an effective action plan for achieving the goal, as well as embracing many other features of a goal-focused approach, such as the need to brainstorm for creative solutions and the requirement for the client to achieve the necessary skills and strategies. In orientation, too, relationship coaching is broadly forward focused, although it gives greater weight to understanding the lessons from past experiences, where appropriate.

However, unlike goal-focused coaching, relationship coaching is also highly developmental insofar as it aims to foster personal development and attitude change in addition to skills development. In keeping with a developmental approach, the focus is on sustaining results over time, rather than achieving a 'quick fix'. Yet, whereas personal development is generally not instantaneous or even discernible, relationship coaching needs to achieve clear progress pretty quickly. While development is gradual and organic (Cox and Jackson 2014), relationship coaching cannot be a lifelong process.

While goal-focused coaching aims to help clients to modify their actions (external), developmental coaching aims to help them change their attitudes (internal) – to transform their perspectives. This distinction shares some similarity with Summerfield's (2006) division between 'acquisitional' coaching (acquires a new ability) versus 'transformational' coaching (undergoes personal change). In the same vein, Brockbank (2008: 133) distinguished between coaching that is functionalist and operational (equilibrium) versus transformative and engagement (disequilibrium). The former seeks 'to enhance performance in a given function' rather than seeking to achieve fundamental change. By contrast, 'transformative' coaching involves radical change and looks to question fundamental assumptions and prevailing discourses. We would therefore argue that relationship coaching also needs to use techniques from transformational coaching, which Hawkins and Smith (2014: 228) described as enabling clients to create 'fundamental shifts in their capacity through transforming their way of thinking, feeling and behaving in relation to others'.

Relationship coaching thus shares with goal-focused coaching an interest in analysing and solving a problem, but it also recognises that the route to a positive outcome travels through personal development territory (Ives 2012). Whereas goal-focused coaching is essentially about raising performance and supporting effective action, developmental coaching focuses on addressing feelings and generating deep reflection (Ives and Cox 2012) in order to achieve transformation. In the following sections, we give a little more background to these two main approaches.

Goal-focused coaching

Goal-focused coaching has been defined as 'a systematic and collaborative helping intervention that is non-directive, goal-focused and performance-driven, intended to facilitate the more effective creation and pursuit of another's goals' (Ives and Cox 2012: 26). Its primary function is fostering the client's self-regulation, 'helping individuals regulate and direct their interpersonal and intrapersonal resources to better attain their goals' (Grant 2006: 153). The primary method is assisting the client to identify and form well-crafted goals and develop an effective action plan (Ives 2008). The role of the coach here is to stimulate ideas and action and to ensure that the goals are consistent with the client's main life values and interests, rather than working on helping the client to adjust his or her values and beliefs. In this conception, coaching primarily aims to raise performance and support effective action, rather than to address feelings and thoughts, which it is assumed will be indirectly addressed through actual positive results (Grant 2003). It aims to achieve results in a comparatively short space of time and normally focuses on a relatively defined issue or goal. Goal-focused coaching does not attempt to stimulate psychological change (Cox 2010), nor is it driven by a desire to eradicate psychological dysfunction (Bachkirova 2007), but it is a tool to improve performance. Although psychological change may occur, in goal-focused coaching it is a byproduct (Ives 2011; Ives and Cox 2012).

Unlike some approaches to coaching – such as the humanistic approach of Stober (2006) or the holistic approach of Gray (2006) – goal-focused coaching does not advocate an integral or systemic approach to achieve its purpose; rather, it focuses on encouraging effective action. It does not stimulate internal change (Hudson 1999) but works instead to integrate change processes into daily modes of behaviour. Goal-focused coaching adopts a forward focus, directing attention towards practical steps to move the client ahead. Doing this leads to a reduction of anxiety and makes the task seem more manageable. It further enhances buy-in by rendering goals more real, thus energising the client (Ives and Cox 2012). Ives (2010) found that applying a forward focus through goal setting and action planning engenders acceptance of self-responsibility, encouraging the client to focus on trying to improve what he or she can, rather than complaining or making ineffective demands on others. In goal-focused coaching, negativity is addressed by redirecting attention towards something more concrete – focusing on a small, practical, desired outcome (Szabo and Meier 2009). By setting a clear goal, clients will be focused on attaining the goal and are less likely to engage in marginal activities that distract from its attainment.

The forward-focus in goal-focused coaching is not to the total exclusion of considering the past, and looking for solutions is not at the expense of gaining a proper understanding of the problem. However, the main focus 'is on the client's present and preferred future' (O'Connell and Palmer 2007: 280). Initial action by a client, even if small, is necessary to create the platform for progress and the client's 'self-efficacy is built upon previous successful experience' (Cox 2006: 204). Small, concrete actions – what Rogers (2008) called 'quick wins' – create positive experiences that ultimately will lead to more positive choices of action (Parsloe and Wray 2000; Berg and Szabo 2005).

Developmental coaching

By contrast, developmental coaching focuses on self-development rather than self-regulation. It is based on a belief in human capability and potential (Spence 2007b) and provides opportunities to develop that capability and potential. As Cox and Jackson (2014: 215) argued, 'To be developmental the coaching has not merely to focus on problem solving but also to ensure that client capacity is built through that problem'.

Development generally refers to the progressive element of growth and change over time. Thus, a developmental coaching approach, 'as well as addressing immediate needs, takes a longer term, more evolutionary perspective' (Cox and Jackson 2014: 216). Developmental coaching requires a greater amount of time because internal psychological progress is at the heart of the process. This approach is therefore more open to learning from the past and using previous experiences as a platform for personal development, as it aims for significant new awareness and growth opportunities. Cox and Jackson (2014: 215) confirmed that development 'must involve progress and expansion of some kind'.

Depending on the approach or target of development, client progress and expansion could be either very broad or quite narrow, quite long term or more instant. As noted, we consider that transformational coaching approaches (Hawkins and Smith 2014) can be useful alongside extended developmental support because the outcome of transformative learning experiences provide some immediate evidence of the potential to change, which may be appealing to both clients and their partners. We explain in greater detail in Chapter 2 how a transformational approach can benefit relationships coaching, helping to jumpstart a client's growth in the short term while supporting longer-term development.

The developmental coaching approach has two strands. The first is rooted in life-course development theories, as described by Palmer and Panchal (2011). This approach takes account of how motivation changes across the lifespan and suggests that coaches need to be aware of this and other life-course issues. The second adult development approach is based on constructive-developmental theories, which claim that as people develop they become more aware of and open to a mature understanding of authority and responsibility, and they display greater tolerance to ambiguity. Coaching from this perspective is predicated upon the idea of stages of development, and it suggests that coaching at each stage needs to focus on issues related to the stage of development (Bachkirova 2011; Bachkirova and Cox 2007; Berger 2006). In Chapter 2, we examine further how both life-course and constructive-developmental theories can enhance relationship coaching.

Contexts for relationship coaching

This book addresses three contexts for applying relationship coaching: to help single people to form and secure sustainable relationships, to assist couples seeking to enhance their relationship, and to support parents looking to improve their relationship with their children.

Singles context

For an increasing number of single men and women, lasting relationships are simply not happening. They may have been involved in dating for ten or twenty years and have met often dozens, even hundreds, of potential partners without success. Some flit from relationship to relationship with little understanding of why their relationships keep coming to an abrupt end. Others invest heavily in longer-term relationships, which fail to result in lasting commitment. Some find they repeatedly reject their partners, while others find that they are often rejected. Regardless of the cause of relationship failure, parties in this continuous struggle end up frustrated, despondent, and confused.

Yet, from our experience, there are usually small adjustments that can make all the difference to people's chances of forming and securing a lasting relationship. Normally, simple awareness of what is tripping them up is sufficient to radically improve their ability to navigate their way around the problem. Although the nature of the issue may have been largely concealed from the client, once this has been revealed clients are typically highly motivated to capitalise on their newfound insight to improve their relationship chances. Ongoing support at crucial moments is often all that is needed to transform a string of failures into an exciting success story.

Couples context

The challenges facing couples in our fast-changing society are manifold. In the west over recent decades, women who were once expected to stay at home and bring up their children for a good portion of their lives are now expected to return to work after a relatively short period following childbirth. Men, who once shunned any domestic chores, now share the cooking, washing up, laundry, and ironing. In addition, both sexes are expected to be fully dedicated to their employers, often working at home in the evenings and at weekends to show commitment.

It is little wonder then, that couples can feel as if their own relationship has been neglected or that the quality of their relationship has deteriorated. In this fast-paced environment, with so many calls on their energies, some couples see their relationships suffer. Paradoxically, people also have greater expectations for a fulfilling relationship and so are more ready to leave a relationship that they consider no longer works for them. Finding time for a fortnightly or monthly coaching session can provide the quality space needed to explore issues in a relationship and to help it grow as the couple matures. Relationship coaching provides an opportunity for focused reflection on the most important aspects of our lives – our connections with the ones we love.

Parenting context

The culture of long working hours and multiple pressures from housework, financial strains, the daily struggle of juggling childcare, commuting, and working from home, together with the school run and ferrying children to various clubs, are amongst the many demands that put added pressures on parents. Added to this are the demands that children are under, which can make them difficult to manage, especially as they enter the teenage years. These demands include academic pressures to excel, peer pressures to conform, as well as social pressures emanating from the media and internet.

Many parents feel overwhelmed by the demands of parenting and find themselves responding to immediate events rather than working to a longer-term parenting goal. This all leaves some parents wracked with feelings of guilt and failure as they worry that they are not being effective in raising their children. Coaching can help by creating a safe platform to discuss and plan parenting strategies, consider and determine priorities, and ensure their parenting values and parenting practices are aligned.

About this book

Despite the central importance of relationships to our lives, relationship coaching is an area that has not attracted significant attention in the coaching literature so far. In the counselling literature, there are some books, notably Nelson-Jones (2006), where coaching is seen as a way of supporting couples to manage their relationship issues. However, Nelson-Jones' book is mainly focused on marital breakdown and the use of coaching skills to help in this situation. By contrast, this book adopts a preventative and positive approach, addressing how to achieve and strengthen relationship success. In this way, we hope that relationships will now benefit more greatly from the insights coaching can generate.

The book explains how the fundamental elements of different approaches to coaching are customised and adapted to meet the needs of relationship enhancement. Specific coaching processes and techniques are introduced along with practical case studies that illustrate a range of applications of relationship coaching.

There are ten chapters in this book. In Chapter 1, this introduction, we have provided a brief background to relationship coaching and introduced the relationship coaching approach. The chapter recognised the boundaries between coaching and other approaches to relationship support and highlighted some limitations. It discussed how relationship coaching draws on developmental and goal-focused approaches to coaching in order to facilitate raised awareness and the enhancement of relationship skills. The other chapters in the book are described briefly:

- *Chapter 2 – Working Towards Personal Development in Relationship Coaching:* This chapter focuses on the importance of the personal development of clients. By development, we mean raising awareness and enhancing perspectives through the expansion of horizons and the fostering of maturity. Learning and unlearning are key aspects of this transformative process. The chapter therefore includes a discussion of adult development theories and a practical exploration of how relationship coaching incorporates a personal development element through a range of perspective-enhancing techniques. It explores the role of the coach in facilitating the growth and development of clients and how the theoretical concerns of developmental coaching translate to specific relationship contexts.
- *Chapter 3 – Working to Achieve Relationship Goals:* Acknowledging the key aspects of goal-focused coaching and using a case study example, this chapter examines how the coach can support individual clients and couples in clarifying their goals and taking effective action towards achievement of the goal. There is an emphasis on the motivation and accountability necessary in this process.
- *Chapter 4 – Psychological Approaches and Relationship Coaching:* This chapter examines the relevance of a range of psychological theories and therapeutic approaches for the relationship coaching context. Guided by the recent idea of integrative coaching practice (Lee 2014), Chapter 4 discusses the kinds of theoretical models or approaches, such as attachment theory or solution-focused brief therapy, that might be useful in relationship coaching, as well as considering more generally the role of such theories in a coaching paradigm.
- *Chapter 5 – Relationship Coaching in Practice:* Using the theories expounded earlier, this chapter sets out our framework for relationship coaching, stressing the role of the coach in facilitating the growth and development of clients as well as helping them to achieve their goals. Using illustrative case studies, we discuss the role of the relationship coach and examine the imperative for building rapport. We also examine the use of other fundamental skills, such as listening and questioning.
- *Chapter 6 – Coaching Single People for Relationship Success:* This chapter sets out a model for coaching with singles, based on a goal-focused methodology, and presents a six-part framework of typical singles issues that explores how the coach can help the client to understand the impact they may be having on their relationships. In particular, the chapter proposes that coaching can provide a valuable method of addressing avoidance and anxiety issues for singles. Using real case studies, approaches for helping clients to address a range of key issues will be explained.
- *Chapter 7 – Coaching Couples:* Drawing on relevant theory, this chapter explores how coaching can be deployed to enhance dyadic relationships

through encouraging openness in communication and an understanding of oneself and others, suggesting that coaching can be effective as a preventative, but also a life-enhancing, approach. A framework for coaching practice in this context is introduced and practical examples and case studies are presented of how coaching can work with the dyad to help them to strengthen their relationship. This chapter also illustrates how relationship coaching can be used with couples to overcome relationship difficulties through cognitive-behavioural and solution-focused coaching approaches. The chapter concludes by explaining the role of coaching in helping with a decision to dissolve the relationship.

- *Chapter 8 – Coaching with Parents:* In this chapter, we focus on how coaching can be used to help parents better manage their role of raising children and young people. Because children change enormously as they grow older, the role of the parent also alters dramatically. Thus, the chapter addresses coaching with parents of children (until 10 years) and adolescents (11 years and older). Coaching can help parents understand, manage, and even change situations and enable them to take responsibility, feel stronger, and have the necessary confidence to help their children face challenges at school, in youth groups, and in other areas of their lives. Coaching can provide parents of older children with insight and techniques to support their teenage children through struggles such as feeling misunderstood, lacking confidence, peer pressure, misunderstandings with parents, or a fear of the future. The chapter considers the way coaching can facilitate addressing a wide range of critical aspects of parenting, including the role of parents as role models, family dynamics, parenting with values, and parenting with emotions.
- *Chapter 9 – Professional and Ethical Issues:* Relationship issues give rise to particularly challenging professional and ethical dilemmas. This chapter is designed to sensitise and forewarn coaches about the complexities of relationship coaching and the range of ethical dilemmas common to coaching in the relationship context, including such key issues as confidentiality, conflict of interests, and professional integrity. Examples will be given of where referral to other services could be necessary. In particular, the relationship coach needs to be fully cognizant of the boundaries between coaching and other approaches to relationship support, such as psychotherapy and sex therapy, which are especially important when there are mental health issues or other specific issues to surmount. These and other topics of concern are discussed.
- *Chapter 10 – Conclusion:* The final chapter summarises the book and the main points it has raised. It also discusses the issue of the extent to which the coach needs an understanding of the context in which the coaching is taking place.

Chapter 2

Working towards personal development in relationship coaching

Many coaches have overtly based their coaching approach on theories of adult development that adopt a structured approach towards the cognitive growth and maturity of the client (Fitzgerald and Berger 2002; Berger 2006; Laske 2006), theories based on life stages (Palmer and Panchal 2011), or ego development (Bachkirova 2011). However, Sugarman, in the foreword to Palmer and Panchal (2011: xiv), suggested that 'coaching has *always* adopted a developmental stance – if sometimes only implicitly' (our emphasis). She confirmed how coaching 'looks forward rather than backwards and is less concerned with restitution and more with prospective work to forestall future misdirection or stagnation'. From this perspective, it could be argued that developmental coaching, whether implicit or explicit, works towards the growth of the whole person into all that he or she could be (Cox and Jackson 2014).

From this implicit developmental stance, adult development could be described as a natural output of our thinking. It is a lifelong process of transformation that occurs with or without coaching. It occurs as a result of change and expansion in outlook and attitude as we work through our experiences of life. Development is what normally happens as a result of life events. It occurs when new learning from experience becomes absorbed and included in who we are, becoming part of our prereflective experience (Cox 2013). Taylor et al. (2000: 10) summed up adult development as 'a process of qualitative changes in attitudes, values and understanding that adults experience as a result of ongoing transactions with their social environment'.

In this book, we take development to mean just this type of awareness-raising: the perspective enhancement and changed attitudes achieved through expansion of horizons and fostering of different ways of forming judgments. This type of thinking is developmental in that it enlarges what Mezirow (2000) called our 'habits of mind'. Development takes place when this expansion process leads us to discard or modify a habit of mind, to see the alternatives, and as a consequence to act differently in the world. Our mind expands as it becomes genuinely able to see more points of view.

We believe that taking account of client development is important in relationship coaching because it enables people in relationships to be open to differences in people's perception and opinions. A relationship is about making connections with other people, so being open to others' perspectives is vital. Therefore, in addition to a better understanding of aspects of themselves, clients achieve greater understanding of other people.

Developmental coaching is a key element of relationship coaching, and it works in tandem with the goal-focused approach that will be discussed in Chapter 3. In developmental coaching, life is seen explicitly as a journey of continuous improvement that can be supported, enhanced, and perhaps even accelerated through the process of coaching. During their journey, clients can be encouraged and supported to think about different viewpoints and to have their own understandings of events challenged in order to expand those viewpoints. Learning and unlearning are key aspects of this process, and mindfulness also plays a part. Ryan and Deci (2000) pointed out how mindfulness is important in separating people from their automatic thoughts, habits, and unwanted behaviour patterns, suggesting it could play a role in fostering an increase in informed self-regulation – something that is associated with the enhancement of well-being.

This chapter focuses on the role developmental coaching plays for clients needing support with their relationships. For most people, when their relationships are not working well, they just want to feel better about it. They are not concerned at that point with their development. However, thinking about the nature of their relationship and thinking about the situation differently, from different perspectives, can help people develop, as well as help them to feel better as they begin to do something about their situation.

This chapter begins with a review of theories that emphasize the course of adult development. Then, we explore integrating strategies to boost development in relationship coaching to demonstrate how the theoretical concerns of developmental coaching translate to specific relationship contexts. We end with an exploration of case studies showing how coaching incorporates a developmental approach.

Theories emphasising the course of adult development

In this section, we review a number of theories about how adults develop. We divide the theories into two broad categories: the ego development and life stage theories of development, which are concerned with the psychological development of the individual; and life event and transition theories of adult development, which encompass sociological triggers for learning and development. We will discuss each category in turn before examining how they intersect and how life events are developmental, especially with the help of a relationship coach.

Ego development and life stage theories of development

Ego development and life stage theories of development include sequential models of psychological development, such as those developed by Erikson (1959),

Table 2.1 Erickson's and Levinson's age-related stages

Erikson	Age and stage	Conflict (resolution)
	0–18 months (infancy)	Basic trust vs. mistrust (hope)
	1–3 years (early childhood)	Autonomy vs. doubt (will)
	3–6 years (play age)	Initiative vs. guilt (purpose)
	6–12 (school age)	Industry vs. inferiority (competence)
	12–18 years (adolescence)	Identity vs. confusion (fidelity)
	19–40 years (young adulthood)	Intimacy vs. isolation (love)
	40–65 years (middle adulthood)	Generativity vs. stagnation (care)
	65+ years (maturity)	Integrity vs. despair (wisdom)
Levinson	Age and stage	Tasks at each stage
	Identify formation (18–22 years)	Following a dream, forming mentor
	Getting established (22–28 years)	relationships, developing an
	Wavering and doubt (28–32 years)	occupation, forming love relationships
	Getting settled (32–40 years)	
	Midlife transition or crisis (40–45 years)	Reappraisal of early adult commitments, modifying the dream
	Commitment to tasks (45–50 years)	
	Questioning and modification (50–55 years)	Preparing for retirement and late adulthood, coming to terms with being old
	Culmination and fulfillment (55–60 years)	

Levinson (1978), and Kegan (1982, 1994). Erikson and Levinson present life as a series of major life stages that are bounded by certain age-related dilemmas and responsibilities. In Erikson's theory, people go through a series of age-correlated conflicts, and the outcome of each stage depends on how they handle these challenges. For instance, he proposed that during adolescence the formation of individual identity arises from a process of exploration and commitment to the identity or peer group. Levinson's theory, based on his research with men in North America, includes a midlife transition in which dreams formed in early adulthood are reappraised and modified. Erickson's and Levinson's age-related stages are illustrated in Table 2.1.

All life stage theories appear to have some form of end point where the adult becomes more autonomous, attaining a more universal perspective or increased wisdom of some form. In Erikson's theory, successfully passing through each conflict involves achieving a healthy balance between the two opposing dispositions. For example, between the ages of 19 and 40, the dilemma is to resolve the conflict between intimacy and isolation. The quest is for love. If people negotiate this stage successfully, they may experience intimacy on a deep level; however, if they do not find it easy to create relationships, then they may experience (crippling) isolation. Later, between the ages of 40 and 65, there is a need to be creative and productive in ways that will contribute to future generations. There is an emphasis on creating one's legacy for the future. Here, the conflict manifests as a struggle between generativity and stagnation, with 'care' being seen as the resolution of the two. For Erikson (1969: 395), the concept of care suggested that, at this stage, people should have 'defined for themselves what and whom they have come to care for, what they care to do well, and how they plan to take care of what they have started and created'. Care could include such things as giving something back, writing a book or a memoir, or becoming a mentor or a grandparent.

In Levinson's research, the importance of the 'modification of the dream' cannot be underestimated. A dream is forged in early life, often as early as the identity formation stage (18–22 years). However, if this dream is not followed or is thwarted for whatever reason, the midlife period can be traumatic. In relationships, the desire – or indeed, the inability – to modify the dream can manifest as uncharacteristic behaviour observed by the partner, such as the desire to move house or jobs and do something entirely different, having extramarital affairs, or taking up some risky pastime. The need to modify the dream – to make it realistic and attainable rather than something to chase regardless – provides some explanation for the archetypal 'midlife crisis' (Jacques 1965) and can enable us to understand why people 'grow apart' from their partners, or why they sometimes get depressed or do uncharacteristic things when they reach around age 45 (give or take 10 years!).

Thus, midlife presents a variety of problems for couples because one or the other partner (or both) may experience the crisis of meaning associated with this phase (Jacques 1965). A developmental approach can help them each to understand the concept of a midlife crisis and the physical and psychological challenges that can pose. Partners who perceived that they had grown apart could be helped to identify areas of interdependence that might ultimately enhance their relationship. For single people, it may be that the early dream of the ideal partner is unrealistic and, at some point, there has to be a taking stock of what characteristics a prospective spouse can realistically offer.

The theories proposing that psychological changes proceed in stages throughout a lifetime can therefore be useful in trying to understand many relationships. For example, if as a parent we realise that teenagers, according to the theory, have to establish their identity amongst their peers, we begin to understand why following fashion – no matter how outrageous or unconventional – is something our sons or daughters feel they absolutely need to do in order to feel part of the crowd, or sometimes to stand out from the crowd. We put it down to being part of growing up, but in fact Erikson's theory also supports our observations.

There are problems with the theory of age-related stages, however. As can be seen in Levinson's findings, situational factors may actually impact the age ranges within stages. With the advent of the rise in retirement age in the United Kingdom and other western countries, it is likely that what Levinson terms 'culmination and fulfilment' may occur later than age 55–60 years. Certainly, the preparation for retirement and coming to terms with being old may shift well into the 70s or even 80s for some people. There are other limitations too, because life events can sometimes thrust people into a conflict stage sooner than indicated by the calendar. Thus, there are criticisms of these stage theories in that the age ranges can vary substantially and transitions occur all the time. For coaches, it is just useful to be able to help the client understand that there may be a generational aspect to the difficulty and that it can be worked through. Knowing that other people are undergoing similar transitions can be hugely comforting. Development, though, is often painful and it is frequently a long time coming as we continue to resist change.

By contrast to the life stage development theories, cognitive developmental theories, such as that proposed by Kegan (1982, 1994), show stages, or orders of mind, that are only age-related until adulthood is reached. Kegan builds on Piaget's (1962) child development work, suggesting that when we are very young we understand everything as 'self' or as 'me' and have no conception of ourselves as differentiated in the world – everything is 'subject'. As we grow, we begin to identify with our individual sensations and needs, and our range of objectivity or 'object consciousness' grows. Our subjective consciousness, which includes the self-concepts to which we are still attached, shrinks and we can step back and see more objectively. In Johari window terms (Luft and Ingham 1950), these self-concepts are not blind spots; they are actually unknown and unknowable to us at the present time. We are 'subject' to them and cannot know or work with them until they become 'object' in later stages of development. Kegan's stages or orders of mind are shown in Table 2.2.

Kegan claimed that, during adulthood, most people reach the third-order or 'interpersonal self' stage, where the emphasis is on mutuality and fitting in with others. However, not all people, according to his research, will move to the 'institutional self' of the fourth stage, where personal values, identity, and autonomy are paramount, nor to the 'inter-individual self' of the fifth stage, where personal systems are emphasised.

In the interpersonal stage, which is usually reached during the teenage years, personal needs and desires can be looked at objectively, but relationships remain subject. People at this stage may be reluctant to express feelings such as anger because of the threat to mutuality. They think that if they upset others, they will not be liked. So, direct conflict is avoided because it is a threat to self-identity

Table 2.2 Subject/object development (adapted from Kegan 1994)

Developmental stage/order of mind	Subject/object development
First order: The impulsive mind (2–6 years)	Seen as object: reflexes Subject to: impulses, perceptions
Second order: The imperial mind (6 years to adolescence)	Seen as object: impulses, perceptions Subject to: needs, interests, desires
Third order: The interpersonal, dependent mind (post-adolescence)	Seen as object: needs, interests, desires Subject to: interpersonal relationships, mutuality
Fourth order: The institutional, independent mind (age variable, if achieved)	Seen as object: interpersonal relationships, mutuality Subject to: authorship, identity, ideology
Fifth order: The inter-individual, interdependent mind (typically age 40+, if achieved)	Seen as object: authorship, identity, ideology Subject to: the 'interpenetrability' of self-systems

(Kegan 1982, 1994). In the institutional stage, the commitment to or reliance on others, which was hidden, is now object. People recognise their previous dependence and make efforts to regulate any competing interpersonal demands that others make on them. However, personal standards and value systems remain subject. It is not until individuals reach the inter-individual stage that these become object, and the individual can become mindful of how their own ideologies and identities impact. This shift is illustrated in Figure 2.1. It shows a growing independence from others and greater discrimination, culminating in the interdependence of the inter-individual mind – the acceptance of others based on a sound sense of self as volitional consciousness.

Thus, Kegan (1982) identified that people have two great yearnings that exist in lifelong tension: to be included and to be independent. His theory hinges on the assumption that, as we develop, there is an imperative to separate from others and to construct an identity of our own. Paradoxically, however, there is also the need to be connected to others and see ourselves in relation to them. Recognition of this need is important, particularly in relationship coaching. Most of us manage the balance well. However, for those single people who want to find a partner but find it difficult, the need to feel included can become overwhelming. Similarly, for those who feel stifled in a relationship, the need for independence can lead to frustration. For parents, there is often apprehension when teenagers show a third-order dependence on seemingly undesirable peer groups where they can realise their sense of identity.

Although theoretically development models, such as Kegan's, are interesting to contemplate, there are no reliable measures through which to formally assess development because all rely on verbal or textual creations and interpretation. However, Bachkirova (2011: 125) claimed that there is no need for formal assessment to

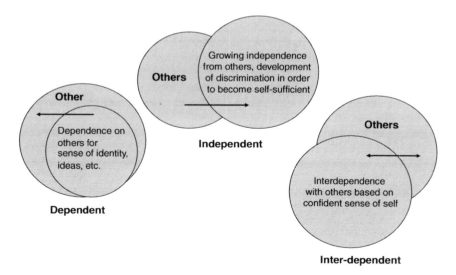

Figure 2.1 The move from dependence through independence to interdependence

calculate the developmental stage of the client; instead, she suggested, the coach should allow for 'full engagement with the theme chosen by the client, but with the knowledge and understanding that this theme is developmental'. The theme or topic, she argued, may itself be characteristic of four developmental stages: unformed ego, formed ego, reformed ego, and ego with a soul. This classification is similar to other accounts. For example, Wade (1996) labelled the stages as conformist, achievement, authentic, and transcendent. However, unlike in other accounts, rather than development progressing linearly through a series of prescribed stages or phases, Bachkirova sees it as a form of organic change – a continuum. She defined development as the 'combination of changes in the organism manifested in a sustained, increased capacity of the client to engage with and to influence their environment and to look after their internal needs and aspirations' (2011: 77).

Bachkirova's main thesis is that developmental themes are ego-based and are 'what clients bring to coaching, formulated from their own perspective of their overarching needs and challenges' (2011: 77). In practice, this may mean focusing on a specific aspect of the person, such as emotional development or critical thinking. The parameters of the coaching should depend specifically on the requirements of the client and the situation.

We propose that it can be useful to consider that there may be some organised progression in our development and to think about the impact that such evolution may have on our relationships. For example, where a couple comprises two dependent people, sometimes life goes on quite quietly. Expectations and 'habits of mind' (Mezirow 2000) are not challenged, and both partners respect (or at least tolerate) family or cultural differences for the sake of their partner. Differences arise when outside influences clash. If partners are from different social sectors or cultures, there may be differences that cannot be reconciled. Demands on the couple from authorities outside their relationship might never be resolved, despite enormous efforts at compromise. Tensions rise and arguments ensue as each of the partners defends his or her 'own' perspective. Such couples can be encouraged to reflect on the influences of work, relatives, peers, advertising, etc., to question those influences and compare them with other positions. Challenging in this way will help them think for themselves and build the self-efficacy needed for development (Bachkirova 2011: 142). Sharma and Cook-Greuter (2010) confirmed that individuals should be supported to move towards more inclusive, 'both–and', rather than black-and-white thinking. The role of the relationship coach here is to facilitate such development.

The independent partner is sometimes difficult for a dependent partner to accommodate and understand. The dependent partner may be threatened by the new autonomy that the partner displays. The shift to independence happens to most people as a natural part of maturity. For example, if a woman is moving to a more independent stage – wanting to make her own decisions, find a job (or a new job) – it may seem as if she is neglecting her partner, leaving him behind. In such situations, the partner could be coached to understand the needs of the independent stage of development and subsequently to consider his own needs.

He may feel he is being unfairly treated or that he is being put upon by the fact that his partner wants him to take on more domestic responsibility. He might feel his confidence is being undermined, or that he is not earning enough to ensure his partner is satisfied with what she has. By contrast, the life-partner is focused on achieving her long-term aim of developing her career and gaining the recognition she feels she deserves – themes that are indicative of the 'formed ego' (Bachkirova 2011: 149).

When partners have reached the interdependent stage, there could be a sense of acceptance. The interdependent husband or wife can live with uncertainty – bearing it. Where there are problems in a marriage, for example, either or both partners might be adept at living 'one day at a time' (Nace 2010). This involves acceptance and forgiveness. Thus, two interdependent people should get along really well, being able to see each others' perspectives and face challenges in a calm way. This configuration can lead to a very productive relationship, but only where both are pulling together in tandem towards the same life goals (Ives and Cox 2012: 36). If the couple are striving to achieve different overarching outcomes, it could lead to major disagreements, with the result that the couple grow apart.

In theory, couples who are both at the interdependent stage should never argue. Wilber (2001: 29) contended that when opposites are realized to be one, 'discord melts into concord, battles become dances, and old enemies become lovers. We are then in a position to make friends with all of our universe, not just one half of it'. Thus, when we can see our disagreements with our partner, or our differences or preferences, as just two sides of the same coin, we allow our partner to have different opinions and tastes, and these do not interfere with who we are or what we want to do. One of the ways in which the coach can help couples in relationship coaching is by encouraging acceptance, both of themselves and the other through the development of such enhanced perspectives. In the next section, we highlight how development is also prompted by life events.

Life events theories of adult development

The life events approach to development is dependent upon many overlapping variables. It suggests that individual development depends not only on life events and individual adaptation to life events (i.e. how people cope with the transitions generated by life events) but also the socio-historical and social context. In the life events model, specific individual events such as marriage, divorce, bereavement, and death all have impact, as well as generational factors such as economic fluctuations, natural disasters, or wars. According to Santrock (2008), the contemporary life events approach is an alternative to age-related stage development theory (discussed previously). In this model, life events such as marriage and divorce cause varying degrees of stress, while mediating factors such as physical health and family support can help reduce anxiety and tension and facilitate a more effective coping strategy. All are viewed as driving a person's development. They all give shape and direction to a life (Sugarman 1986). This perspective views such events as opportunities for growth, development, and change.

The life events theory is useful because it does not focus purely on events as crises or dilemmas to be overcome. It provides a helpful way of approaching life events – seeing them as opportunities for individual development, based on strengths and so enabling self-understanding. In Figure 2.2, we show how socio-historical and individual factors, together with life events, combine to influence individual development. It can be seen how development is made possible through a very idiosyncratic process of appraisal that is not just dependent on age, context, or another single factor. Development therefore depends on the following:

- Life events, such as meeting someone new, marriage, or divorce
- Individual attributes, such as physique, mental ability, and personality
- The socio-historical context, such as economic recession, fear of war or terrorism, or a global viral epidemic
- Life/ego development stage: The developmental age or stage of individual development
- The individual's appraisal of the situation and adaptation to the life event, such as whether the individual is prepared, having been in this situation before
- Whether there is sufficient support from family or from a coach to encourage coping strategies.

An example of this intersection and the support a coach can provide is illustrated in the following case.

Case study: Mabel and Robert

Mabel and Robert divorced after 24 years of marriage. Both were at what life stage theorists might call the midlife stage, so each was affected by the same life event and each was ostensibly at the same life stage. However, Mabel and Robert were at different developmental stages and had different individual attributes. Mabel was quite independent, forging a well-paid career for herself in a pharmaceutical company. She was also quite extroverted. Robert, on the other hand, was more introverted and seemed quite dependent on Mabel, despite his responsible job with the city council.

The relationship coach saw Mabel and Robert together because the divorce was proceeding amicably and they wanted to discuss how to ensure they could remain friends, not just for the sake of their two children (aged 23 and 21). It was evident to the coach that Mabel was driving this decision and that Robert was taking it much harder. He was less sure that it would be possible to stay in contact. His friends had told him that it would not work, suggesting that any meetings would result in a kindling of old desires or animosities.

The coach, being aware of developmental theories, encouraged Robert to appraise the situation by exploring his values and setting out a range of 'staying in contact' options, from meeting regularly at social events with the family, right through to just exchanging Christmas cards, and then to ask Mabel to accept his choice of friendship option. This coping strategy was aimed in just a small way at helping Robert develop as a person so that his decision-making would become easier.

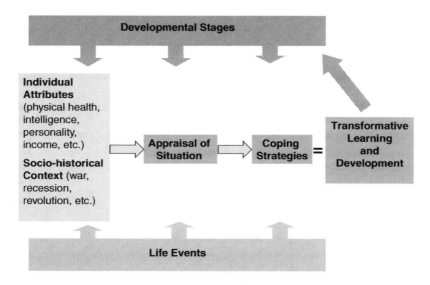

Figure 2.2 Adult development and life events framework (adapted from Santrock 2008)

Figure 2.2 shows the iterative process of ongoing development that influences our developmental 'stage' and so affects our appraisal and coping capacity.

In the next section, we discuss the role of the coach and how the appraisal process leads not only to coping strategies but also to transformative learning and then to development.

Transformative learning

For Mezirow (2000: 19), transformative learning occurs in the following four ways, all of which involve reconstruction of the stories we tell ourselves – what Mezirow called 'dominant narratives' – which then becoming critically reflective of our assumptions, our habitual responses, and 'taken-for-granted beliefs':

- By elaborating on existing frames of reference (reflecting critically on current experience)
- By learning completely new frames of reference (broadening our range of different experiences)
- By transforming points of view by 'trying on another's point of view' (Mezirow 2000: 21), examining what it would be like to think in another way
- By transforming habits of mind, examining our assumptions about why we act or respond in certain ways and being open to change.

Mezirow described transformative learning as awareness about 'the values that lead us to our perspectives' (2000: 8). He suggested that our values and sense of self are 'anchored in our frames of reference' providing a 'sense of stability, coherence, community, and identity' (18). Consequently, Mezirow suggested that 'they are often emotionally charged and strongly defended' because the points of view of others are judged against standards set by our own points of view. Transformative learning, then, refers to 'the process by which we transform our taken-for-granted frames of reference to make them more 'inclusive, discriminating, open, emotionally capable of change, and reflective so that they may generate beliefs and opinions that will prove more true or justified to guide action' (Mezirow 2000: 7).

Mezirow also explained how the crucial part of transformative learning is 'becoming critically aware of one's own tacit assumptions and expectations and those of others and assessing their relevance for making an interpretation' (2000: 4). These tacit assumptions or 'habits of mind' form one dimension of our complete frame of reference or 'meaning perspective' (16). The other dimension is the 'point of view', which the habit of mind engenders as shown in Figure 2.3. So, a habit of mind acts as a filter for interpreting the meaning of experience and governs our 'point of view' within a particular frame of reference.

Habits of mind come in different varieties. For example, we all have habits relating to how we view culture, ideologies, social norms, morality and ethics, sensory preferences, religion and philosophy, self-concept, emotional response, fantasies and dreams, values, tastes and attitudes, as well as other aesthetic judgments. To become aware of such tacit 'habits', the practice of mindfulness can be helpful. Mindfulness separates people from their automatic thoughts (Ryan and Deci 2000); it involves 'bringing our awareness to the body and the environment in which it is currently situated' (Cox 2013: 127). Mezirow discussed how mindfulness allows us to have an implicit awareness of more than one perspective, as opposed to mindlessness, which he says 'involves relying on past forms of action or previously established distinctions and categories' (2000: 7).

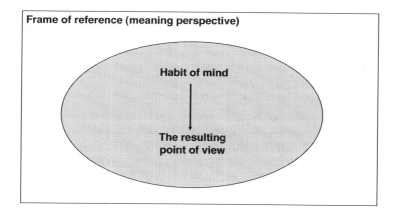

Figure 2.3 The anatomy of a meaning perspective

At start of the transformative process, when they are at the 'horns' of what Mezirow (2000) called a 'disorienting dilemma', people begin to question their values and beliefs and review their previous habitual responses to events. Thus, also linked to transformative learning is the need to 'unlearn'. Delahaye and Becker (2006: 8) suggested that 'one of the key challenges for those involved in facilitating lifelong learning is to understand how to also facilitate unlearning'. For successful unlearning, the old habits need to be challenged, critically reviewed, and emphasised as being necessary to be unlearned (or at least put aside). Coaches will need to support clients in playing an active role in consciously letting go of old habits, ensuring that the old behaviours are not used. For example, parents who are designing a better relationship with their child need to ensure they no longer criticise and only compliment the child. The challenge for unlearning is that the existing habits of mind have been heavily rehearsed and are well entrenched. Therefore, in unlearning the habits, a client must make certain that the old habit of mind is not practiced. This will contribute towards a natural decaying process – forgetting. Hedberg (1981) suggested that a phased or spaced approach to changing existing habits encourages 'overwriting'. Accountability to a coach would be beneficial during this process (Cox 2013).

Mezirow also championed the need for critical reflection in transformative learning. This involves 'weighing the supporting evidence and arguments' and 'examining alternative perspectives'. Critical discourse is the 'process in which we have an active dialogue with others to better understand the meaning of an experience' (2000: 14). He further explained that reflection can be at three levels: content reflection, which is focused on what happened; process reflection, which focuses on dynamics and the process by which the event occurred; and premise reflection, which involves looking at assumptions. It is this last level of premise reflection that achieves perspective transformation and is thus the work of the relationship coach: helping clients, through critical discourse, to make a critical assessment of their assumptions and so leading them towards a better understanding.

Mezirow (2000: 13–14) explains that, to fully participate in transformative discourse, people must have the following:

- Accurate and complete information: The coach can help clients obtain accurate and complete information. Questions may include, 'Have you got all the information you need?' and 'Do you think that is right?'
- Freedom from coercion and distorting self-deception: This includes a nonthreatening environment, where anything can be said.
- Openness to alternative points of view: Empathy and concern about how others think and feel (listening to the other's point) are emphasized. In the case of coaching with couples, this is a vital element of the coaching process.
- The ability to weigh evidence and assess arguments objectively and the willingness to seek understanding and agreement.
- Greater awareness of the context of ideas and, more critically, reflecting on assumptions including their own: Clients can be helped to see how an

assumption may be right in one context, but a different context may alter its effectiveness.

- An equal opportunity to participate in the various roles of discourse (this is particularly important when coaching couples).

For example, in the case study, Robert's friends assume that a divorced couple can never be friends. However, Robert's premise reflection with the coach on different levels of friendship might enable him ultimately to have an agreeable ongoing connection with Mabel.

Sometimes, appraisal of a situation triggers what Mezirow (2000) called a 'disorienting dilemma' triggered by events that do not conform to our expectations. The dilemma occurs when events surprise us and generate more than usual self-reflection and soul-searching. Thus, dilemmas are tremendous learning opportunities, but they can be painful or even traumatic. As Mezirow (2000: 6) pointed out:

> Transformative learning, especially when it involves subjective reframing, is often an intensely threatening emotional experience in which we have to become aware of both the assumptions undergirding our ideas and those supporting our emotional response to the need to change.

At these times, people need some support, which may usefully come in the form of coaching. Although appraisal of such dilemmas happens to some extent without the help of a coach and sometimes family and friends can fulfil the helping function, often a nonbiased outsider is best. Especially where relationship issues are concerned, working with a coach who specialises in this area can alleviate much frustration by helping clients to make sense of their experiences. For example, for single and married people, arguments within a relationship can be reframed as a chance for learning and an opportunity to gain a new perspective on life rather than being the end of that relationship.

According to Mezirow (2000), transformative learning may either take the sudden ('epochal') form of the disorienting dilemma, or it may take an incremental form. In the epochal form, the dilemma is 'a state of cognitive dissonance where the individual faces the indisputable fact that he or she is wrong, experiences stress and reduces that stress by changing so that the old knowledge is at least put into parenthesis if not immediately overwritten' (Delahaye and Becker 2006: 8).

It is interesting to note that in Hawkins and Smith's (2014) popular model of transformational coaching, the transformation is epochal: the challenge created through that model aims to generate a transformational shift right there and then in the coaching room. In the incremental form, the client's outlook changes gradually so that old habits are progressively overwritten. In the case of Robert, the exercise undertaken to appraise the situation and explore different options for remaining friends with Mabel was used to challenge his frames of reference, as part of an incremental transformation.

Transition

In Figure 2.4, we have mapped Mezirow's ten steps of transformative learning on a transition curve to show how a life event might provoke a disorienting dilemma and be followed by a period of self-examination and ultimately reorientation. Thinking of transformative learning as a transition can be useful, providing chronology for the process and an explanation for the emotional dynamics inherent in transformation. In Figure 2.4, internal and external energies are mapped on the vertical axis to show these dynamics.

According to transition theory, when a life event occurs, it provokes a shift. Transition is a process of disorientation and reorientation that Bridges (2001) suggested marks the turning point on the path of growth. Palmer and Panchal also noted that transitions are good opportunities for learning and development and suggest that developmental coaching involves 'supporting individuals to negotiate transitions, and therefore grow and develop' (2011: 4).

Bridges defined transition as an internal experience of gradual, psychological reorientation occurring as we respond and adapt to change. His model of transition begins with the ending of one 'event', then moves to a neutral zone, a seeming 'no-man's land between the old reality and the new ... a time when the old way is gone and the new doesn't feel comfortable yet' (1991: 5). The final phase is the beginning of something new, where a new aspect of life is begun.

If we take the example of getting divorced as one life event, the change associated with the ending of being married is a time of considerable uncertainty and transition. If the end came suddenly, then the intensity of the life event may trigger

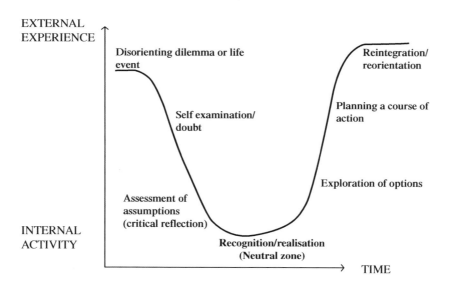

Figure 2.4 Transition model of transformative learning using Mezirow's (2000) ten steps

a disorienting dilemma. The break with the status quo of married life is then followed by a neutral period (which may last some years), an uncertain time where partners may each miss the comparative stability or companionship of their married lives to varying degrees. The final phase is where the divorced state is accepted as the norm and gradually becomes a more comfortable way of life.

Implications for relationship coaching

Within this fundamental model of transformation, transition, and development, many reflective and critical thinking tools and techniques can be used. In this section, we give two examples of developmental coaching that illustrate specific work with relationship issues. In these case studies, clients are helped to appraise their situation by looking at current coping strategies and finding new ways of thinking. Coaches challenge beliefs, values, and meaning perspectives in order to help the client arrive at the best way forward for them.

Kochi, a single parent

In her autobiographical novel, Alice Koller (1981) observed that she appears not to have a life of her own and talks about how she just uses up her days. She explained how she has only been someone for someone else. She has spent her entire life living through 'the other'. This state of affairs is common and could happen, for example, in people who marry young and have not had an opportunity to develop their independence.

Like Koller, Kochi also believes that she does not have a life. Kochi was 34 years old when she first came for coaching. She has two children with her ex-partner, Bill, and at that time she was living alone for the first time in her life. She was trying to cope with raising two small daughters, keeping a small apartment, and working as a hotel receptionist. Her mother was helping out temporarily with childcare.

Kochi has spent all her adult life in relationships. She has always done what had been expected of her by her parents, her different male partners over the years, her employer, and her children. She told her coach, 'I don't know who I am any more. I thought I knew, but since Bill has gone out of my life, I am nobody and I don't know what to do now or where to turn.' Kochi looked up to Bill, idolised him. However, for some reason, this kind of 'living in the shadow' of another person can have an adverse effect on partners, who are sometimes drawn towards a flirtation with a self-sufficient, independent-minded partner. Bill left Kochi for a successful marketing executive.

Kochi now considers that part of her life has ended with the break-up of the relationship and she now dedicates herself to working and raising her family – using up her days in the way Koller described. When asked what she wants from the coaching, Kochi explains how she never wanted anything for herself – she had always wanted to be a better mother, a better partner, a better daughter, a better employee.

As a single mother, she struggles daily with the expectations her culture places on her not to become a drain on society.

A coach with an understanding of Kegan's stages of adult development might be able to recognise the need for a shift from a focus on mutuality or dependence toward personal autonomy. The 2008 film *The Women* also gives an example of a woman, like Kochi, who lives through and for her family. In the film, Mary has a successful financier husband, a young daughter, and a caring mother whom she can go to for advice. It is only when her marriage is thrown into disarray by her husband's infidelity that she begins to realise that she has never done the things she wanted to do. She then begins to think differently and to challenge authority, and ultimately she builds her own successful design company. Unchallenged habits of mind together with a reliance on authority appear to go hand in hand with black-and-white thinking. The shift to independence requires the broadening of perspectives and openness to the possibility that authority figures, such as parents or bosses, can be challenged.

Kochi can benefit from relationship coaching with its emphasis on development, as she can be helped to see her current dilemma as part of a maturation process and begin to believe that whatever she does for herself at this point in her life will lead to a more equal and 'independent' relationship with the next person she chooses as an intimate partner. With the support of a coach, it would help Kochi to examine literature and films that show women working through their separation from a partner so that she can have access to role models. Reflection on vicarious experience can be a valuable technique in developmental coaching. Once she recognises this pattern of dependence in herself, she can move on to exploring options for a new life.

Another way in which Kochi might expand her options is through some form of continuing education, as adult education is well known for its developmental potential (Daloz 2012). A coach, therefore, might help Kochi to explore different options for study. Any learning that involves reflection and critical thinking will broaden Kochi's horizons and enhance her future relationships.

Katherine and Karl

Katherine and Karl had been married for 22 years. They had been happy bringing up their children: the eldest was now in the armed services and the youngest had just started a university course. Karen was conscious that the children had been the main shared focus of the marriage, and she was worried that she and Karl may grow apart now that focus had gone. Karen was a midwife, working shifts and long hours, while Karl had built a successful career as a head teacher of a primary school. Now that the children were no longer at home, it seemed that she and Karl had very little in common and their conversation was limited. The divisions between them meant they just went their separate ways, rather than uniting to build stronger relationship.

Relationships thrive or flounder at all levels of development, but studies show that couples who marry young – when they are at what Kegan (1994) called the interpersonal stage of development – sometimes have a higher risk of relationship breakdown than couples who marry when they are older. Oppenheimer (1988) described this as a 'maturity effect'; at younger ages, people are still developing and thus may grow apart. Frequently, guidance for such couples suggests they have to work at their relationship. This 'work' can be greatly enhanced when a relationship coach supports the process.

The role of the coach in a relationship such as Katherine and Karl's, where the couple are both independent people, can be to help the couple to acknowledge the need to create joint interests and challenges that can enhance their connection with each other. They will need to integrate tensions that result from their different work foci and the perception of leading separate lives. Sharma and Cook-Greuter (2010: 25) suggested working to shift 'polarities' so that each client sees interdependencies between elements of their lives that until now have been held as separate. For example, Katherine and Karl may notice that what brings them together is their link with children – their own and other people's. Also, there may be other areas of their daily lives that require cooperation and hence have the potential for mutual sharing and understanding. Sharma and Cook-Greuter suggested that developmental tasks can be framed in terms of polarities by including and integrating the opposite of what is currently being privileged (e.g. union). In the case of Katherine and Karl, integration of the seeming differences between their occupations would be an initial way forward, while if the two of them then paid attention to the opposite of 'division' – the state that is currently being privileged – this would give scope for interesting conversation and, ultimately, togetherness.

Summary

In this chapter, we have described the role of development in enhancing relationships. Developmental theories were discussed and related to examples where clients brought relationship issues to coaching. We argued that an awareness of the client's stage of life development can help coaching to be more effective. Often, a developmental perspective can help individuals or couples who come to coaching to begin to understand the different challenges they face in their lives. A developmental perspective can also help people who are not in relationships to consider alternatives to their present situation and particularly to their habitual responses to situations.

We saw how a single mother, trapped in a cycle of dependence on others, might be helped to develop her autonomy and become a more independent and critical thinker, and how an independent couple can reframe how they think about their relationship.

Whatever approach to developmental coaching is adopted – whether it is the developmental stage theory or a gradual whole life path – of vital importance is the coaching philosophy of openness between coach and client (Cox 2013). Indeed, Bachkirova (2011: 80) cautioned against undertaking developmental coaching 'under the radar', recommending that explanations of developmental theories be part of the work with clients.

In the next chapter, we focus on how goal setting can be used to help enhance relationships. We will consider how coaches can support individuals and couples to clarify goals and maintain effective action towards achieving those goals.

Chapter 3

Working to achieve the goal

Looking for a life partner, or seeking to enhance an existing relationship with a loved one, is a clear and focused goal. Like any goal, it benefits from effective goal setting and action planning. While goal setting may come naturally to many people, it can be a challenge for others. Whereas in the previous chapter we explored the role of the coach in facilitating the growth and development of the client, in this chapter we examine how the coach can support the client to clarify his or her goal, take effective action to pursue it, and help the client stay motivated throughout this process.

The client's goal is a key means of self-regulation, and the nature of the goal is likely to play an important function in governing and motivating future behaviour. Although relationship coaching is primarily a developmental form of coaching, it is still important that the coach helps clients to set clear goals, plan effective action, and secure commitment and motivation. There are three main aspects of goal construction (Ives and Cox 2012): goal setting (the 'what'), action planning (the 'when and how'), and motivation (the 'why'). This chapter will be divided into three main sections that reflect these aspects.

From a coaching perspective, many relationship issues have a practical component. Although relationship challenges often stem from unhelpful approaches to relating or poor awareness of how people function in relationships, in part at least they can be addressed through changes in behaviour. People with a possessive relationship orientation, for example, can be helped to set realistic levels of inter-action with their partner, seek clarification from partners about their needs instead of anticipating them, and maintain friendships outside the relationships. People with an avoidant, distant relationship orientation can be helped to set healthy amounts of time together to sustain the relationship, regulate time at work to make space for the relationship, or learn to take advice when the relationship runs into trouble. Such steps are all measurable goals that can be specified, organised, and monitored. However, even non-behavioural changes can be set as goals, as we illustrate in this chapter.

Making tough choices, setting learning targets, and setting time limits for making decisions are also heavily goal-related. To illustrate this, consider the following real-life scenario, which we will work through during the course of this chapter.

Case study: Mark

Mark is a 36-year-old divorcée who has been separated for five years from his ex-partner, with whom he had a short marriage. For the last three years, Mark has been officially dating, although he has gone through long periods with little dating activity. Mark is serious and mature and describes the dating scene as 'frustratingly shallow'. Nevertheless, he has developed a few potentially serious relationships over the last three years, the most serious of which was with Shelley, a mother of two small children. However, Mark did not feel he could commit to being a father as well as a husband and left that relationship. Since then, Mark has met several other people, but he feels that none are as suitable as Shelley. From the coaching conversation, it emerges that Mark attributes part of his interest in Shelley to her being a mother, which he feels 'gives her a more real perspective on life'. Yet, it also becomes clear that he feels overwhelmed by the thought of 'instant fatherhood'.

From the unfolding coaching dialogue, it becomes evident that Mark has not managed to get Shelley out of his system, and feels that the other women he meets 'aren't as real'. What is clear from this is that Mark is going to have to make some tough choices (goal setting). Whatever his choices, he will need to learn how to adjust to them (action planning), and he is likely to find the transition challenging and will need a great deal of motivation and commitment to see it through.

Goal setting

Goal setting is a graduated process in which the activity of setting the goal contributes to the ultimate achievement of the goal (Skiffington and Zeus 2008). In fact, some clients will not arrive at the coaching with a clear goal, and they may be rather confused about what they want to achieve. There are two main levels of goal clarification, and effective goal setting can only occur at the second level. The first level of clarification is establishing a 'meta goal' (Carver and Scheier 1998), whereby the client establishes what he or she is hoping to *become* or arrive at – what has been termed a 'dream goal' (Whitmore 2003) or the 'future perfect' (Jackson and McKergow 2008). This level of goal abstraction is akin to the constructs of 'current concern' (Klinger 1975), 'personal project' (Little 1993), 'personal striving' (Emmons 1986), and 'life task' (Cantor and Khilstrom 1987). The second level relates to defining the goal in operational terms – what the client wants to *do*.

In our scenario above, if Mark was unsure whether he wanted to pursue a relationship and was thinking that 'perhaps relationships are just not for me', coming to a decision on this fundamental principle may itself be a significant process. (Yossi has experience with people coming for relationship coaching, but through coaching concluding that they would prefer not to pursue a relationship.) If Mark decides that he does want to pursue a committed relationship, he then needs to work out what kind of person he is looking for (based on his own experiences of the kinds of people he feels are suitable for him: the 'carefree' or the 'responsible' types). So, at the first level, Mark is deciding what he wishes to accomplish. At the second level, he is refining and solidifying his goal to focus on the option that he has determined is most appropriate. Stelter (2009: 207) similarly advises that 'it is not always beneficial to define a goal at the beginning of the coaching session, but to allow narratives to unfold'.

It is helpful to understand that these levels of goal clarification vary in their flexibility. The more high level a goal is, the more likely it is to remain unchanged, unless there are radical changes to the client's circumstances. By contrast, the more concrete the goal is, the more it will be increasingly subject to change, and it will need to be adjusted or replaced according to circumstance. In the scenario above, Mark is less likely to change his mind about his desire for a life partner, but he may well reconsider the kind of partner he is searching for.

Additionally, the higher level the goal is, the less it will be associated with a specific timescale. At the highest level of goal setting, the issue is about establishing the principle; it is not essential that it has an explicit timeframe because its main purpose is to set out a vision and basic direction. Therefore, the aphorism 'a goal is a dream with a date on it' is only true at the level of a concrete goal, where committing to a specific timeframe is critical to ensuring that the goal is reached.

Consequently, it is not always possible or suitable to begin relationship coaching by trying to set a specific, concrete goal, as the client may not have a clear goal in mind (Dembkowski and Eldridge 2008). As Pemberton (2006: 36) noted, 'Goals are outputs, not the starting point'. Before embarking on setting a specific goal, it may be necessary to broadly establish what the client wants to achieve. Thus, Pemberton (2006: 67) advocated beginning with 'fuzzy vision', which 'validates people for not knowing precisely what they want by encouraging them to talk about how they would like things to be different, rather than setting a precise outcome'. Securely establishing this more abstract goal is often a prerequisite to an action-oriented goal.

In forming a clear (concrete) goal, there are three main factors for which it is essential to strike the right balance: goal specificity, goal proximity, and goal difficulty. As each client and each situation is unique, there can be no absolute formula for determining the optimal level of specificity, proximity, or difficulty of the goal (Locke and Latham, 1990). What can be said is that rarely, if ever, would an extreme be appropriate. Thus, the work of goal setting is matching the prevailing circumstances and the characteristics of the individual to a desirable and achievable goal.

Goal specificity

Goal specificity (Locke and Latham 1990), or goal clarity, enables a clear standard against which to measure attainment, which research suggests is increased through coaching (Moen and Skaalvik 2009). 'Doing my best' or having no goals allows a person to settle for the lowest standard, with no price to pay in terms of self-concept (Latham 2007). Bandura (2001: 8) likewise suggested that 'general goals are too indefinite and non-committing to serve as guides and incentives'. As a result, we agree that the *S* in SMART goals needs to stand for *specific*, as suggested by Rubin (2002), and not simple, sensible, or significant, as others have suggested.

Designated specific outcomes must also be observable and measurable (Bandura 2001). They 'must be stated in sufficient clarity that both parties [coach and client] will be able to recognize them as occurring or not, and also be able to discern what progress has been made toward them' (Flaherty 2005: 119). Alexander (2006; Alexander and Renshaw 2005) described coaching as a precision tool that asks clients to define their words more precisely: what exactly do they mean, in comparison to what, etc. A single person may say, 'I need to be more focused on choosing the right person' or a couple may say, 'We need to learn to communicate better', but neither of these is a goal – they are merely aspirations. A more useful goal would provide specific issues to be addressed, such as 'I'm going to do a bit of homework before dating someone' or 'We will make a point of interrupting each other less'. A parent may say, 'I shall always give a compliment to my child when she is helpful'.

Goal proximity

Goal setting and action planning are two separate stages in goal activity, and each involves goals of different proximity. Goal setting involves setting distal (long-term) goals, whereas the setting of proximal (short-term) goals is part of the action-planning stage, as discussed in the next section. Proximal goals need to be preceded by distal goals, what Miller and Brickman (2004) termed immediate versus future goals and Bandura (1986) called sub and end goals (although the distal goal may itself consist of two stages, fuzzy and clear, as mentioned previously). In coaching, these are sometimes termed end versus performance goals (Whitmore 2003). Focusing too early on proximal goals clouds or confuses the distal vision; action planning is appropriate once the distal goal is established. Proximal goals generally emerge over time, unlike distal goals that are typically set in place at the outset and remain fixed unless there is a significant change in circumstances. Selection criteria for a one-off date, for example, are typically different than those for seeking a long-term relationship (Bredow et al. 2011). The coach should help the client ensure that a long-term goal guides immediate dating choices. Distal goals need to be in concordance with the client's values and aspirations; by contrast, proximal goals may be more instrumental, aimed at a practical outcome.

Distal, long-term goals – or what Miller and Brickman (2004: 15) called 'personally valued future goals' – are objectives where success in performing the current task does not immediately produce the desired end result. It is the initial commitment to a valued distal goal that instigates the process of developing the current, proximal goals (Nuttin 1984), and the progress towards reaching the distal goal is what motivates subgoal achievement (Carver 2007). In real life, people are normally only motivated to strive for proximal goals that are tied to a longer-term objective (Miller and Brickman 2004), such as finding time for one's spouse because maintaining the marriage is regarded as important in the long term.

Establishing a clear, overarching goal is therefore important to guide future action (Khan and Quaddus 2004). According to Arriaga and Rusbult (1998: 928), focusing on a long-term objective or goal enables effective self-regulation, as 'immediate, self-interested preferences are replaced by preferences that take into account broader concerns, including considerations to some degree that transcend the immediate situation'. This focus on 'action control' was found by Busch and Hofer (2012) to promote the development of generative concerns that increase purpose in life. Moreover, Vallacher and Kauffman (1996) suggested that people who construe their actions solely in short-term goals are typically in a state of relative disorder, guided by immediate considerations that are quite restricted in scope and transitory in application, such as getting into a relationship rather than focusing on a finding a long-term partner.

By contrast, proximal goals generate detailed action plans and infuse immediate tasks with relevance (Miller and Brickman 2004; Manderlink and Harackiewicz 1984). They offer more immediate evidence of progress, thereby raising self-efficacy (Bandura and Cervone 1983), and they provide criteria to monitor for self-evaluation, thus enabling more effective feedback (Locke and Latham 1990; Bandura 1991). Latham (2007) described how the self-regulative effectiveness of goals wanes as they are projected further into the future, whereas proximal goals, given their immediacy, are more effective at mobilising self-influencers. The goal of improving the relationship with teenage children is a long-term objective that provides the basis for more practical goals for parents, such as setting individual time with each child.

Given the varying strengths of distal and proximal goals, it is necessary to combine both goal types in the coaching process (Weldon and Yun 2000). Coaches should help clients to link short-term strategies to long-term goals (Scamardo and Harnden 2007; Skiffington and Zeus 2008). A primary task of the relationship coach is to help clients align their long-term goals and their short-term interests. Some clients may state that their goal is a serious committed relationship, yet in practice they seek out fun, recreational partners and have failed to spot the discrepancy (Dion et al. 1972; Langlois et al. 2000).

Goal difficulty

Progress is primarily made when clients set challenging goals (Locke and Latham 1990). However, it is essential that clients consider the challenges to be attainable and realistic. Difficulty is not an objective measure against a universal standard, but it refers to the judgment of the individual in question: Are they at the limit or close to the limit of the person's capabilities (Bandura 1986)? The coaching needs to encourage the client to maintain goal difficultly at an optimal discrepancy level – sufficiently stretching to motivate action but sufficiently narrow to be considered attainable. If the goal is too easy, there is insufficient discrepancy between the current reality and the desired change to stimulate action. If it is too difficult, there is too much discrepancy and it will lead to inaction. Ford (1992) called this 'the optimal challenge principle'.

Goals do not motivate directly but through the self-engagement with the task that they engender (Bandura 2001) and the self-engagement value of easy goals is negligible. However, conversely, Brown et al. (2005) found that goals only had a motivational effect when the person was not already experiencing overload. Thus, motivation will be highest when tasks are at an intermediary level (Pintrich and Schunk 1996) to ensure they are manageable but not boring (Nakamura and Csikszentmihalyi 2002; Kauffman 2004). If a goal is perceived as unattainable, there is likelihood of disengagement; 'high commitment is attained when the goal is perceived as being *attainable*' (Grant 2006: 158). Carver (2007: 28) similarly argued that goals that are perceived as unattainable are usually downgraded or abandoned: 'Sufficient doubt about goal attainment results in an impetus to disengage from efforts to reach the goal and even to disengage from the goal itself.' Clients will use their anxiety levels as a guide for moderating the ambitiousness of their goals. 'Keep looking' is too easy a goal, typically involving little new effort of mind or body; 'get married in the next six months' is likely to be too difficult a goal, which will probably be quickly abandoned as unrealistic.

Several coaching texts (Kemp 2006; Cox 2010; Cox and Jackson 2014) present the role of coaching as stretching the client to spur both learning and growth. Coaching aims to push the client to the 'edge of chaos' (Cavanagh 2006). It is the task of coaching to help the client strike a suitable balance between the extremes of proximity, difficulty, and specificity, in accordance with the needs of the situation, the characteristics of the client, and the stage of the goal-setting process.

In Mark's case, a goal such as 'I want to find a life partner' or 'My aim is to meet someone nice' is too general and vague. It is acceptable for the first level of goal setting, but it is insufficient to guide future action. Instead, Mark needs to clarify a more specific goal: What kind of person is he looking for? What are his criteria for a suitable spouse? What exactly does he mean by 'nice'? At this stage, he needs to set out his ultimate goal and his general strategy, without getting bogged down in the tactics and detailed actions. What issues he needs to deal with, what methods he will adopt to try to meet the right person, and so forth, are proximal goals that will come later at the action-planning stage. The coach should be pushing Mark to challenge himself to take positive action and, if appropriate, set himself a target for achieving it. However, it would be counterproductive for Mark to set unrealistic ambitions that will undermine the coaching and success. So, if Mark needs to address some underlying emotional issues or if he is entering a particularly busy patch at work, these things will need to be considered when setting a goal. For example, he may agree to aim for six dates in the next month, which may be unattainable given other pressures or personal issues.

Feedback

Feedback from the coach, but more importantly from the actual reality of the client, is fundamental to coaching (Grant 2006). Feedback is helpful for informing the client of the results of his or her actions, which leads to more effective goal-setting and resultant actions. There are two main types of feedback, both involving the collation and analysis of knowledge:

- *Long-term feedback*: The linking together of information that informs the person as to the likely consequences of actions. This knowledge becomes a guide to inform action under similar conditions. This process is called 'learning' (Carver and Scheier 1998).
- *Short-term feedback*: The immediate feedback from actions that inform the person whether or not to alter the course of action. Short-term feedback emerges from the task itself, as 'performance itself is feedback' (McDowall and Millward 2009: 61).

Both types of feedback are equally vital to relationship coaching (unlike in goal-focused coaching, which is primarily about short-term feedback, or in therapeutic coaching, which is primarily about long-term feedback).

Feedback is vital to inform clients how closely their performance approximates or deviates from the intended task and to ensure accurate information is available upon which to base decisions (Locke and Latham 2002). As Du Toit (2006: 53) asserted, 'In order to develop self-awareness the individual must have access to honest feedback'. Also, the more specific the feedback, the more useful it will be, as it aids learning and development. Coaching is most effective when it incorporates a means of monitoring and evaluating performance so that it can demonstrate progress. While Grant (2006: 154) expected 'observable concrete behaviours that are clearly discernible to the client', in relationship coaching, change is also measured by newly acquired skills sets and changes in attitude. Coaching could, for example, explore what kind of reaction the client gets from dressing in smart casual attire or making changes towards complimenting a child for her cooperation.

The coaching process can be viewed as a recursive, cyclical process in which clients monitor the effectiveness of their strategies, which, where necessary, generates a goal that directs future action (Zimmerman 2000). Coaching provides a safe environment to explore and analyse the effects of the client's strategy and to decide what new goal to set next. Accurate feedback is thus empowering, as the client has insight on which to base decisions, rather than groping in the dark. To be clear, feedback is only as useful as the changes the client makes as a result (London et al. 1997). Feedback is most powerful when it leads to concrete and future-directed goals, as McDowall and Millward (2009) suggested. When a coach does provide feedback, it should be nonevaluative (Chase and Wolfe 1989) and certainly nonjudgemental.

Feedback from the coach should aim to be empowering, but vitally it must be accurate, rather than trying to boost self-esteem by giving exaggerated praise

(Blumenfeld et al. 1982). Where there is a skills deficiency, clients should be helped to understand this (Pintrich and Schunk 1996). Invalid praise or inaccurate feedback only leads to the fostering of unrealistic feelings of efficacy (Pintrich and Schunk 2002), whereas targeted praise and supportive encouragement are sources of positive feedback. Praise needs to be informative, providing substantive comments on the coachee's qualities, abilities, and accomplishments that the coach has identified (Jackson and McKergow 2008), while extravagant compliments risk sounding condescending.

Research within positive psychology suggests that excessive positivity – exclusive praise with no critical feedback – results in reduced efforts (Fredrickson and Losada 2005). Feedback is needed to guide the choices and actions of the coachee and to foster his or her meaningful learning. If the feedback is implausibly positive, it may generate unrealistic future expectations and could stunt learning and development, result in the setting of inappropriate goals and a missed learning opportunity. Any short-term positive effect will be more than undone by the long-term negative consequences. Furthermore, when positive feedback is never moderated with constructive criticism, the praise ceases to be believed (Linnerbrink and Pintrich 2002). Elsewhere (Ives and Cox 2012: Chapter 9), we explain that the self-regulatory mechanism that controls human behaviour is determined by the information the person has about what is happening in reality by comparison to the desired outcome.

Action planning

Action planning comes after a clear distal or long-term goal has been set. It is 'the process of developing a systematic means of attaining goals' (Grant 2006: 159). Breaking down the long-term goal helps clients to feel more confident about their ability to complete tasks, thereby raising task-related self-efficacy. Hunt and Weintraub (2007: 52) argued that 'helping the individual being coached to articulate a personal learning agenda' is a key to coaching success and, according to Reeves and Allison (2009: 147), it 'is the very spine of the work coaches do with clients'.

The purpose of planning is to reduce the various options open to the client to a single action plan. In a study by Gollwitzer and Bransdstatter (1997), participants who specified a time and place for implementing a writing project were more likely to complete the project than those who had not, as 'planning the when, where, and how of initiating goal-directed behaviours furthers goal attainment' (Gollwitzer and Schaal 1998: 124). McDowall and Millward (2009: 74) similarly advise that the goal should be 'unpacked into a hierarchy of concrete criterion-based sub-goals against which shorter timescales could be mapped'. So, if the coaching has identified that a key issue for Mark is a lack of understanding about parenting and a high level of apprehension about children, which is preventing him from pursuing his relationship with Shelley, then this is an area of personal development that would benefit from a structured plan.

Action planning will often be an evolving process, with new issues arising on an ongoing basis. If, say, Mark decides to restart dating Shelley, he may discover that he is uncomfortable with commitment or that she is finding him too argumentative. As noted earlier, proximal goals are more readily subject to change: 'Thus, it makes sense to plan in general terms, chart a few steps, get there, reassess, and plan the next bits' (Carver and Scheier 1998: 256). As noted, these practical goals are more transitory in nature (Carver 2007). Mark may overcome his issue with commitment, but the long-term goal of settling down with a permanent partner remains.

According to the Rubicon model of action phases (Gollwitzer 1996; Heckhausen and Gollwitzer 1987), a person's level of goal commitment rises as they transition from a 'deliberative' to an 'implementation' mindset. The initial careful examination of competing options that characterises the deliberative phase is replaced with a determined focus on implementing the selected course of action. At the goal-setting stage, clients are in a more reflective, contemplative mode and are inclined to look into the horizon. By contrast, at the implementation stage, they typically get down to the more immediate tasks. Thus, at this planning stage, it is necessary to specify when, where, and how to take action (Achtziger and Gollwitzer 2008). This involves disaggregating the goal by dividing a problem into component parts.

Coaching texts generally emphasise the importance of relating goals to specified timeframes. While in relationship coaching there is the obvious factor of another person, working within a framework of time is often important. If Mark says he will register for online dating or will register for dance classes, the coach should be asking him when he will do so, how often he will go onto the website or how often he will attend class, and so on. Clearly, it may not be possible for Mark to give a date by which time he plans to be married, but he can set out a timeframe for many of the tasks that emerge from coaching. Doing this has the benefit of holding Mark to his commitments and ensuring that he is setting suitably challenging and realistic targets. Doing this will also help him to consider how to juggle various demands and to choose his priorities wisely.

Options

Given many clients' inexperience with some of the tasks required in pursuance of their goals, they may need to generate new options that are not part of their normal repertoire of activities. This is why some coaching texts promote the use of brainstorming and the creative pursuit of solutions in order to ensure that positive action is not hindered by an absence of ideas (Whitworth et al. 2007; Rogers 2008). Dembkowski and Eldridge (2008: 202) similarly advocated that the coach helps the client to 'develop a wider range of ways of achieving the goal'.

Helping clients to review their options enhances their commitment to the planning process by clarifying that their strategy is sound. It also helps them to recognize the unsuitability of some options, which results in greater confidence in their ultimate choice. As Achtziger and Gollwitzer (2008: 274) argued, the more thoroughly an individual has weighed the consequences of his or her choices, 'the closer he or she comes to the belief of having exhausted all possible routes'.

In relationship coaching, brainstorming for options should not be limited to the existing repertoire of the client, as it is recognised that the client may need to acquire new skills and reconsider aspects of their perspective or approach to relationships. Some ideas may be genuinely unsuited, but others present a growth opportunity (Dembkowski et al. 2006; Wasik 1984). Mark may consider himself unable to handle a more easygoing kind of person, but in fact it may be important for him to learn to better understand such personality types. A client may be tempted to reject a goal because it is regarded as impracticable; the coach's role is to ensure that important development is not avoided in this way.

Strategy

Action planning involves identifying strategies for achieving tasks; good intentions are not enough. Kanfer and Ackerman (1989) showed that without the requisite skills and knowledge, setting difficult goals can have a deleterious effect. Latham (2007: 68) explained that 'goal attainment on tasks that are complex for people requires that problems associated with getting started and persisting until the goal is reached are effectively solved'. It is through such strategies that the client is enabled 'to recognize, direct and modulate her or his own behaviour' (Skiffington and Zeus 2008: 87).

If there are gaps in skills or thinking, it is necessary to first establish with the client an effective strategy for attaining those skills or knowledge. When a client takes on a demanding goal without having an effective strategy, it triggers a mindless trialling of strategies, instead of systematically searching for ones that are effective (Latham 2007). 'Trying harder' to please one's spouse makes no sense if it entails doing more of whatever manifestly has been unproductive.

Mark has decided that finding a life partner is a top priority for him at this point in his life, and he has put himself under pressure to make this happen. This may result in him trying to make it work with Shelley without addressing the causes of the previous problem. Alternatively, he may seek to date other women without learning from past experiences and without ensuring that he has a plan that could be more successful for him. In practice, this could mean going for therapy, registering for a carefully selected online dating service, changing work patterns, working on his social skills, changing attitudes or behaviour regarding sex – a potentially unlimited list of possible options. The role of the coach is to facilitate an exploration of the individual client's needs and help him to identify the hopefully most effective route to success.

Action planning may often reveal that in order to maximise the chances of success, the client needs to seek the help or support of others. 'Adaptive help-seeking' (Newman 1998) is often a central element in action planning (Ives and Cox 2012). Some studies suggest that men in particular have difficulty requesting assistance (Addis and Mahalik 2003), but doing so may be essential for a successful outcome.

For this reason, systemic approaches to coaching that adopt a broad perspective have become increasingly prominent (Peltier 2009; Cavanagh 2006; Jackson and McKergow 2008).

By setting out a strategy, it is possible for Mark to focus on implementation, rather than continuously remaining in the deliberative stage. So, instead of each night Mark having to consider whether going to the nightclub is an appropriate choice or whether he would be better off joining a bridge class or perhaps going online to meet people, he can rely on the plan he had already set out. This is incredibly more efficient and also more effective. Mark will spend less time racked in doubt, trying to decide what to do – and often then doing nothing. He will also be more likely to act because he has already primed his mind about what he plans to do (Gollwitzer et al. 2007; Mone and Shalley 1995). We explained elsewhere (Ives and Cox 2012) how the role of coaching is to help clients optimise their attention, by differentiating between those decisions which should be always be made consciously and those which should be put into motion and carried out with a high degree of automaticity. From time to time, clients can reflect on the effects of the strategy and consider making changes – and coaching can be an effective facilitator of this process.

Flexibility

For all the careful thought that may go into creating an action plan, it should be understood that reality has no respect for action plans! Changes in the life of the client, in the life of a dating partner, or the broader context may add significant new complications. For example, the client may lose his or her job, changing the priority to finding new employment. The client may have started an overseas relationship, and the airfares to that destination double in price or direct flights are cancelled.

An action plan must, therefore, be flexible (de Haan 2008; King and Eaton 1999). As Carver and Scheier (1998) confirmed, it is neither possible nor appropriate to plan in great detail too far into the future, as circumstances are liable to change. Bandura (2001: 6) likewise noted: 'Future-directed plans are rarely specified in full detail at the outset. It would require omniscience to anticipate every situational detail.' However, this should not stop the coach and client from formulating plans, unless there is overwhelming uncertainty. Action planning is a flexible process, and it can be made even more flexible if conditions warrant this. Importantly, even if the circumstances change and the action plan has to be scrapped, it would still have typically given rise to valuable clarity of thought.

Motivation

Many clients are impatient for solutions. They have spent years struggling, and now that they finally have come for help, they are eager to get a speedy outcome. In coaching, we expect progress to be quick, but it rarely is instant; therefore, the coach cannot promise immediate results. However, the coach can and should galvanise the client's impatience as a goal-setting device: 'I can see how eager you are to get going with this. When would you like to see some change by?'

However, while many may think that clients would always be highly motivated to do what is required to maximise their chances of relationship success, this is often not the case. A client may say they will buy a book that could help with a better understanding of relationships, but months later the book has not even been bought, never mind read. Many coaches report that clients repeatedly cancel coaching sessions or just do not turn up. Similarly, during coaching, clients may decide to spend quality time with their teenager, book a romantic weekend break, go to a singles event, or register for online dating, but they still put up major resistance. Thus, relationship coaching is not a special case; the coach still needs to be adept at helping clients find motivation that will ensure they act on their goals.

Hollenbeck et al. (1988) defined performance as the interaction between cognitive ability and motivation. This means that the client may be aware of the need for change (i.e. cognitive recognition), but without the requisite motivation it will not result in any. However, unlike cognition, which once established remains relatively stable, motivation is typically inconsistent and unstable (Kanfer and Ackerman 1989). Managing motivation is therefore an ongoing requirement (Bandura 1986). Before a decision is made, the main faculty is that of cognition – weighing all the options and making smart choices. Once the decision has been made, what is most crucial is commitment and motivation (Achtziger and Gollwitzer 2008).

Coaching approaches advocate a variety of motivational strategies. Neurolinguistic programming practitioners, for example, have led the way in developing a colourful array of motivational techniques (Grimley 2014). Narrative coaching (Drake 2008; 2014) is another example of how to personalise and internalise change. In this chapter, given its goal focus, we highlight two approaches to raising motivation: identifying the benefits of achieving the goal through benefits questions and ensuring commitment through commitments questions. These two approaches have their origins in solution-focused coaching, which is discussed in more detail in Chapter 5.

Benefits questions

Benefits questions involve using a motivational interviewing approach to asking questions (Miller and Rollnick 2002), which brings into awareness the benefits of change and verbalises how change could be beneficial in order to raise motivation (Passmore and Whybrow 2007). Motivation can be fostered by asking clients to articulate the benefits to them from achieving their stated goal (Passmore 2007). Ford (1992) argued that aligning a performance target with a benefit reinforces the goal through a synergistic effect. This becomes most important when it comes to securing commitment for change or for challenging tasks.

As Pemberton (2006: 9) explained, to create real impetus, 'the challenge is to unearth what the other's motivations are, and then to use them to lever the performance you need'. For a goal to sustain persistent motion, it needs to capture the person's deep aspirations – what Bandura (2001) calls people's 'valued futures'. It is motivational for the client to talk through the specific benefit he or she hopes will accrue from attaining the goal. For example, Mark may be motivated by saying, 'If I make the effort to attend dance classes, it will enable me to meet the kind of person who is suited to me. At this point in my life, this is of crucial importance to me.' Similarly, Burns (1990) advised that the client should conduct a cost–benefit analysis, as commitment to the goal is more likely if benefits are then found to be important (Allan and Whybrow 2007; Locke 1996).

However, when considering deploying a benefit question as a means of raising motivation, it is worth noting this may be alienating to the client. Not all clients will respond positively to being asked to articulate the benefits of achieving their goal. They may regard it as superficial or embarrassing (Ives and Cox 2012). It should also be noted that the motivational benefits of this technique are comparatively short-lasting. It is more useful to gain cooperation from the client for accepting the need for change than for long-term sustained motivation.

Commitment questions

Goal commitment refers to the strength of the individual's endorsement of his or her goal (Locke and Latham 1990). The benefit of a goal is entirely dependent on the strength of the commitment to it (Seijts and Latham 2001), particularly if the goal is perceived as difficult (Klein et al. 1999).

One method of rating and bolstering commitment is for the coach to ask the client to rate, on a scale from 1 to 10, 'their intention to carry out' the actions to which they have committed (Whitmore 2003). Verbalising commitment is said to increase the likelihood of the person actually carrying it out (Dunbar 2009; Spence 2007). If the client gives a low rating of their likelihood of carrying out an action, the coach should ask 'What was preventing it from being a 10?' A low rating may also suggest that adjustments are required to the goal or plan to render it more accessible. Based on the Rubicon model of action phases (Achtziger and Gollwitzer 2008), we suggested elsewhere (Ives and Cox 2012) that the motivation and commitment questions add volitional strength, which foster the will and determination to implement the goal.

Summary

Desire and effort are both requirements of goal achievement, but while necessary they are not sufficient. Many people invest huge efforts over a long time to successfully achieve what they come to conclude was the wrong goal. Other people struggle to achieve the right goal, but discover after much frustrating effort that they were pursuing it in the wrong way. Then, there are people who – despite pursuing the right goal in decidedly the right way – lack the motivation to implement the plan with sufficient persistence to accomplish it.

The key relationships in our life are of vital significance to us. Success and fulfilment in our close personal relationships bring much happiness; failure and disappointment can be the cause of much upset and misery. In this chapter, we provided some key pointers on how to clarify and set important goals, put in place an effective action plan, and encourage goal-directed motivation. Combined with a strong emphasis on personal development – discussed in Chapter 2 – and effective coaching skills – addressed in Chapter 4 – a relationship coach has the vital means with which to support clients to relationship success.

Chapter 4

Psychological approaches and relationship coaching

In this chapter, we explore some of the psychological theories and approaches that have particular usefulness for relationship coaching. The chapter is divided into three main sections. First, we address cognitive behavioural theory with its focus on how rational thinking can help overcome relationship problems (Williams et al. 2014). Next, we present solution-focused approaches, where the emphasis is on change and results rather than problems, which we suggest has particular application in coaching couples. Finally, we explore attachment theory, initially developed by Bowlby (1951), which is particularly helpful for work with single people and parents to understand how attachment orientations influence our relationship behaviours and, in particular, how we form relationships. Each section provides a case example to illustrate how the theory has been used in relationship coaching settings.

Cognitive behavioural coaching

The cognitive behavioural approach is one of the most popular psychological approaches and is highly relevant to relationship coaching. It is one of the most researched models of therapy, with many studies that validate its efficacy in a therapy setting (Butler et al. 2006). Like coaching, it is integrative, drawing on 'cognitive, behavioural, imaginal and problem solving techniques and strategies within a cognitive behavioural framework' (Palmer and Szymanska 2007: 86).

González-Prendes and Resko (2012: 14–15) explained how cognitive-behavioural approaches are 'rooted in the fundamental principle that an individual's cognitions play a significant and primary role in the development and maintenance of emotional and behavioural responses to life situations'. Cognitive processes 'in the form of meanings, judgments, appraisals, and assumptions associated with specific life events, are the primary determinants of one's feelings and actions in response to life events and thus either facilitate or hinder the process of adaptation' (14). Beck (1976) argued that many psychological problems are not necessarily the product of deep-seated issues, but are rather the result of confused and distorted information and ideas about reality.

The cognitive behavioural approach is premised on three basic assumptions (Dobson and Dobson 2009). Firstly, emotional processes can be known and, with practice, people can become aware of them. Secondly, thinking can mediate the way that we react to our environment; the way people think about their reality can affect our emotions and our behaviours. Thirdly, our thinking can be intentionally focused and modified. When thinking is changed and becomes more rational, realistic, and balanced, problems are lessened and there is increased functionality. Similarly, underpinning cognitive behavioural coaching is the view that feeling and emotions are the product of one's thoughts: a person's perceptions, interpretations, mental attitudes, and beliefs (Auerbach 2006).

These assumptions are evident in rational emotive behaviour therapy, the most commonly used cognitive behavioural strategy. This strategy uses the ABC model proposed by Ellis (1958, 1985; Dryden and Branch 2008) to explore emotional reactions and change behaviours, which was later expanded to the ABCDEF model (Ellis 1985; Palmer 2002; Williams et al. 2014).

In the ABCDEF model, an Activating event (e.g. the end of a relationship) arouses certain Beliefs or thoughts in the client ('I can't ever have a long-term relationship: there must be something wrong with me'), which have behavioural or emotional Consequences that hinder or frustrate the client in some aspect of their life (e.g. the client stops going out to meet people because there is no point or prematurely rejects a partner to avoid getting hurt, as in the case of Gavin below). The client presumes a causal link between the activating event and consequences, whereas with further analysis it can be seen that the link is merely being mediated by the beliefs about the event. The next step is to Dispute or challenge those beliefs, which makes it possible to Effect a change in behaviour. Having overcome the negative belief, this model encourages a spotlight on the Future, where the client focuses learning from the ABCDE process and goes on to set a more positive goal.

Based on Ellis's (1985) work on cognitive behavioural coaching, here are some examples of the kinds of unhelpful thinking a relationship coach may face:

- *All-or-nothing* – Imperfection means total failure: 'My relationship with my child has problems, so it is a disaster.'
- *Overgeneralization* – A single negative outcome is seen as continuous failure: 'My partner sometimes says very hurtful things, so he or she is a nasty person.'
- *Myopia* – Failure to put a negative within a more balanced context: 'Even though the hurtful comments are generally said when my partner has had a stressful day, I see them as typical of his or her attitude.'
- *Exclusive negativity* – Downplaying of positives: 'I don't think it's relevant that my date has some good points; from my point of view, the negatives are what matters.'
- *Mind reading* – Reading negative intentions into others' actions without evidence: 'He forgot to pick up the newspaper for me, which was clearly intentional because he knows how much it winds me up.'

- *Fortune telling* – Predicting a negative outcome without sufficient reason: 'Whatever I do will be pointless, because I know he will only twist it to his advantage.'
- *Catastrophizing* – Exaggerating the importance of a minor event: 'He forgot to give me an anniversary card, which shows that he doesn't even regard himself as married anymore.'
- *Emotion as fact* – Treating negative feelings as evidence of something wrong: 'I hate it when she comes home late. To me, keeping to a schedule is basic. Her lateness is inexcusable.'
- *Unrealistic demands* – Unachievable expectations, leading to anger when not met: 'I know that if he wanted to enough, he would have been able to find the money for that holiday. He just doesn't care enough.'
- *Labelling people* – Rather than having a problem, a person is the problem: 'She is a total disaster, a fashion tragedy on two legs. She is a total embarrassment.'

The coach can help clients to be aware of how they perceive reality through such attribution schemas, preconceived notions, and a particular 'knowledge' of reality, which can hold them back from making things better. Helping the client overcome these maladaptive perceptions should be framed positively as an opportunity to develop. In practice, this means that the coach can work with the client or clients for improved thinking, therefore avoiding actions and interactions that lead to further relationship deterioration and introducing actions and interactions that will serve to build or restore the relationship.

Case study: Rational emotive behaviour coaching

Gavin is a 34-year-old music executive who has had several medium-length relationships. He came to coaching because he was concerned about his failure to hold down a relationship for very long. His successive abrupt relationship terminations have raised significant doubts in Gavin's mind, leading him to shy away from relationships, which has only deepened his sense of despair. The clue to understanding what was going on for Gavin came when he explained the most dramatic breakup, which was also his last. He was – as had become the pattern – already beginning to question whether his then-partner was really suited for him and was becoming increasingly anxious about it. Once, in middle of the night, Gavin awoke in such a state of panic about his relationship that he decided to end it. Since then, he has lost his self-confidence about forming a new relationship. It became apparent from the subsequent dialogue that nothing in the terminated relationship seemed to justify that extreme fright. It began to dawn upon both coach and client that his difficulties in adjusting to the relationship were being interpreted more severely than seemed warranted.

Gavin began to realise that his reactions were the product of his mind registering real concern, which he was not subjecting to reasoned questioning. During coaching, he was encouraged to consider: Was his relationship concern quite that frightening? Was it the case that such legitimate concerns necessitated the relationship to breakup? Was there an alternative reaction that made more sense? Gavin's panic was all too real, but in a sense it was entirely fictitious – based on automatic negative thinking and a muddled process of causation. He began to consider that perhaps a better reaction to his panic would be to question it: 'Why am I panicking? Is it really something to do with the perceived faults of my partner, or something to do with how I react to commitment and loss of autonomy?' Gavin declared that 'coaching has changed my entire thinking' and was convinced that while it may take some time to work things through, he would now challenge his thinking before making such major decisions.

The coaching session ended with Gavin making a future plan to reconnect with a girl he previously knew, renewed in his optimism that he could break the cycle of panic and breakup.

Williams et al. (2014: 43) argued that cognitive behavioural coaching is a powerful intervention 'wherever a client is disturbing or limiting him/herself by unhelpful thinking, or engaging in self-defeating behaviours that undermine their performance'. The authors suggested that it will help clients reduce the tendency to blame others or their circumstances; instead, they begin to accept responsibility for their thoughts and actions and start to own their self-limiting beliefs and habits.

Solution-focused brief coaching

In contrast to the cognitive behavioural approach, the solution-focused approach does not centre on problems; instead, the focus is on helping people construct solutions (Grant 2006). According to de Haan (2008: 220), whereas cognitive approaches are broadly a 'thinking' style, the solution-focused approach is typically more reliant on 'intuition'. There is no emphasis on cause and effect; instead, the approach demands that clients focus only on the desired outcome and what it would feel like to achieve that outcome. It is therefore particularly suitable in relationship coaching situations where couples are often 'at odds' with each other.

Solution-focused brief therapy grew from the clinical practice of de Shazer and Berg and others who were working in the United States in 1980s. Cavanagh and Grant (2014: 52) described how practitioners working at that time found that 'a focus on solution talk, strengths and resources, rather than problem talk, was very effective for a large range of clients' and can be effective for a variety of issues. Follow-up studies in the mid-1980s (e.g. de Shazer and Berg 1986) reported significant success rates where individuals had either met their goals or felt that significant progress was being made. Studies since have supported the effectiveness of the approach when applied to coaching (e.g. Green et al. 2006).

The basic assumptions underpinning the approach is that a small change can lead to a bigger change: once we know what works, we can do more of it. Small changes can be amplified to great effect and result in a broad impact through the effect on the overall person (Jackson and McKergow 2008). It is not necessary for clients to undergo a significant personality change to see meaningful differences in the reactions they elicit from others. Reeves and Allison (2009: 148) confirmed that initial action by the client, even if small, can create the platform for progress and that a single action by the client can yield a strong return.

Solution-focused coaching also involves helping the client to discover solutions based upon their existing skills and prior success. It is not necessary to investigate the causes of problems in order to develop solutions; there will always be exceptions to the problem (days when things are better), and all perspectives are valuable. Pemberton (2006) suggested that the approach aims to develop principles of effective behaviour derived from the person's own evidence – how each person already successfully brings about change in his behaviour. Furthermore, unlike some other types of therapy, the solutions focus does not require an 'expert' position to be taken in relation to the client. Thus, its similarity with coaching can immediately be seen.

Elliot and Harackiewicz (1996) confirmed a fundamental point of solution-focused coaching: focusing on the problem only exaggerates its impact, whereas a focus on finding solutions reduces the crippling effect of the problem and increases the likelihood of a solution being found. Drawing on O'Connell (1998), Grant (2006) suggested that key concepts in solution-focused coaching include the following:

- Use of a nonpathological framework; problems are seen to stem from a limited repertoire of behaviour
- Focus on constructing solutions, rather than trying to understand the problem; future-oriented
- Based on the client's own expertise and resources
- Action-oriented; the client is expected to work on change
- Clear and challenging goal setting
- Short-term; the expectation is that change can occur over a short period
- Personalised; coaching is designed for each person

MacDonald (2011: 85) also identified several key elements from strategic therapy that apply to the solution-focused approach:

- A non-expert stance
- Emphasis on the client's language

- The number of sessions is kept to the minimum necessary
- Change can be small and incremental
- Recognition that the problem and the solution may not be connected

Cavanagh and Grant (2014) suggested that self-regulation is an important part of the solutions-focused approach, where the role of the coach is to assist clients in their journey through a cycle of planning, action, monitoring, evaluation, and ultimate goal achievement.

Techniques for achieving the goal centre on changing how clients perceive the problem (as a problem to be solved) via imagining and planning for a new future without that problem (Jackson and McKergow 2008). Strategies include the following:

- *The 'miracle' question*: Clients are asked to imagine the first thing that they would notice if they woke up tomorrow morning and the problem had by some miracle disappeared forever. It is important to ask clients to focus on how they would feel and what would be different, so that they can become aware of and rehearse the positive feelings. This may be extended to include perceptions of other people.
- *Scaling questions*: Clients are asked to score their progress towards their goal on a scale of 1 to 10. This technique enables the client to mark incremental progress and to recognise and celebrate even small achievements. Such questions may help clients to identify relevant differences that can point to more options for solving or improving a situation.

A less publicised technique is *normalising*, which helps to allay people's concerns that their problem is unusual and insurmountable (Visser and Schlundt Bodien 2009). If their concerns are reframed as normal and it is emphasized that other people also experience such difficulties and overcome them, it helps clients to feel more relaxed and more solution-focused. Acknowledging the problem and the client's response as normal diffuses the situation. In the following case study, George may have felt that his jealously was abnormal and that he therefore had a deep underlying problem. Normalizing helps to stop the problem from escalating into something pathological. By acknowledging the jealousy, George can be helped to relax and hopefully to move on from it.

Cavanagh and Grant (2014: 51) explained that 'deconstructing the chain of cause and effect that led to the current state of affairs, or apportioning blame, is often a waste of time and energy'. In relationships, they suggest, identifying how the problem arose rarely helps us decide how it might be solved. The solution-focused approach is underpinned by the idea that the articulation of causal explanations only constrains the client and the coach in their work together, limiting any potential solutions rather than creating them.

Case study: Solution-focused approach in relationship coaching

Lydia and George had married very young and had a child soon after marriage. George was in the armed forces, so he was sometimes away from the family home for quite long periods during active service. The couple was very happy while the child (George Junior) was a baby and a toddler. Lydia had plenty of army wives as friends and there was an active social life for young mothers. However, once George Junior started school, Lydia felt that she ought to find a job; this appears to be when the problems for the marriage had started. Initially, George joked that he was concerned that his attractive young wife might meet lots of men when he was abroad on duty, while for Lydia the real problem was dovetailing working with being a mother and the tiredness that brings. As time went by, she was often nonresponsive to George's advances because of tiredness, which George began to interpret as rejection. Soon, he started making accusations that Lydia must be being unfaithful; despite her attempts at denial, all of Lydia's reassurances fell on deaf ears.

The couple came for coaching wanting to regenerate their earlier happiness. In the solution-focused coaching that followed, the coach worked with the couple, first asking them each to describe what a really happy day would look like for them (the preferred future). They were asked to respect and listen to each other's answers without interrupting or disputing. Following this, they were asked to recall previous really happy days (past success questions). Lydia and George found it refreshing to focus on the good times, rather than the bickering and silences that had dominated their relationship recently.

The advantage of using the solution-focused approach with couples is that the coach can ask the same question to each partner, and each can listen and begin to understand the perspective of the other. There is minimum focus on problems and thus a reduced chance that partners can get into conflict. They are asked to practice putting the problem behind them and focus on the common goal of being happy again. As a couple, they begin to construct a joint picture of a happy day or reflect together about what was good in the past. They each chose specific small steps that served to reduce tension and build closeness.

Another technique that the coach used particularly successfully in this setting was to ask Lydia to try and overcome the urge to push George away when she felt tired, and for George to resist the temptation to display any jealousy. During this process, both parties have to pay attention to and observe what they actually do when they overcome the urge. This exercise in self-awareness helps them to develop additional self-understanding.

Attachment theory

Attachment theory is a psychodynamic theory that sheds light on the struggles that people face in all kinds of personal relationships and, in particular, offers valuable insights into the difficulties that many single people face in forming and securing lasting relationships. It suggests that our first close relationships give us the template for future relationships, which is then used throughout life to develop our relationships, particularly when we form romantic bonds and later when we become parents. Attachment is a special kind of emotional bond, the need for which is wired into our brain as a survival imperative. The human brain codes isolation and abandonment as danger and the touch and emotional responsiveness of loved ones as safety – a safety that promotes optimal flexibility and continual learning. When attachment instincts are not well-enough formed, a person can struggle to respond constructively to their own and others' emotional needs.

Bowlby (1958, 1973) developed attachment theory by studying the relationship between children and their caregivers. He concluded that children develop two main expectations from their many interactions with caregivers: whether they are accessible and whether they are likely to be responsive. This expectation is based on one or both of the following judgements:

> (a) whether or not the attachment figure is judged to be the sort of person who in general responds to calls for support and protection; (b) whether or not the self is judged to be the sort of person towards whom anyone, and the attachment figure in particular, is likely to respond in a helpful way.
>
> (Bowlby 1973: 238)

These expectations, derived from attachment experiences with a principal caregiver, become internalised as a working model of attachment or a 'generalised attachment representation' (Bowlby 1988). This 'operable' model serves to 'regulate, interpret, and predict both the attachment figure's and the self's attachment-related behaviours, thoughts and feelings' (Bretherton and Munholland 1999: 89). These will typically persist unless new experiences occur that demand an adjustment to the model.

Hazan and Shaver (1987) later suggested that attachment theory could be applied to adult romantic relationships in a variety of ways. First, they showed how, in many respects, romantic partners display similar features in their relationship to that of a child with a caregiver:

- They seek to be close to one another.
- They feel comforted when their partners are present.
- They are anxious or lonely when their partners are absent.
- They provide a secure base that help partners to face life's challenges.

Models of child attachments thus served as a base for understanding attachments later in life, although there are several important caveats to this comparison – most notably that, unlike in adulthood, attachments in childhood are not reciprocal.

Second, Hazan and Shaver (1994) showed how attachment patterns influence the mental representations or schemas that we hold about people and relationships between them. These attachment orientations typically form into 'working models' that persist into adulthood and play themselves out in people's romantic attachments. While adult attachment theorists differ on many points, there is broad agreement on the following:

- The working models that people form about relationships in childhood are relatively stable, such that their close relationships reflect their attachment histories.
- Individuals form relationships based on the expectations and beliefs they have about relationships.
- While working models of attachment are stable, they are subject to change based upon new life experiences and social conditions.
- Problematic attaching orientations can lead to relationship complications, which are sometimes quite debilitating.

Case study: Attachment theory in relationship coaching

Natasha is a 40-year-old woman who is slim, athletic, outgoing, and cheerful. She has seldom been involved in a serious relationship. A male friend described her as ice cold, dismissive of men, and ambivalent about relationships, despite the fact that she firmly asserted that marriage is an important goal in her life. Another friend of hers described her as unreachable and a lost cause in terms of relationships.

From a brief discussion of her relationship history with her coach it emerged that Natasha was uncomfortable getting close to people. She was distrusting of people in general and men in particular, and she had a habit of getting involved in unhealthy relationships with partners suffering from psychological problems. The coach asked her to consider why she thought this was happening, and she tearfully disclosed a painful chapter in her childhood. Natasha perceived that her uncle felt threatened by her, in part because he thought that she showed his daughter (Natasha's cousin) in an unfavourable light. For some years, the uncle would use every opportunity to harangue her and humiliate her. Natasha considered herself strong and resilient and would defend herself against these attacks, telling her uncle that he had no right to behave in this way – but of course, the insults still hurt. However, here is the attachment issue: She would tell her father about the mistreatment she was receiving, and he failed to ever stand up for her. She was told that it was only words and that she knew how to stand up for herself. The result is that Natasha learned that she could not trust people to be there for her, especially men.

Years later, this distrust persists. She cannot overcome the deep sense of abandonment from her caregiver, whom she looked to but who failed to deliver the protection she craved and needed. The mental models she has developed are to expect to be let down. Her attachment orientation is to avoid close relationships, because they are worthless and disappointing. Understanding this and working closely with the coach will help Natasha to explore the way she currently makes meaning and the impact this has. She will then have the tools and the potential to change her perspective and ultimately her response.

A functional relationship provides each party in that relationship with two vital benefits (Johnson 2004):

1. Knowledge that there is a supportive and available partner who provides security – an attachment figure upon whom we feel we can rely offers comfort and reassurance, which in turn reduces our anxiety and mitigates distress at life's difficulties;
2. The safety we need to then go forward with confidence and explore ourselves and the world, including learning new ideas and making changes to ourselves.

Natasha was deprived of a supporting attachment figure during her formative years, leading her to doubt herself and others and rendering her cautious and afraid when venturing into adult relationships. Her reaction to her mistreatment was important in helping her to defend herself at the time, but it now has become an unhealthy defence mechanism against exaggerated threats. Her attachment orientation is so highly avoidant of abusive closeness that it is now 'protecting' her against any closeness.

The process of reworking in Natasha's mind what happened to her as a youngster and connecting that to her grown-up relationship experience achieved two important outcomes. Firstly, Natasha was able to release some of the self-blame and confusion as to why she reacts the way she does to potential partners. This helped her to gain greater confidence about her ability to overcome her issues, given that she felt she now had a plausible explanation for her situation. Secondly, she was able to use her new awareness to question and critique her reactions and, upon reflection, make a conscious choice to not to project onto other people her resentment at being mistreated at the hands of her uncle. Changing a deeply ingrained habit is not easy and normally takes time; but with this awareness Natasha had turned a corner towards greater control over her reactions.

Attachment styles

Based on recent interpretations of attachment theory (e.g. Bartholomew and Horowitz 1991), it may be said that there are broadly four styles of attachment orientations. In this section, we show how these styles can be related to how partners in a relationship negotiate their own needs and those of the relationship (Rahim 1983), including whether they put first their own needs or those of the relationship (Feeney and Noller 1996).

Secure

Secure people find it relatively easy to get close to, trust, and depend on their romantic partners. They perceive themselves as loveable, establish a long-term commitment, and are comfortable that their partner depends on them. They are tolerant of differences and are responsive to their partner's needs. Secure partners express feelings, articulate needs, and are willing to reveal their vulnerabilities. In a relationship context, this person will look to find a way of solving the problem, so that the relationship is not harmed but their own needs are not left behind. They look out for both their interests and that of the relationship.

Dismissing

People with a dismissing style prefer to be self-reliant, neither seeking nor accepting support from their romantic partners, even when this is harmful to the relationship. They maintain emotional distance, struggle to articulate emotional feelings, and are reluctant to acknowledge their need for others. They become anxious with closeness and find trust challenging. Typically, their partners seek more closeness and connection than they are able or willing to provide. This person seems to care little about self or the relationship and in a problem situation will simply withdraw.

People with a dismissive attachment orientation are often controlling of their partners and their relationships. Not only do they generally want to be in charge of every aspect of their partner's life, but feel that they *need* to be. They are desperate to ensure that they are not swallowed up by the relationship. To justify a controlling tendency, they convince themselves that their partner could not manage without them and believe that things would be much worse if they were to let go. Such people take the view that one is either in control or being controlled. They find it difficult to relate to the concept of parity. People with this relationship orientation may be over-competitive, and they are typically poor at compromising.

It may initially be comforting to have a partner take care of everything, but it can soon feel suffocating. Many people will recoil at surrendering all important decisions to the control of another person, and they will reject the idea that someone else always knows better than they do what is best for them.

Anxious

Anxious people are filled with worry and uncertainty about their romantic relationships. They suspect that they will not be loved and supported, and they often demand reassurance – sometimes aggressively so. They can become rather jealous and blaming, and often end up scaring their partner away. While they have a profound need for closeness, they distrust the emotional availability of others. This person cares about his or her own self but not so much about the needs of the relationship, such that they will be aggressive to achieve their goals in the relationship, even if the net result is damage to it.

Those of an anxious relationship disposition are the ones who most often and most intensely fall in love. They are typically characterised as being hungry and needy for love and are highly concerned about their partner's response to them (Hazan and Shaver 1987). A similar pattern was found with people suffering from low self-esteem (Dion and Dion 1975).

When someone experiences acute insecurity in their relationships, they respond with anxiety, possessiveness, and jealousy. Constant fear of losing their partner despoils them of the happiness they could enjoy from the relationship. Ultimately, the continuing pressure for reassurance proves too burdensome for many and they leave the relationship through exhaustion. While initially some people may be attracted to an insecure partner, because it allows them to feel valued and important, when no amount of affirmation is sufficient it leaves the other party feeling frustrated.

Some romantic partners feel the need for constant closeness to their partner and can struggle to function normally when separated from them. It has been called lovesickness (Hindy and Schwartz 1985), limerence (Tennov 1979), and desperate love (Sperling 1985). This can be a totally normal phase for some people at the beginning of a relationship (Hazan and Shaver 1987), but it could be seen as dysfunctional when it persists long-term.

Fearful

Those with a fearful style are ambivalent, desperately wanting closeness on the one hand but being afraid of it on the other hand. They perceive themselves as unworthy of love and are afraid that they will be rejected. Thus, they vacillate between attachment and hostility. To their partners, they appear highly inconsistent and unreliable, seemingly unable to stick to a relationship without escaping, often for contrived reasons. A fearful person will try to do anything to restore calm and will make sacrifices to preserve the relationship, even at the expense of his or her own relationship needs.

People with fear of intimacy are also typically seeking it; otherwise, they would not be in the relationship. What they often do not realise is that they want it and fear it at the same time. Thus, their relationships are characterised by a dynamic of drawing close and pulling away. This kind of dance is often intolerable for the partner who struggles with the inconsistency and volatility of the relationship.

Moreover, fearful people know from their own relationship experiences that they cannot easily handle intimacy, and thus live in constant fear of both increased closeness and the collapse of the relationship. They are both afraid of having the relationship and of not having the relationship, meaning that to anyone but themselves (and often to themselves as well) it comes across as highly confusing and indiscernible. People with this orientation are more likely to be pessimistic about other areas of life, which can be a drain on the relationship (Gunther 2010). This issue only arises once the relationship becomes close, so initially the other partner will have no reason to suspect a problem.

In transactional analysis, Harris (1976) similarly characterised people by whether they think they and others are 'okay', which closely parallels the four relationship orientations:

1.   I'm not OK, you're OK (anxious).
2.   I'm not OK, you're not OK (fearful).

3. I'm OK, you're not OK (dismissing).
4. I'm OK, you're OK (secure).

These four orientations suggest that people's mental models of relationships (frames of reference in Mezirow's terminology) are influenced by two elements: how they generally think of themselves (self-esteem), and how they generally think of others (sociability). Those with secure and dismissive attachment styles typically display higher self-esteem when contrasted with anxious and fearful attachment styles (Bartholomew and Horowitz 1991). People with secure and anxious attachment styles, on the other hand, typically demonstrate greater sociability than dismissive or fearful attachment styles.

Because they emerge within a typically long-term family situation, mental models are generally stable. As the reactions based on these mental models become habitual, they tend to operate entirely outside of conscious awareness, which makes them more difficult to change. Moreover, mental models are continually reinforced through the direct consequences they produce (Feeney and Noller 1996). For example, an avoidant person will trigger responses that will confirm their initial hesitation about relationships. Alternatively, overly anxious people will often fail to get the desired degree of the implausibly high demand for reassurance and connectedness, confirming their original anxiety. Alerting the client to these models can foster transformation. In Chapter 2, we discussed how, during relationship coaching, challenges to thinking can enable a client's outlook to change so that ingrained habits get progressively overwritten: challenging the client's frames of reference enables either sudden or incremental transformation.

In Figure 4.1, we identify some common relationship attitudes and behaviours associated with the four main relationship orientations described above. Clearly, these are generalisations; not all people with the particular attachment orientation will display all of these features or to the same degree. Similarly, it may be possible to shift attachment style through awareness and changes in outlook.

Using this attachment classification during coaching, the coach can help a client recognise how mental schemas foster damaging attitudes and practices. For example, Natasha recognised that she was fearful of relationships. She became aware of how she found open communication stressful, even in the coaching setting. She also shared her confusion that she found the very thought of a relationship as both attractive and a trap. In particular, she considered the idea of intimacy or passion quite frightening.

Relationships between insecure partners may suffer from low levels of supportive behaviours and experience more conflict (Treboux et al. 2004). As we shall explore in later chapters, the attitudes and behaviour that arise from less than optimal relationship orientations can be addressed by raising the clients' awareness to their existence and the impact they may be having. A relationship does not need to be perfect to be effective, so the coach should help the client to ensure that problematic attitudes and behaviours are brought to a sufficiently workable level that does not strain the relationship to a breaking point.

Low	Sociability	High
High		
	Dismissing	**Secure**
	Displays intense criticism and anger Lacks empathy Rarely views others as altruistic, is suspicious of motives Relationships feel threatening to sense of control Compulsive self-reliance Avoids intimacy, engages in casual relationships Perceives relationships as imbalanced Rapidly breaks up relationships	Respects partners space Supports partners autonomy Open about vulnerabilities Expresses feelings Negotiate differences Willing to compromise Willing to seek and accept help Reluctant to break up, but does so if the relationship isn't working
Self-Esteem	**Fearful**	**Anxious**
	Mood swings Feels relationships are not worth the effort Passive withdrawal Low levels of perceived support Fear of closeness Views partner as desirable but unpredictable Perceives others as difficult to understand Negative and pessimistic	Possessive and jealous Sensitive to rejection or blame Highly self-critical, views self as unlovable Low levels of perceived support Compulsive caregiving, idealizing of other Desire for extensive contact and declarations of affections Overinvests emotionally in a relationship Heavily dependent in relationships Break-up involves intense loss
Low		

Figure 4.1 Attachment styles related to self-esteem and sociability

The relationship coach could benefit hugely from a thorough understanding of how attachment issues play themselves out in relationship choice, compatibility, and challenges. Some personality combinations may initially work well, but they begin to suffer later because underlying issues surface. For example, someone with an anxious attachment style may, ironically, work well with a dismissing partner because such a person has a strategy for coping with their demands. However, this balance can be upset when something happens to shake up the relationship, such as illness and loss, which serves to highlight the imbalance that exists in the relationship.

Coaching attachment issues

While attachment theory argues that a person's relationship schemas are stable, research suggests that negative attachment orientations are subject to change for a variety of reasons. Firstly, over time, people's attachment orientation can change as a result of life experiences (Feeney and Noller 1996). Secondly, people may have more than one orientation, each activated depending on the circumstances or the particular individual (Baldwin and Fehr 1995; Baldwin et al. 1996) or triggered by external social cues (Davila and Sargent 2003). Thirdly, adult relationships can influence attachment orientations. Baldwin (1992, 1997) showed how, as adults we continue to develop relational schemas based on the interaction we have with close partners. Depending on what happens during these interactions, we form a view of our own lovability, the lovability of others, and likely responses from close partners. People who have had positive adult relationships are likely to more be at ease when starting a new dating relationship (Carnelley and Janoff-Bulman 1992). Finally, attachment styles may be challenged and adjusted through personal development (Feeney and Noller 1996), in particular through a person gaining increased clarity about their interpersonal style of behaviour and the beliefs and perceptions that gave rise to them (Davila and Cobb 2004).

In the case study of Natasha, we saw how attachment theory was used to raise a client's awareness of the influences of her childhood and how this helped move her forward. Natasha explained how she was reacting in particular ways that she was not aware of; during the coaching session, she began to talk about how there was a 'monster' lurking in her head that would attack any potential partner, reacting to him as if an automatic threat. This 'monster' was ostensibly acting to safeguard her, but it was now becoming apparent to her that it was in fact a major liability. It would take over her persona, preventing the real Natasha from making a more reasoned judgement about the trustworthiness of another. Learning to recognise this reaction and learning alternatives methods of responding was a key achievement for Natasha and allowed her to begin to regain control over her reactions and choices.

Attachment styles learned in a person's formative years can therefore be changed; more secure attachment styles can be adopted, which can reshape how relationships are formed and maintained as well as enable the repair of an existing relationship. Moreover, over time, the learned new orientation can become the person's automatic relationship response (Davila and Cobb 2004). Coaching can help the client develop an adaptive relationship orientation and the practices that flow from that. Coaching can help a client change a damaging cycle of behaviour and discover and adopt effective ways of nurturing a successful relationship.

Contrasting the therapeutic and coaching approaches

Relationship coaching addresses attachment issues primarily by raising awareness about the client's attitudes and behaviours, rather than the therapeutic approach, which focuses on changing emotions (Greenberg and Goldman 2008). Coaching works primarily with cognition (and the resultant behaviours), while therapy works primarily with emotion (and the experiences that gave rise to them). Coaching seeks to harness reason to foster personal development and adaptive behaviour, rather than aiming to transform negative emotions at their root (Greenberg 2004).

Coaching focuses on the regulation of attitudes and behaviours, rather than regulation of the person's deep psychological processes.

While coaching is less suited for enabling what Greenberg (2010: 37) termed 'enduring emotional change', coaching helps people to 'learn to understand that certain emotional or somatic reactions are erroneous interpretations of what is occurring or belong to the past and are now irrelevant' (Greenberg 2004: 6). Coaching helps the client to identify and understand their negative emotions and discover ways of handling them, rather than accessing, venting, or re-experiencing those emotions through therapy. Thus, if a client is experiencing particularly strong emotions, a therapeutic approach is most likely more suitable.

While therapy would tend more towards reducing the unpleasant affect to mitigate its impact on people's reactions, coaching looks to help people understand that their negative affect may not be a reason to avoid something. People can live with negative affect if they realise what is happening. They can often override their instinct to avoid pain if they understand that either it will subside or it is unavoidable. While addressing the emotional issue may be a more fundamental manner of addressing the cause of the problem, it is not always a realistic option.

Similarly, whereas therapy often has as its central activity addressing unfinished business, such as traumas from previous relationships, coaching concentrates on dealing with the current or future relationships. Coaching aims to enable the person to gain clarity around issues and it can help to map out likely consequences, so clients can be aware of their behaviour and why it is happening. Through this, clients can also recognise the triggers of the behaviour and take action to avoid reacting in a maladaptive manner. However, coaching is not designed to address the unfinished business itself.

Another key difference between coaching and therapy lies in the role of the professional helper and the interaction with the one being helped: Davila and Cobb (2004: 151) suggested that the benefits of therapy are most often attributed to the impact of the therapeutic experience itself, including the values of the relationship with the therapist life stress model. By contrast, the benefit of coaching lies mostly in the change to cognition and growth in personal development. Purnell (2004), writing from a psychotherapeutic perspective, argued that the provider of help acts as a secure base from which it is possible to embark on self-exploration. However, whereas in therapy the client–therapist relationship is itself used to develop and model alternatives models of relating, in coaching the emphasis is not on the relationship between the coach and client as the main mechanism for change (Ives and Cox 2012).

Summary

In this chapter, we have considered that relationship attitudes and behaviours are influenced by our perspectives on ourselves and others. We saw how relationship difficulties can emanate from distorted thinking and how a cognitive behavioural approach might help. We also reviewed the use of a solution-focused approach that emphasises constructing solutions rather than unpicking problems. Finally, we explored attachment theory and how parts of the unconscious mind are in constant struggle, also noting how our behaviours and feelings as adults may be rooted in our childhood experiences. We also saw how, by combining these ideas with a coaching approach, significant change can be brought about for the client.

Even though these are established therapeutic approaches, each with its own merits, there is a role for these approaches within coaching to address issues in adult relationship contexts. Coaching typically provides a fairly brief, collaborative, and pragmatic intervention, mostly addressing cognition and behaviours. Its role is not to engage in emotional repair work, although this may result. Rather, it adopts a forward-focused developmental approach to enable people to see how they can improve their relationships. The next chapter will discuss how the relationship coaching process is managed and will address the core coaching skills necessary for effective coaching in this context.

Chapter 5

Relationship coaching in practice

In previous chapters, we set out the theory underpinning relationship coaching. We examined how psychological theory, developmental theory, and a goal-focused approach all contribute significantly and have a particular function within relationship coaching. In this chapter, we bring those theories together in a framework and tease out what relationship coaching is in practice: what skills are needed and what approaches or techniques could be used. Thus, this chapter elaborates a distinct model or framework for relationship coaching built from appropriate theories and models of practice.

The first part of the chapter focuses on the relationship coaching framework and how the elements of theory work together, illustrating this with some case studies. The second section looks at the role of the coach and the relationship with the client built through rapport. The third section then considers the fundamental skills of listening and questioning that are employed during coaching, considering particularly how they are used in relationship settings.

A framework for relationship coaching

The theories and approaches discussed so far in this book can be seen as contributing to a useful way of working with people with relationship issues. The issues may be related to formation of romantic alliances (as discussed in Chapter 6), the enrichment of a continuing close relationship (Chapter 7), or the creation of improved understanding between parents and their children (Chapter 8). We consider that the blend of theories and approaches culminates in a practice that is appropriate for working with many of the issues that singles, couples, and parents face. Figure 5.1 summarises the combination discussed so far in this book.

In the case studies that follow, we demonstrate how the different coaching approaches are integrated in practice. The first case is an example of perspective transformation, achieved by discussing an unproductive attachment orientation and the developmental theory of 'mini-selves' discussed by Bachkirova (2011). The second case draws on the life course development theory of Levinson (1978), where the importance of 'the dream' is emphasised. Again, coaching aims to enhance perspectives and results in a solution-focused plan for achieving a cherished life goal.

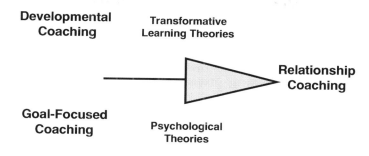

Figure 5.1 A framework for relationship coaching

Case study: Stacey

Stacey is an attractive and intelligent 31-year-old woman, who said her greatest priority in life is getting married and starting a family. She said she has had dates with over a hundred men, around forty of whom were interested in pursuing a relationship with her, but she was disinterested in all of them. Her explanation at the outset of the coaching was that she was 'being set up with the wrong type of people'. During the early stages of coaching, it became clear to Stacey that she may have developed a dismissive attachment orientation (see Chapter 4), perhaps resulting from the callous behaviour of her father, who divorced her mother when she was a very young child. Her father's womanising behaviour may also have led Stacey to distrust men in general. This, she came to realise, led her to think that no man was good enough. Moreover, her father was highly charismatic; consciously or not, she both admired and despised her father and was attracted as well as repelled by men she identified as similar to him. She was in a sense torn by two mini-selves (Bachkirova 2011), each pulling her in a different direction.

For Stacey, thinking about this resulted in what Mezirow (2000) termed an epochal transformation – an 'a-ha moment' – during which her presumptions were disrupted, opening up a key learning opportunity. This enabled the coach to work with Stacey to challenge well-entrenched habits of mind and explore new perspectives. As part of this process, Stacey used critical reflection to re-examine her assumptions about what she was looking for in a partner and the motives upon which she made her judgements. She was now better able to decouple her past traumas from her future choices. To help with reframing relationship attitudes, the coach adopted a cognitive behavioural approach where Stacey was challenged to reconsider her tendency to 'overgeneralise' (men are all good or bad) and her practice of 'exclusive negativity' (some faults mean the person as a whole is no good).

While quite draining for Stacey, the process was also exhilarating. She was now free to date potential partners without being overcome with negative emotions. She now had a clearer goal: to find a partner who was suitable for her healthy, positive self and to prevent the hurt, negative self from sabotaging future relationships.

> Given how deep-rooted are the sources from which the negative feelings come and considering how long these have played themselves out, Stacey needed to create an action plan and a support mechanism to allow her to stay on track as she implemented her new awareness in her dating life. She identified that even with her new-found clarity, making the right choices was still very tough. She therefore agreed with her coach that before making difficult dating decisions, she would call to review. She considered further that this would help her stay on track and not return to her previous patterns of thinking that had not worked for her until now.

Bachkirova (2011) discussed how personal goals, such as the need for confidence or self-esteem, can be detected in the declared issue that prompted a client to seek coaching. These goals can be related back to what she called the 'developmental themes' prevalent in developmental theories – the unformed, formed, and reformed ego (Bachkirova 2011). There thus appears to be a subconscious effort by clients to meet their implicit developmental needs through their explicit articulated goals.

In Stacy's case, it is evident that one part of her (unformed) ego is still being influenced by her father through an unexamined, subconscious process of attachment that holds her back in an important area of her life. Through exploration with a coach and thinking critically, new ways of looking at and understanding the situation have resulted in considerable development and enhancement of her life.

Case study: Neil and Norman

Neil and Norman are both in their late forties. The theme or task for their first coaching session was to rekindle the togetherness that they had when they first met twelve years ago. Since that time, they have grown apart – mainly because work demands pulled Neil to undertake more overseas travel in his role as the European director for a large corporation.

Norman, on the other hand, preferred to be at home, apart from cycling holidays, and had always wanted to find a plot of land for a self-build project. Dissatisfaction and disagreement between them had now increased, especially because Norman had looked at a number of building plots while Neil was on a business trip to Cologne and Hamburg. Norman had also begun drinking every evening and was cycling less – two things that were totally out of character.

In discussions with the coach, Neil and Norman explored how the self-build project was a dream Norman had nurtured since his early adult years. He still longed to fulfil this dream. The coach shared Levinson's (1978) life course theory in the session, with the result that both men realised this kind of aspiration was normal. In further exploration, Neil revealed how his dream was in fact being fulfilled by his work – heading up a large division in his organisation and travelling

> to meet interesting people and see interesting places. He realised that to get in the way of Norman's dream was not fair.
>
> As part of the coaching process, Neil and Norman were able to create a 'perfect future' using scaling questions as part of a solution-focused approach (Jackson and McKergow 2008) and setting out an action plan that would help Norman to achieve his dream while preserving Neil's – and preserving their relationship.

As discussed in Chapter 2, if a dream is not followed, it can manifest as uncharacteristic behaviour, as witnessed in our case study. A combination of life course development and goal theories resulted in the normalising of Norman's lifetime ambition and the recognition by both partners that a plan to achieve the self-build, while supporting Neil's career, would also serve their shared desire for a happy, fulfilled relationship.

Getting to coaching

The core of relationship coaching is working with the client to identify where an obstacle may lie or where an area for personal development may be useful to clear the path towards the goal of relationship success. However, before the main coaching activity can begin, it is crucial to establish the coaching relationship. Under ideal circumstances, this is a simple matter of clarifying expectations, elucidating the aims and limitations of coaching, and making the basic effort of getting to know the preferences of the client. When this contracting goes well, it enables a warm and productive coaching alliance, so that that the proper task of relationship coaching can begin in earnest.

Regrettably, there could be all kinds of reasons why, in practice, establishing the coaching relationship runs into difficulty. While in relationship coaching we may fairly assume that the clients come to coaching voluntarily, this does not mean they appear entirely without compulsion – especially in couples coaching, where one partner may be threatening separation if the other does not agree to some outside intervention. Even when a client is under no pressure to be coached, various resistances may manifest that can present stern barriers to the progress of coaching. Getting to the point where the coaching can begin may require considerable skill, effort, and time (Ives and Cox 2012), and a focus on forging an open relationship between coach and client is then vital.

Relationship with the coach

Coaching is a dyadic relationship; therefore, much depends on an effective connection between the client and coach (Cox 2012a, 2012b). Ensuring an adequate coaching relationship is particularly vital at the outset (Fillery-Travis and Lane 2006) to set the coaching on a sound footing. Ives (2008, 2011) argued that the importance and nature of the coaching relationship varies depending on the coaching paradigm. Within goal-focused coaching, the coaching relationship itself is less central to coaching success than in therapeutic coaching, with developmental coaching being somewhere in between. Relationship coaching is a combination of developmental and goal-focused coaching. Therefore, while rapport between the coach and client is important, closeness is not of the greatest significance. Relationship coaching is often a comparatively short process, and therefore it does not lend itself to the deeper relationship necessary for more therapeutic approaches. Indeed, the deep, long-term relationship required in the psychodynamic approach, where the helper works *'through* the relationship' (Stober 2006: 20, emphasis added), is typically unsuited to coaching.

Furthermore, Bordin (1979) proposed two levels of bond in the therapeutic alliance: a broader, *affective* bond, and a more defined *work* bond, aimed at facilitating goals and tasks. From this account, it would appear that relationship coaching is closer to the goal-focused paradigm. Still, in any form of coaching, the coaching alliance remains a central pillar (Stern 2004; Peterson and Hicks 1996; Wasylyshyn 2003; Cox 2013), as trust and openness are critical. Minimum relationship requirements still involve respect, courtesy, and understanding (Kilburg 1997), but with less emphasis on the more humanistic aspects of relationships such as empathy, authenticity, and unconditional positive regard (Stober 2006).

Relationship with the coaching

Even with a firmly established coach–client alliance, the coaching will falter if the client does not engage with the coaching – if the client fails to 'buy in' to the process. There are numerous possible reasons why a client may be reluctant to engage, a few of which described here.

Negative self-belief

Despite arriving for coaching, it is entirely possible that the client is unconvinced that he or she can be helped. Deeply wedded to pessimism, clients may regard themselves as a hopeless case. For example, they may be driven to seeking help because being in a relationship is a powerful aspiration, but in their hearts, they do not believe it will ever happen. Cognitive behavioural approaches to coaching as described in Chapter 4 would be helpful to challenge and overturn such negative attitudes, which will dissipate the motivation to succeed in both the coaching and real-life relationship work. A developmental need may also be at play here, in that the aspirations of such clients may be influenced by other people (family, peers, etc.) rather than coming from a considered place of self-understanding.

Difficulties Trusting

Some people want to be coached but have difficulty being open about their personal issues. The reluctance could stem from embarrassment or perhaps a fear about confidentiality. Some clients may want to present a positive image of themselves and may be unwilling to be frank about their past relationship experiences. This is especially the case in coaching couples. Coaching is dependent on trust (Cox 2012a), which is the quality most cited by clients as important (Luebbe 2005; Jones and Spooner 2006) and most vital for coaching success (Lowman 2007; O'Broin and Palmer 2009). The coach needs to ensure that the relationship is capable of supporting the demands of the coaching process. Again, a developmental theme could be relevant: openness comes from not taking ourselves too seriously and acknowledging that there may be many different perspectives on the same situation.

Procrastination

Many people who seek relationship coaching have busy and fulfilling careers, and while they profess that investing in a relationship is a priority, in practice it gets squeezed out by other more pressing matters. This is especially true about some single people who are quite ambivalent about their desire for a relationship. The coach may therefore find that coaching sessions are sometimes postponed or cancelled, or that when clients appear for sessions they have their mind elsewhere. The coaching process is operating within the clients' broader context, and apathy may result because clients have other priorities that they cannot seem to juggle effectively. Learning to separate work and play, as well as managing a better work–life balance, may be necessary before clients will feel ready to fully engage in relationship coaching. Clients may consider other matters to be more critical to satisfying their needs, which could lead them, in final analysis, to view relationship coaching as comparatively unimportant. As Flaherty (2005) suggested, if the client's mind is engaged with more pressing matters, coaching cannot function properly.

Indecisiveness

Similar to the foregoing, some clients are highly volatile in their level of commitment to pursuing their relationship goals. Although this indecisiveness plays itself out in their personal relationship activities, it also affects their attitude towards the coaching itself. The coach may start to form the impression that the client is not entirely sure that securing a lasting romantic relationship or enhancing their existing relationship is always that important to them.

Dependency

Some clients are looking for a quick fix, and they come to coaching with the intention of finding it. Such clients are seeking advice, rather than trying to explore. When the coach puts the onus back on the client, this may not be met with great enthusiasm. Such clients want to be told what to do, instead of seeking to gain deeper awareness and enhanced life skills. The coach must ensure that misconceptions about the purpose of coaching and the role of the coach are addressed, and should avoid making assumptions about what clients think is the status of the coach and the purpose of the coaching (Ives and Cox 2012). De Haan (2008) highlighted that the client may bring a range of presumptions and urged the coach to explore the perceived role of the coach.

At the heart of coaching is the need for personal responsibility (Whitmore 2003). To avoid this, clients may resort to blaming others for their current situation, playing the victim, and looking to be rescued. However, relationship coaching is largely nondirective. The purpose of the coach is not to offer advice, but to support clients towards a higher level of achievement. It is the client who 'holds the ultimate responsibility for, and ownership of, the desired outcomes' (Gray 2006: 479). As Flaherty (2005: xviii) put it, coaching 'is not telling people what to do; it's giving them a chance to examine what they are doing in the light of their intentions'.

These and similar resistances are what we call 'barriers to coaching' (Ives and Cox 2012); they do not allow the coaching to begin (Cox 2010; Garvey et al. 2009). Clients either fail to believe the coaching can help them or will not make the effort to give it a try. They may accept they have a problem or issue that requires coaching, but paradoxically they do not accept coaching as a solution. Therefore, establishing the relationship with the coaching is as important as establishing one with the coach. Addressing barriers to coaching can be time consuming (Berg and Szabo 2005) and represent the early work of many coaching interventions (Flaherty 2005; Cavanagh 2006; Jackson and McKergow 2008; Dembkowski and Eldridge 2008); in some cases, it could take up the 'bulk of the time' (Alexander 2006: 63). They are also not unique to the relationship domain. For example, procrastination is a well-known obstacle to weight loss and improved fitness, and dependency emerges in the casebook of many coaches.

Acceptance of coaching as a solution is enhanced when the client sees the clarity that the coaching brings. Commitment to and faith in the coaching process is likely to strengthen as the coaching shows potential for practical improvements.

Underlying issues

Sometimes difficulties in establishing an effective coaching alliance may be due to deep-seated issues that need to be confronted before the core relationship coaching can take place. For example, if the client has very low self-esteem, is still deeply sorrowful due the breakup of a previous relationship, or is riven with guilt because of absence during a parental illness, these issues may well need to be tackled before focusing on developing enhanced relationship attitudes and skills.

Often, although not always, the intervention at this stage will need to be therapeutic in nature. Whether the coach is able to use a humanistic (Stober 2006) or a cognitive behavioural (Williams et al. 2014) approach to addressing these issues will largely depend on previous training and orientation, as well as the requirements of the issues at hand. Although these issues may directly affect the client's relationship, aspirations, and efforts, we argue that this is not the core business of relationship coaching. Unless the coach is suitably trained, these issues are best tackled by referral to a counsellor or therapist as a prerequisite to relationship coaching.

Coaching skills

Numerous coaching texts have addressed the core skills required for coaching (e.g. Whitworth et al. 2007; Starr 2007; Rogers 2008), and we will not provide an exhaustive review here. However, rarely do such texts acknowledge the diverse applications of these skills and the subtle but important alterations required to tailor them to the coaching paradigm and approach. We will therefore briefly summarise the key coaching skills with particular reference to the requirements of relationship coaching.

Rapport building

Some coaches lay great store on building rapport with the client, in some cases making this a centrepiece of their coaching practice. The basis for this position is the view that coaching work is conducted in close and intense interaction between the coach and client, and therefore the quality of that relationship will determine the outcome of the intervention. For certain types of coaching or for some issues this is probably true, but we would argue that relationship coaching's core activities are reasonably pragmatic and nontherapeutic and so the role of rapport should not be exaggerated.

What is clear is that in any form of coaching, 'a successful client–coach relationship is critical to coaching effectiveness' (Boyce et al. 2010: 21). More specifically, the coaching process necessarily requires a trusting relationship in particular to deal with initial resistance, which we have highlighted earlier. Coaching also works because it provides a supportive environment. The client feels he or she can speak the truth rather than cover up for fear of blame or ridicule.

In addition, the coach should show empathy and interest in the client's concerns. Rapport is about giving the client the feeling of being totally accepted (Starr 2007), and it needs to be built and worked on, which is why it is usually necessary to allocate time at the beginning of the coaching relationship to become properly acquainted. This is certainly true in relationship coaching, where the subject matter is often quite personal and clients need to feel comfortable opening up to the coach. Rushing too quickly to 'get down to business' risks alienating clients just when the primary goal is to form a friendly working relationship.

There are several aspects to rapport building. It is important to get to know clients beyond simply to obtain the factual information about the issue at hand. It is likewise important that the coach gets to understand the work and life context of clients, to understand what key forces are acting upon the presenting issue

(Kombarakaran et al. 2008). This is especially true in relationship coaching, where broader information about the person is likely to provide useful clues into the client's character. Clients should be allowed time to talk, especially at the beginning of the coaching. Such informal comments could provide valuable information that may help towards a mutual understanding of the coaching issue.

Rapport is thus about achieving and maintaining a harmonious state in the coaching relationship, 'when the coach and client connect, understand each other's perspective, and appreciate each other as people' (Hart 2003: 5). Hart added that in addition to rapport there is a need for what he termed 'collaboration' (2003: 6), which is when the coach and client work together as equals and exhibit respect for each other's knowledge and views.

It is also important for coaches to take the time to clarify what the coaching will entail and to obtain agreement for the process they plan to facilitate with the client. For example, if a coach expects the client to do 'homework' or undertake neuro-linguistic programming (NLP) exercises, it is best to explain this at the outset. Hart (2003: 6) referred to this as gaining the commitment to the coaching relationship, in which the 'client and coach mutually pledge to follow a course of action to fulfil their respective responsibilities in the coaching relationship, persevere through setbacks, and celebrate successes'. Coaching handbooks (e.g. Starr 2007; McMahon and Archer 2010) emphasise that simple courtesies are crucial to achieving good rapport, such as being punctual and prepared, carrying out promises, and ensuring no interruptions. Needless to say, the most fundamental aspect of rapport is the maintaining of high professional standards, such as respecting confidences and not becoming deflated if clients experience failure.

'Getting into rapport' is an NLP term (Zamfir 2011) for the process of breaking down barriers that may prevent optimal communication. People have vastly different ways of experiencing and therefore understanding the world. For example, people may have a visual, auditory, or a kinaesthetic preference. The client will be providing clues as to their preferences, personality, strengths, and limitations. It is argued that people like people who are like them, and that fitting with the client's styles helps to gain trust and understanding. While it is true that the better the perception of the client, the better the coach is able to actively get into rapport, it is by no means essential for a relationship coach to have mastered these techniques to be able to establish adequate rapport with the client.

However, even without categorizing the client into one type or another, there are simple techniques that the coach can adopt to send subliminal messages that he or she is in tune with the client. Discreetly mirroring and matching the client's mannerisms helps put the client at ease and make him or her feel understood (Dembkowski and Eldridge 2003). It can be done by matching pitch of voice, pacing the speed of the clients' talk, and matching complexity and length of sentences. Critchely (2010) even addressed what he termed 'psychogeography', such as the optimal level of proximity to the client and the angle and positioning of the coach.

The limits of rapport

It must be emphasised, though, that while ensuring effective rapport is crucial, coaches must not be so afraid of losing rapport that they avoid challenging the client (McLeod 2004). Handling rapport is about knowing when it is appropriate to push and when not – creating the optimal level of stretch for the progress of the client. Coaching is intended to stretch the client beyond his or her comfort zone to generate learning and growth (Kemp 2006; Cox 2013; Cox and Jackson 2014; Reeves and Allison 2009). Cavanagh (2006) stated that coaching seeks to help clients 'maintain themselves at the border between chaos and sameness – a place complexity theory calls the "edge of chaos"'. Coaching then seeks a 'sustainable instability' or a 'dynamic equilibrium' (Haines 1998; Stacey 2000), a 'bounded instability' that seeks sufficient flexibility to sustain growth and change, while preventing breakdown and chaos (Cavanagh 2006: 319).

As a developmental approach, relationship coaching should not shirk from challenging clients to address issues vital to their development. Hart (2003: 6) similarly argued that developing the relationship is not the end goal:

> If the coach does not use the relationship to turn the client's attention to his development and performance, then the client may make little progress, achieve minimal results or not be sufficiently challenged on substantive issues. Moreover, if the coach becomes overly invested in maintaining a harmonious relationship or the relationship becomes too personal, the coach may find himself [or herself] reluctant to challenge the client.

We concur with McLeod (2003, 2004) that, contrary to the view of some who think that rapport is focal to the coaching intervention, in fact the main value of rapport is in helping to establish an effective coaching alliance. At times, the coach needs to risk being less popular to push clients forward to achieve their potential. Asking challenging questions could weaken rapport, but this is sometimes a risk worth taking (McLeod 2010). As Greenleaf (1996) pointed out, rapport is needed as a bedrock to enable the coach to constructively challenge a client, so it should not be used as a reason to avoid it. Borrowing from attachment theory (Bowlby 1969), we may think of rapport building as establishing the secure base from which the coaching can go forth in the confidence that the adventure is backed up by a firm relationship. In our view, rapport is established in large part by addressing the barriers to coaching discussed in the previous section.

Transference and countertransference

Coaching itself may be the forum in which some of the client's relationship dynamics are played out. Lee (2014: 23) suggested that understanding transference is one of the ways in which coach and client can begin to explore 'potentially limiting interpersonal strategies'. Transference occurs when we transfer learning or habits unconsciously from one context to another. For example, people often respond to senior management people in their organisation in the same way as they did to their teachers, or they interact with partners in the same way as they did with their parents. This transference can also extend to the coaching relationship itself. Countertransference relates to the behaviours and feelings that can arise for the coach in the coaching session, such as when the coach responds to the client's behaviours, from their own unconscious.

In transference and countertransference, habitual responses are restimulated and projected into other current relationships. How the other person in the relationship reacts is often to counter the response with a similarly unconsciously driven reply, and this continued re-enactment can significantly affect the coaching relationship. Therefore, it can be useful for the coach and the client to be aware of where transference and countertransference are occurring. In relationship coaching, attachment or transference are merely noticed in existing relationships, not expected to be explored in depth as part of the coach–client relationship.

Listening

Effective listening skills are vital for establishing trust (Skiffington and Zeus 2003; Rogers 2008), whereas poor listening appears uncaring (Goleman 1998; Cox 2013). Listening begins with silence; while we talk, we cannot listen. Silence creates the space in which another can speak. Effective listening includes clearing one's mind of external and internal stimuli to allow full concentration on what another is saying. Instead of listening to our own inner dialogue, our response to what we hear, we surrender our mind solely to hearing what the other person is saying. In fact, Pemberton (2006: 74) distinguished between type A and type B listening. Type A listening is 'where the listener signals that they are giving the other person their full attention'. In relationship coaching, it is necessary to have Type B listening, which picks up on emotions, personality, and beliefs. This advanced listening 'is focused on understanding what extra information the other person holds that could be helpful to the conversation, which they may not articulate' (Pemberton 2006: 82). Furthermore, the coach needs to adopt a posture of 'not knowing' (Anderson and Goolishian 1992), in recognition of the reality that he or she most likely does not know what the client is thinking or what is best for him or her.

Silence is important not only when the client is talking, but also when the client is thinking. Greene and Grant (2003: 128) urged the coach to 'hold the silence', and resist the temptation to break pauses. If unsure whether the client needs the question to be repeated or explained, the coach should consult before rushing in. Silence gives the client the time to reflect and dig deeper for fuller and more meaningful answers. Respecting silence will also put the client at ease.

Whitworth et al. (2007: 34–39) distinguished three incremental levels of listening:

1. *Internal listening* is concerned with the content of speech, whereby the coach is listening to guide the next question.
2. In *focused listening*, the focus is totally on the client. The listener reflects back what comes from the client and is also aware of the impact the listening is having on the client.
3. *Global listening* involves being observant of the full range of body language and mood alterations.

Given the sensitive nature of what is being addressed in relationship coaching, the coach should strive to manage all levels of listening to ensure the coaching is calibrated to the emotional experience of the client. Hawkins and Schwenk (2010: 208) listed four increasing levels of listening, which have some overlap with the levels described above: attending, accurate listening, empathic listening, and generative empathic listening. We propose that empathic listening is more suited to therapeutic forms of coaching that seek to garner insight into the psychological state of mind of the client (Cox 2013). In fact, we suggest that only in therapeutic coaching is it necessary for the coach to convey that he or she '"got" what it feels like to be in their situation', as Hawkins and Schwenk (2010: 206) argued.

Cox (2013) claimed that the empathic approach is essentially reproductive, whereas coaching should be seen 'a "production" or an "authoring", where meaning is created through what two people (client and coach) bring to the alliance'. She claimed that this type of listening would offer clients 'an experience of their paradigms as constructed realities as opposed to absolute reality' (Cox 2013: 58). Cox's notion of authentic listening is seen as the more congruent approach for use in coaching because it is openly and mutually interpretive.

Active and holistic listening

Active listening gives the client the *experience* of being 'listened to', making the client *aware* of the listening and a feeling that the coach values the listening experience (Brockbank and McGill 2006; Cox 2013). Active listening has two main features. First, it involves adopting postures and making gestures that demonstrate that we, as listeners, are fully engaged – what Hawkins and Schwenk (2010: 208) termed 'attending' – including eye contact, focused attention, and verbal and hand gestures that encourage open communication. Second, it means ensuring that we have been listening correctly, that we understand the message of the client by summarising and reflecting back to the client (Collins and O'Rourke 2008). Passmore and Whybrow (2007: 165) called this 'reflective listening', where 'the coach checks, rather than assumes, the meaning of what the client has said'. This ensures both that the coach understands correctly and that the client feels understood.

The coach should also exert what Mason (1993) termed 'authoritative doubt', which involves taking the risk of venturing an interpretation of the client's words while leaving it wide open for the client to correct or clarify. Rosenberg (2003) proposed a similar approach as a compassionate form of communication.

Holistic listening (Rowan 1986) goes further still, involving looking out for verbal and nonverbal clues, such as changes in tone and language patterns: a monotone may indicate repetition of old ideas, excitement usually suggests the emergence of a new idea, negative terms indicate disbelief, while childish language could mean lack of confidence. Body language is also a good indicator and is a more reliable source of information about how clients are feeling than possibly their words (Ives and Cox 2012). During phone coaching, it is even more vital to attend to verbal cues. If the client has to ask, 'Are you still there?' then the coach has failed to listen sufficiently actively.

It is also necessary to listen for what is not being said, such as underlying emotions (Collins and O'Rourke 2008), 'awareness of the feeling behind the words, and sharpening ... sensitivity to the context of the conversation' (Whitworth et al. 2007: 33). Finally, active listening should include encouraging and motivating of the client by exuding a spirit of positivity and confidence in the client, what we have termed 'authoritative belief' (Ives and Cox 2012).

Questions

In coaching, questions are asked in order to stimulate deeper thought, foster creative ideas, and raise awareness. There are no right or wrong answers – only honest and dishonest ones (Whitmore 2003). Questions in relationship coaching are intended to raise client awareness, as they 'enable the client to explore the situation from different standpoints and generate new perspectives and possibilities' (Hawkins and Smith 2010: 239). Questions also aid clarity; they are 'the precision tools in the coach's toolkit' (Bresser and Wilson 2006: 18). However, in relationship coaching, questions are also expected to stimulate deeper reflection. 'Insight-driven questions' such as 'If you were to change your view of the current situation, what would that allow for?' and 'What may be possible if you were to make the change you are describing?' prompt clients to rise beyond self-limiting beliefs and thought processes (Kemp 2008: 42).

De Haan (2008) distinguished between 'what' type questions, which are technical or objective in nature and can be supplied by a mentor or expert; 'how' type questions that address the application of skills to specific situations, which is the main domain of coaching; and 'who' type questions, which deal with the personality of the individual. Relationship coaching will use all of these types of questions at various stages of the coaching process.

Drawing on Argyris and Schön's levels of learning, Skiffington and Zeus (2003) described three types of questions. Single-loop questions, they suggest, are those that explore issues at a superficial level. They concentrate on the actions clients perform to resolve a problem. Double-loop questions look at deeper assumptions in order to question why a situation has occurred and what factors may have contributed to them. Triple-loop questions explore the underlying values that shape the client's sense of being that guides choices. Again, all three types of coaching are appropriate in relationship coaching. Triple-loop questions will challenge meaning perspectives and encourage development and thus are powerful in the relationship context.

The purpose of asking a question is to create an opening for the client to explore his or her thoughts; therefore, the best questions are generally those that leave the widest space for the client to examine his or her own opinions and experiences. However, in relationship coaching, questions must also be used to challenge the client's assumptions. Questions therefore can at times be proactive and robust.

Questions may therefore be used for the following purposes:

- *Clarifying the goal* – Is seeking a committed relationship a current priority? Is perhaps the client acting under pressure (internal or external)? What exactly is the goal? Does the client know what he or she is looking for?
- *Synchronising the goal* – Does the goal fit with other goals the client has? Does it accord with the client's own values and other life priorities?
- *Planning action* – What choices are available to the client? Has the client truly considered all options? What are the preferred methods and are these also likely to be the most effective?
- *Securing motivation* – Is the client ready to put in the work and make the effort required for success? Will the client be motivated to keep going outside of the coaching session?

Questions are building blocks for both the coach and the client to progress to ever greater awareness. Small questions provide input to be used to generate broader and deeper questions. As Cox (2013: 109) explained, 'a seemingly small question may turn out to be influential in generating a larger, more important question later in the coaching sequence'. The purpose is not to aid the awareness of the coach per se; rather, the evolution of the coach's understanding serves exclusively to help the client rethink their understanding.

Relationship coaching is primarily developmental and therefore attaining knowledge is a key objective; thus, questions should be designed to generate maximum insight. Questions are the key method of stimulating perceptual reorganisations. They do this by generating a desire for greater clarity and by drawing attention to the current ambiguity, thereby triggering an interest in closing that gap. Before the question is asked, the client may only be aware of his or her dissatisfaction with the current situation and not be aware at all of any lack of clarity. However, questions 'stretch' the clients (Grant 2006; O'Neill 2000), widening their purview to incorporate aspects hitherto overlooked. Questions help clients to form a picture of their current reality as well as imagine a new one, thus closing what we might call the 'dissatisfaction gap'.

Types of questions

The coach needs to maximise the thought-provoking qualities of a question and avoid questions that deprive the client of the full benefit of asking. In our view, there are three main criteria for questions in relationship coaching:

1. *Short and simple* – Long-winded or multipart questions are confusing, and the client will often struggle to remember the first part of the question. Questions should also be specific, as this attracts a more detailed response and generates a higher level of attention.
2. *Open questions* – As Whitmore (2003: 44) suggested, 'Telling, or asking closed questions, saves people from having to think; asking open questions causes them to think for themselves'. Open questions provoke fuller responses and exploration of the issues and, importantly in coaching, allow for a follow-up question. Open-ended questions encourage speculation and offer greater potential for shared thinking. However, during action planning, closed questions can be used to tie down the client to a specific action and times, so they are useful when following up on goals.
3. *Challenging* – Questions help the client to piece together a coherent understanding of what is really going on for them. Querying the cause, motivation, or consequences of relevant events in the client's life help probe below the superficial layer of reality to help gain a more profound understanding (Graesser et al. 1995). While 'why' questions can be understood to indicate disapproval (Sintonen 2004), and some coaches have cautioned against their use (Brockbank and McGill 2006; Nicholson et al. 2006; Berg and Szabo 2005), when carefully and selectively used, they stimulate challenge and reveal assumptions that need to be uncovered (Cox 2013).

Whereas with some forms of coaching asking leading questions would be considered unacceptable, in the case of relationship coaching we propose that the situation is more complex. We distinguish between 'rhetorical' questions and 'guiding' questions: Rhetorical questions are not questions at all, as they only invite a prescribed 'answer' (e.g. 'I suppose you're sorry now?'). Such questions are widely acknowledged to be inappropriate in coaching (Nicholson et al. 2006; Hawkins and Smith 2010). By contrast, 'guiding' questions are used to draw attention to seeming inconsistencies in the client's thinking (e.g. 'You've told me that you often keep him waiting. How do you think he feels about that?').

Although relationship coaching uses factual questions to gather relevant information stored in the client's memory that is useful to informing the coaching process, it primarily uses conceptual questions that are largely creative and call upon the client to imagine possibilities that are not currently a reality. Some factual questions are quite probing, as they ask clients to draw deeply on the inner recesses of the mind to recall rarely accessed data about themselves or their environment. For example, the coach may ask 'What was it about Lucy that most attracted you?' This is a question that does not get asked on a day-to-day basis, and it may require some serious thought and reflection, requiring higher-order memory processes in order to answer it (Munch and Swasy 1983).

Factual questions include what Tomm (1988) termed 'lineal questions' (which seek clearly defined causes of explanations of actions, events, or feelings) or 'circular' questions (which explore recurring patterns rather than lineal causality). These may include some closed or 'why' questions to enable the coach to clarify a chain of events relevant to understanding the client's situation.

By contrast, conceptual questions ask clients to contemplate unknown situations. For example, a coach may ask, 'What do you think would happen if you told him how you feel?' Here, the client is being asked to 'speculate' on the likely reaction to a course of action, which cannot be answered purely factually. Or a coach may ask, 'What obstacles might you meet if you reached out to your daughter?' to pre-empt challenges the client is likely to face. The answers to such questions are more tentative and therefore cannot be backed up with the same certainty as answers to factual questions; closed and 'why' questions are therefore generally unsuited to this line of questioning.

In Tomm's (1988) classification, 'strategic' questions build on the information revealed by answers to lineal or circular questions; they generate predictions to aid planning a future course of action. More conceptual still are what Tomm called 'reflexive' questions, which marshal the client's problem-solving resources by allowing clients to reflect on their beliefs and reframe their thoughts. In relationship coaching, reflexive questions are used to help clients explore their perspectives and to ensure they have the internal resources to go forward.

Incisive questions encourage creative thinking when the client is stuck. Bramson (1984: 123) suggested the use of what he termed 'detours', which suspend the negative view for long enough for the positive view to avoid suffocation. An example of creating a detour in a coaching scenario is for the coach to say something like, 'I realise that this probably won't be what we'll end up with, but could we take a few minutes to see if there may be anything useful there at all?' Incisive questions ask the client to suspend judgement and to think uninhibitedly.

Summary

In this chapter, we began by exploring how the different theoretical underpinnings of relationship coaching work together in practice. We presented two case studies that illustrated these theories in action. We also discussed how relationship coaching can only begin in earnest once clients have embraced the coaching process and have overcome any barriers stopping them from taking ownership of the situation, such as procrastination or indecisiveness. We examined how rapport enables an open and exploratory coaching alliance to be formed, and how in this way clients are comfortable being open and sharing their thoughts, their hopes, and their ideas. This discussion included mention of transference and countertransference as ways in which rapport can be interrupted. We concluded the chapter with an examination of the two key techniques used in all coaching – listening and questioning – and suggested how different approaches to listening and questioning can be used to different effects both for the attainment of goals and the development of the client.

Chapter 6

Coaching single people for relationship success

Some single people make a choice to remain independent. However, many singles invest incredible efforts, time, and money into finding a life partner. Many are in great distress as this goal eludes them. Society does not help such people by telling them that they are fine unmarried and that they do not need a spouse to be happy or fulfilled.

A relationship is not just something that happens to us; our thoughts and actions play a decisive role in how we experience relationships and how we participate in them. That is why David Steele (2007: 68), an experienced relationship coach, advised: 'If you're single and would prefer to be in a fulfilling relationship, I believe that the most important question for you to ask yourself is, "Why are you single?"' By 'why?' he means, 'What is getting in the way of your relationship?' This chapter is designed to help coaches to work with clients to identify what is getting in the way of a relationship and what needs to be addressed to maximise the chances of relationship success. As relationship expert Randi Gunther explained (2010: 1):

> Much of the time, relationship saboteurs are left confused, not knowing what they have done to cause their partners to pull away. Because the saboteurs don't understand what happened, they are likely to repeat the same undermining behaviours upon entering a new relationship.

Therefore, this chapter will consider how coaches can assist clients in what Creasey and Jarvis (2009: 296) called 'the way' people initiate relationships.

As a relationship coach, Yossi reports often hearing singles make disparaging generalisations about the opposite gender, such as 'Why are all men so inconsiderate?' or 'Women are so demanding'. Not only do such prejudices have no justification, but coming into a potential relationship situation with this perception is likely to inject undue pessimism and negativity. If we expect rejection, we are less likely to try; we deselect ourselves to avoid others having the opportunity to do so. However, simply telling someone to replace a negative thought or attitude with a positive one is generally pointless, and changing such thought patterns can be extremely difficult.

There is also something highly paradoxical about relationships, insofar as they typically begin as a selfish act. A single person is seeking his or her own happiness, but for it to culminate in a lasting commitment, it must result in a selfless love of another. Moreover, the idea of dating is highly 'acquisitional', whereby typically a person seeks exclusivity over another person; the dating individual seeks to make the other person 'theirs' – 'my boyfriend' or 'my fiancée'. It is rare for someone to date another in order to make the other person happy; dating is a pursuit of self-happiness. Somehow, this selfish act has to transform into a comparatively selfless relationship, in which each seeks the happiness of the other. The exact method by which this happens is unimportant for the purposes of this chapter; it is relevant to know, however, that there are several reasons why this process can get blocked. Where there is a blockage, it could halt the progress of the relationship – or worse – it could break down the relationship altogether. When the people involved are aware of the blockage, it usually can be resolved – sometimes quite easily. However, when this awareness is lacking, the relationship may face a crisis.

The chapter begins by outlining a model for coaching with single people. Following this model, we introduce a number of case examples that illustrate the types of issues facing single people and how a coach might work with the client to address these.

The GREAT coaching model

As a framework for relationship coaching with singles, we propose the GREAT model (shown in Table 6.1) as an informed expansion of the GROW model popularised by Whitmore (2003). This model acknowledges the importance of goal theory. As is true for most coaching models, the stages are not strictly linear and, depending on the situation and the style of the coach, some stages may overlap and interact. In almost all scenarios, coaching is an iterative, cyclical process, in which the various stages repeat themselves as the client progresses towards achieving his or her goal.

Table 6.1 The GREAT coaching model

G – *Goal*	Setting a general and a specific goal; together with any necessary exploration
R – *Reality*	Understanding the current state of play and what has gone on in the past
E – *Exploration*	Gaining a deeper understanding of the client's experiences, perspectives, and attitudes and teasing out the learning from this
A – *Action plan*	Identifying what the client can now do differently and the preparation for creating strategy
T – *Take action*	Implementing a new strategy

A brief description of each stage now follows.

Goal

As noted in Chapter 3, the process of goal setting may often involve two distinct stages (Ives and Cox 2012): the first to clarify a general goal (e.g. whether the client desires to be in a relationship) and the second to identify a more specific goal (e.g. what kind of relationship). Setting the goal at the optimal level of specificity, difficulty, and proximity ensures the goal is most achievable. It is also vital that the goal is consistent with the core values of the client, which can be a complex challenge because the client may have conflicting value sets that have never been explored or resolved.

Reality

Relationship coaching focuses on past events to the extent necessary to plan for the future. It delves into the past only to form a coherent picture of the client's challenge. As a learning approach, relationship coaching draws heavily on understanding the lessons from past experiences, so the coaching requires a thorough fact-finding activity to clarify what has gone on until the present. This stage brings key information to the fore for the client, it directs attention towards facts and away from negative emotions, it enables the coach to get a reasonable understanding of the client's situation, and – crucially, by listening carefully and without judgement to the client's story – to build trust and rapport, which sets the platform for the important coaching work to follow (Whitmore 2003).

Exploration

The coach will be asking quite probing and challenging questions to help the client understand the possible underlying reasons for choices made and the key events in his or her relationship life. Instead of brainstorming for options, at this stage coaches might brainstorm for lessons from past experiences. This is what Goodman (2002: 138) called 'asking for meaning'. Some coaches will find that, part way through the reality stage, they already are finding useful and meaningful 'exploration' questions to ask. We recommend, in keeping with many other coaching texts, to allow for the reality stage to be given due time in order to build trust and gain a complete picture before pressing forward with more robust exploratory questions. In coaching, the order always is listen – then ask.

While the exploration stage may throw up numerous interesting and valuable areas for growth and change, it is the purpose of coaching to zoom in on where the 'issue' lies. The coach is looking to work with the client to understand where the 'blockage' is to enable progress (Peterson 2006). As noted in Chapter 2, learning can occur in a transformational moment, but it may also involve several iterations as the client internalises the insight from the abstract to the practical. To aid this process, the coach may ask the client to maintain reflective and observational logs, experimenting with problem-solving or communication patterns.

Action plan

The aim of relationship coaching is not enlightenment, but enhanced capability to form and secure a lasting relationship. An action plan specifies what changes in attitude and behaviour the client can make. The plan may include additional reading and learning or skills development, as well as practical steps, as we shall see later in this chapter. This is an experimentation process, whereby ideas are tested 'in the field' and the learning is fed back into the coaching process. The coach guides the client towards a forward-focus, directing attention towards the levers over which the client has a measure of control to affect desired outcomes. Working on an action plan reflects the strong commitment to prioritise envisioning and acting to create a better future, and crucially not being dragged down by past frustrations. While the client determines what goes into the action plan, the coach provides valuable insight into planning effectively and offers vital encouragement to adopt adequately stretching goals (Ives 2010).

Take action

Having established credibility and trust, the coach must hold the client accountable for the actions to which he or she is committed. Often, the client will fail to implement the plan as agreed or will do so only in part. The role of the coach is not to become despondent, but rather to view this as a further learning opportunity and to support the client in finding more effective ways of succeeding in implementing the plan (Rogers 2008). Coaching should address if the client is making the desired progress, whether that is in terms of awareness, new skills, or greater relationship success. Furthermore, it has been our experience that the client will often want to come back to the coach to review the situation. Future coaching sessions would provide the opportunity to revisit previous attitudes to explore how they may have changed and whether any adjustments or skills have been sustained.

Relationship issues

We now highlight some key relationship issues that singles may need to address along their relationship pathway. By generating greater understanding about these challenges and their manifestations, we hope to help relationship coaches to work with their clients to uncover the origins of relationship difficulties. We shall expand somewhat in describing these issues, as we view a good grasp of issues singles face to be critical to providing a truly beneficial service.

From the work Yossi has done with singles, it can be concluded that while each person and situation is unique, usually familiar patterns appear. Although it is possible for someone to struggle with a variety of issues, experience suggests that a client will normally have difficulty with one area in particular. Later, we explain that while these issues can emerge at any stage of the dating process, experience to date suggests that they typically appear at different stages.

If it is a different thing going wrong each time something goes wrong, we would probably explain each event as an unfortunate occurrence, each unrelated to the other. When, however, events repeat themselves, we are more inclined to consider that they are connected to a single issue. The role of the coach is to help to identify patterns and to help clients to recognise such patterns. Here, as in all coaching, the coach walks a tightrope. Clients may view their relationship disappointments as unfortunate let-downs from badly behaved partners, whereas the coach may recognise a common thread that leads back to the approach adopted by the client. It is the role of the coach to gently raise the awareness of the client towards greater clarity and a sharpened perspective. When the client is helped to observe a common thread running through their relationship experiences, they normally readily acknowledge it and are relieved to understand why they have experienced such difficulties.

Peterson (2006) presented a constraint model of coaching, whereby coaching is intended to help the client navigate the pipeline towards attainment of a goal. Any constraint or bottleneck in development in one part of the pipeline impedes progress towards effective implementation. Coaching needs to focus on widening the bottlenecks to enable the client to progress, although new bottlenecks may appear further down the line. This is a useful way to think of the role of the relationship coach in a singles context: to help the client to identify where there is a bottleneck in their relationship development. While a client may struggle with more than one constraint, and while constraints may differ depending on the personality of the client's dating partner, many clients will find themselves repeatedly stuck on the same issues.

While issues can arise at any stage before, during, or after the dating process, it may be that they are more typical at particular stages, in the order in which they are presented below. This framework offers a useful tool for the relationship coach to consider where the client's issue lies and how best to help the client.

Impatience and anxiety

Some people have an anxious attachment orientation, leading them to feel insecure in relationships (see Chapter 4). This sense of vulnerability feeds a heightened anxiety that stimulates obsessive or clingy behaviour that can be very damaging to relationships. Anxiously attached people may be unaware of their relationship orientation and the practical consequences thereof, and they are oblivious to its impact on their partners. A barrage of text messages, phone calls, and emails may appear loving and caring, but to the recipient such attentions can feel suffocating. Demands for explanation about a partner's every move may be ostensibly motivated by intense interest in their lover but can be experienced as highly intrusive nonetheless. It is in the nature of the anxious single that when they meet someone they are really interested in, they rush in full force, throwing their heart and soul into the relationship, often oblivious to the pace of their overwhelmed partner. People with an anxious attachment orientation are strong at fostering a sense of closeness and intimacy, but they struggle to allow appropriate autonomy and self-sufficiency (Johnson 2004).

Kevin, a 31-year-old accountant, came to coaching both hurt and perplexed, as yet again a seemingly promising relationship had crumbled. Kevin started dating comparatively late in life, having struggled to emerge from the domination of overbearing parents. He brought some of those attachment issues into his dating life, typically throwing himself headlong into any relationship that seemed to hold some promise. While initially his partners would bask in the attention showered upon them, Kevin began to realise that they soon started backing away. To Kevin, this was profoundly hurtful because he felt that not only he but also his loving nature was being rejected. Kevin did not realise, as Gunther (2010) explained, that flooding a partner with affections and over-intense interest ceases to be endearing and can feel exhausting and overwhelming to the other party, who soon becomes 'burned out'.

Kevin was therefore finding himself entering and leaving relationships in quick succession, as partner after partner backed off from his attentions. The coach helped Kevin to become aware that this was happening and encouraged him to take action to set appropriate limits on the number of interactions he might have with a future partner, to be more cautious about asking intrusive questions, and to create a support mechanism for controlling anxiety-driven impulses.

Kevin needed to learn to set and indeed respect clear boundaries. For example, if his girlfriend asks to go slow, it is unwise and intrusive for him to turn up unannounced at her work with flowers. The coach was able to assist Kevin to gain increased awareness about what was happening and why, in order to enable him to manage his personality. Someone with an anxious relationship style is also prone to scrutinise and overanalyse aspects of the relationship. Small variations in their partner's communication (e.g. signing off an email with 'Best' instead of 'Love') can become an occasion for a complete postmortem. Such behaviour can alienate the partner, who feels interrogated. Some partners complain of too much intimacy, which they feel can be suffocating (Mashek and Sherman 2004) – something that men in particular cite as a major cause of relationship dissatisfaction (Collins and Read 1990; Simpson 1990).

Singer Taylor Dayne pleaded, 'Don't rush me, this love could be so much more, it's well worth the waiting for'. Yet, in an age of fast food and instant coffee, we are often prone to impatience when trying to form relationships – an issue that can be exacerbated by loosening sexual mores and the introduction of online dating. Technology has transformed the dating experience of many singles. However, while the explosion in online dating has enabled us to connect with thousands of potential partners with a few clicks, this ease of dating has only exposed the challenge of forming relationships. New technologies may alter how we date, but not how we fall in love. The rapid march of digital technologies have outpaced what Foucault (1988) termed 'technologies of self'. Rosen (2008: 149) suggested, 'What we need to do is create new boundaries, devise better guideposts, and enforce new mores for our technological age'.

With the pervasive use of technology in finding and relating to a partner, it can be more difficult to establish effective boundaries. Instead of abiding by basic technological etiquette, some lovers bombard their partners with phone calls, send excessively intense emails pouring out all their fears and emotions, or inundate their partners with text messages recording their every move. Rather than fostering closeness, it can be more likely to alienate a partner. For someone like Kevin, with an anxious relationship disposition, technology offers a potentially irresistible invitation for its misuse. Some people report that they have received irate phone calls from their partners, stating, 'It's already twenty minutes since I sent you my text and you haven't responded. Why are you ignoring me?' Singles therefore may need support in acting smart on their journey to relationship fulfilment along a road replete with relationship potholes.

Internet dating affects how we date in another important way. We have been offered the promise of leveraging technology to instantly hit upon the perfect mate. If only it were so! When hoping that the science of psychology will bring us the ideal partner, we can become discouraged from taking greater personal ownership for building relationships.

Jerome, a 34-year-old sales director, was often travelling and turned to internet dating as a way to meet a partner. After two years using a couple of websites, he found that he was no closer to meeting someone suitable. It emerged during coaching that he was making snap judgements based exclusively on the most cursory glances at people's profiles. He at first justified this on the basis of his busy lifestyle, but through coaching Jerome came to recognise the reality that perhaps he was trying to meet people who did not share his interests or values. He began to reconsider his strategy of scanning people's biographies and started focusing instead on his key priorities.

Whereas in the past, courting would involve gradually getting to know someone, we now expect total revelation – instantly. As Rosen (2008: 155) noted, 'Our new technological methods of courtship also elevate efficient communication over personal communication'. However, relationship success is in the personal communication. The reason why coaching is so helpful is because, ultimately, technology and science cannot solve our relationship problems. As Rosen also explained, 'Real courtship is about persuasion, not marketing'.

Jerome was also quick to become physically intimate with people he met online, and he was surprised that the emotional side of the relationship did not keep up the pace. During coaching, it became apparent that he needed to be more patient in identifying and developing a relationship, as his sexual activity was having a bearing on his objectivity when evaluating the suitability of a potential partner. Jerome recognised that his choice of spouse, being possibly the most important life decision, requires clear thinking. Life coach Collette Jones also told Yossi (in a personal communication) that, in her experience, one of the major relationship issues people face is commencing sexual activity before deciding whether they want to be in a relationship with the person.

Furthermore, while the emotions and biochemical stimulants released through sex are often insufficient to cover up gaps in the relationship, they are often sufficient to blur matters so that a couple can quickly find themselves in a serious relationship and are then faced with a full-blown breakup, rather than a casual parting of ways. Steele (2008: 159) advises his clients to set and preserve boundaries around physical intimacy; becoming intimate, he suggests, creates the sense that they are a couple and they start to become attached before they genuinely got to know each other, as 'it is easy to confuse love and attachment'.

The coach should thus be alert to patterns of premature intimacy, which may be a cause of frequent relationship failure for the client. The coach can help the client realise that the biochemical reaction to physical attraction and sex are such that they release stimulants that overpower the brain with intense longing for the other person. Some people imagine that a strong attraction or satisfying sex amounts to genuine love, and place exaggerated emphasis on sexual compatibility. A coach can also help the client recognise that, whereas people with the intent of a long-term relationship are more likely to woo their partners through being supportive and offer sincere compliments, those with a short-term orientation are much more likely to adopt disingenuous methods (Bredow et al. 2011). Thus, delaying sexual activity helps to identify those who are genuinely seeking a long-term relationship.

The coach can help the client to enter a relationship for the right reasons. Some singles rush into almost any relationship, believing that this is their surest route to happiness. Some people start believing that there is a shortage of 'decent people' and that they should take whatever is on offer. Others are motivated by a sense of vulnerability and are searching for someone to rescue them. When a person comes across as needy, they are more likely to provoke pity than real intimacy. Conversely, some people think that their best chance of being in a relationship is to search for some else to rescue, believing that their kindness will be repaid with love. Regrettably, it very often does not work out that way. At best, it results in an unhealthy co-dependency, whereby the relationship is based on solving insecurities instead of on love and affection. At worst, one party will feel exploited and used, resulting in the eventual collapse of the relationship when the rescuer gets exhausted and depleted. As Cagen (2004) wrote, there is no point entering into a relationship solely for the sake of not being alone.

Conflicting or confused priorities

Many singles have aspirations or expectations that do not hold up to rational analysis. For example, Yossi's client, Doreen, cited four features she was looking for in a man: intellectual, higher earner that her (she was a banker), ambitious, and kind. She was flexible about most other things and considered that just four expectations were not unreasonable. However, when she analysed it during coaching, it began to look increasingly incongruous. Is a high-earning intellectual an easy thing to find? Most intellectuals are not high earners. She also insisted that her partner earns more than her, but she is a banker! She is looking for someone who is both ambitious and kind (by which she means kind to her), but most ambitious people (especially if they are high earners) are ambitious about themselves. In coaching, Doreen came to recognise that while these combinations are not physically impossible, they are a comparative rarity and radically reduce her likelihood of success in finding a man. Katz and Holmes (2006) contrasted the sensitive type of man who is happy sharing his feelings with the 'got it all under control' type who allows no chink in his armour and noted that some women seek a partner with both qualities!.

A similar issue arises when people look for someone who is both similar to themselves and yet who offers something different. In theory, it is possible to find a way of reconciling these desires, but this adds significant complexity to an already complicated dating game. Some singles find it extremely difficult to prioritise their most valued qualities and relinquish the others.

People experience conflicting aspirations because their engagement with the world is facilitated by what Ryan and Deci (2003) termed multiple selves and Bachkirova (2011) described as mini-selves, which manifest in relation to specific issues or under particular circumstances. To Jung (1953), real individuality rests in the unconscious self rather than the conscious ego. Rogers (1951) similarly separated the true self from the social one, suggesting that people can become alienated from their true being. Goffman (1959) likewise highlighted the distinction between a person's public persona and his or her inner self. Higgins (1987) more recently recognised that there may be a significant difference between a person's ideal self and actual self.

The coach may need to help a client to recognise that, when seeking a partner, it may not be easy or even possible to please both parts of their persona. Bachkirova (2011: 65) cited philosopher William James (1999: 73), who wrote: 'I am often confronted by the necessity of standing by one of my empirical selves and relinquishing the rest.' These various mini-selves operate mostly unconsciously and therefore are typically unaware of each other's existence. As Bachkirova (2011: 66) noted, 'Each mini-self is responsible for its own engagement with the world'. Similarly, Kegan and Lahey (2009) noted how a person may find their efforts stymied by competing hidden commitments.

A cognitively generated goal, however, can help to countervail unconscious influences (Carver 2007). Relationship coaching can raise awareness and conscious thought to prevent unconscious processes from overtaking. The role of the coach was to help Doreen to recognise the existence of alternative mini-selves and highlight potential conflicts between those elves. As part of this process, Doreen deployed her conscious mind to select which mini-self should be given overriding priority, what might be termed 'coaching the selves'.

So, we can see how unrecognised, unconscious aspects of the person's personality can have a huge but unacknowledged influence on choices and actions. However, the problem can also exist in the reverse, whereby conscious choices based on rational decision-making processes are not in keeping with less conscious aspects of a client's character. Coaching has long recognised the importance of aligning the client's goals and actions with their deeply held values (Whitmore 2003). Ives (2011) argued that the issue of congruence and concordance is central to coaching – namely, that goals must be in synchrony with a person's values, meaning, and purpose or other life and work objectives.

Although a discussion of concordance is often based on a conception of the 'self' as an objective, relatively stable locus of identity, it is compatible with a conception of multiple selves, whereby a strong mini-self will cause psychic obstacles to progress if the goal contradicts its values. Humanistic approaches to coaching also emphasise the importance of values in underpinning personal development (e.g. Stober 2006), and a positive psychology approach to coaching (Kauffman 2006: 227) promotes 'an awareness of the alignment of the client's vision and values'. Besser and Wilson (2006: 20) similarly argued that, for a goal to be effective, it must 'resonate and be congruent with the client's values and personal culture'. The coach should facilitate what Natale and Diamante (2005: 367) termed 'adaptive congruity', where all aspects of the person are aligned and balanced. Coaching can provide an arena in which goal conflict can be explored. It can also assist people to ensure greater concordance between how they present themselves and who they actually are.

Self-presentation

The initial stages of dating involve a high degree of self-presentation, whereby people seek to render themselves appealing to their objects of romantic interest, accentuating such qualities judged to be particularly attractive to the others. As a result, people can find themselves impelled to seek to be liked for what they present themselves to be, rather than what they actually are. People are only likely to be totally open about who they really are in first encounters if they are highly confident that the other will be accepting (Figley 1979). Thus, people commonly present themselves in a manner calculated to arouse a prospect's interest (Bredow et al. 2011).

Mandy, a 32-year-old lawyer turned entrepreneur, was unaware of how she had long ago developed a hyperdynamic persona to mask her internal fears stemming from a rather troubled family situation during childhood. She sought only to date men who were super-driven and larger than life in some way. Predictably, she found herself experiencing a series of dramatic but brief relationships. Mandy recognised how the carefully crafted image cannot be maintained for too long and the real person comes through, resulting in rejection because they could not live up to their profile. Through coaching, Mandy was able to discern that behind the macho externality was a profound insecurity resulting from experiencing rejection early in her life. She made a plan to take steps to present herself as more real and to look for the same in a potential life partner.

The temptation can be particularly acute with online dating, where people feel able to portray themselves in ways that bear the most tenuous of resemblances to their real lives. The coach can help the client to identify such practices and encourage her or him to present an impression that is not too greatly detached from the real person. Many single people complain about being solely evaluated on a solitary – in their eyes, marginal – feature, rather than being valued as a whole person, such as when they are viewed as worthwhile solely on the basis of appearance or income. Yet, often when reflected upon, it becomes apparent that they have contributed heavily to encouraging that impression.

The coach should encourage the client to ensure the persona conveyed on a date is broadly compatible with who they really are. There is a temptation to repackage ourselves in order to be attractive to a potential partner. Some people make implausible efforts to appear more appealing, believing that only in this way will someone be interested in them. Making an effort while on a date is appropriate, but trying to present ourselves as something we are not in order to impress is likely to quickly unravel. When completing online profiles, people are often tempted to present as eye-catching an impression of themselves as possible, even though it feeds into the very reactions they wish to avoid.

Here, we highlight the online profile of Miranda, an attractive 35-year-old mother of one who had qualified as a doctor. This client came to coaching because she felt that she attracted the kind of men who did not treat her or relationships seriously. The following biographical entries are presented with the comments Yossi gave as feedback, along with an example of how Miranda may phrase her entry to be more in keeping with her true personality.

Online form: The one thing I am most passionate about:

Miranda's entry: I like to live a healthy lifestyle. I adore travelling and visiting historical places. In such situations, I feel myself being a small part of an interesting universe.

Yossi's comment: I can see that you are genuinely excited by travel. On the other hand, you are now 35 and wanting to prioritise relationships, so is wanderlust consistent with wanting to settle down? Remember this is the opening line, so it says a lot.

Yossi's edit: I like to live a healthy lifestyle. I love travelling and visiting historic places, but I am at heart a homebody who puts relationships and family first.

Online form: The things I cannot live without are:

Miranda's entry: Summer, music, the arts, dancing, love

Yossi's comment: Are these the real five, or the dating website five? What about other things I know you are care about: helping people, learning, family, friendships, relationships?

Online form: The first thing people notice about me:

Miranda's entry: After being bedazzled by my appearance, you'll be captivated by my velvet voice and charm.

Yossi's comment: You are earning your reputation for humour, but what effect might this statement have on potential dates?

Yossi's edit: To be honest, many men focus on my appearance, but I do wish that they would give equal attention to my loving nature.

Online form: A little more about me:

Miranda's entry: I am intelligent and independent-minded and looking for somebody of a similar disposition. Must must must be fun loving and have a sharp sense of humour … even if it's a bit quirky.

Yossi's comment: You use 'must' three times about fun-loving. What if you supply the fun and they are reliable, loyal, dependent, mature, hardworking, fair, sincere, intelligent, good looking, generous, and amiable? Will you forgive them if they are not super-duper fun-loving? Why is a sharp sense of humour so important? What if the sense of humour is a bit blunt? What if he is a good listener, a strong support, honest and open, well organised, and easy going, but his sense of humour is less than sharp?

Online form: I typically spend my leisure time:

Miranda's entry: I have lots of interests to keep me occupied, including all the 'normal' stuff … playing piano, travel, scuba diving, holidays, cinema, theatre, tennis, quantum physics, remote viewing, chaos theory, cooking, cultural pursuits, etc. etc.

Yossi's comment: What really do you spend your leisure time doing? Limit yourself to five.

The foregoing comments or suggestions are just that, but hopefully they illustrate how a coach can challenge a client who may be tempted to present themselves to a potential date in ways that are inconsistent with who they are and what they are looking for, but moreover are likely to elicit the opposite reaction to the one they seek. This happens especially when communicating through an online dating profile.

Many singles' relationship issues come down to poor self-awareness, resulting in behaviour that provokes an undesirable reaction in potential partners. Sabrina, a 44-year-old publishing executive, is energetic, forceful, and impatient. She complains that she does not meet many men who are of the right calibre. The coach helped Sabrina to adopt the perspective of the men she was trying to date and become more aware of how her opinionated or independent demeanour may be experienced by them. Strong-minded and highly capable women have often not considered that the men they meet may find them a little overwhelming. Sabrina complained that all the men she meets 'seem one-dimensional', but through coaching she came to realise that her approach may be contributing to some men feeling inadequate. Many clients are baffled that people respond to them in ways that so radically contradict their own self-perception. However, with supportive feedback and challenging yet constructive questioning, Sabrina was willing to reconsider and to make adjustments.

The simple awareness of how other people react may be sufficient to achieve immediate enlightenment – the 'penny drops'. The role of raising awareness in relationship coaching is fundamental, but it should be emphasised that clients cannot be given awareness; they can only be helped to take it themselves. The role of the coach is not to tell the client how their attitude or behaviour is likely to impact upon those they date, but rather to hold a candle to it and ask the client how he or she thinks this may impact. The role of the coach is also to ensure that this awareness transfers from a cognitive insight into changes in approach and behaviour. Thus, Pemberton (2006) distinguished between 'support for *thought*', whereby the client has an opportunity to explore his or her thoughts, and 'challenge for *action*', whereby the client is encouraged to translate insight into action. Similarly, Grant (2006: 157) suggests that the coach needs to help the client to 'change his viewing' (an adaptive outlook) and 'change his doing' (enact behavioural change). Role playing is an effective way of helping clients to put their new awareness into practice. However, as Hawkins and Smith (2007) argued, 'real play' is better than 'role play', whereby the client uses their real-life scenarios. This is consistent with an adult learning approach, which suggests that adults learn best when the subject matter is most relevant to them (Knowles et al. 2005).

Jackson and McKergow (2008) argue that small actions should be treated as experiments; small actions are easier and require less of an imaginative leap. It is best to make incremental steps, rather than take major irrevocable actions that may turn out to have different consequences than those imagined. Hence, when addressing the issues in this category, it is advisable to explore and experiment and learn by experience, rather than making far-reaching judgements and changes. The small changes vary entirely depending on each client and the particular circumstance. In the case of Sabrina, who came across excessively domineering, the client was coached to deliberately make space for her dates to come forward and express an opinion. By contrast, highly reserved individuals may make a point of explaining their personality and assuring that, in time, 'I will come out of my shell'.

We would add that in addition to changes in perception and behaviour, for relationship coaching there may also need to be a change in language, as relationship building is so dependent on language. Flaherty (2005) argued that the coach needs to help the client to develop new language that will allow the client to make new observations, and that this language needs to become a permanent feature in the client's 'structure of interpretation'. This new method of observation will then be ingrained in the client and will be independent of the coach, who will be able to respond effectively to new situations. Flaherty (2005: 32) declared: 'Provide new language, plus the chance by practice to have the language become part of us, and new observations, new actions, and a new world will inevitably follow.' How we speak about ourselves, the narrative we tell about our life, is vitally important in how another experiences us.

One client, Jonathan, who had a challenging life story, was asked to complete an exercise that would help to articulate a more positive life story that would feel less burdensome to a new partner:

- Who is Jonathan?
- Tell me the brief story of Jonathan from the beginning until now.

- How would you like the 'story' of Jonathan to continue?
- Describe your life using positive terms. Use two or three descriptors ('My life is/has been...').

Failure to cope with disappointment

Jenny, a vivacious and popular 28-year-old advertising executive, came to coaching after her relationship ended with what she considered was 'the man of her dreams'. When she first met him, she was immediately swept away by this amazingly attractive, charming, and impressive man, but it became apparent that he had difficulty being open and had avoidant tendencies. Jenny was crushed when it dawned upon her that this picture of perfection was illusionary. She cried herself to sleep for three nights over the loss of a perfect relationship. Coaching Jenny, it became apparent that this was a cycle that repeated itself with comparatively reliable succession.

Sometimes two people meet and are really excited about each other; this excitement remains at implausible levels for a few weeks, until reality hits that this 'god' has feet of clay. Cracks appear in the image of perfection. When this happened to Jenny, instead of rationalising that this was only to be expected and accepting that we all have imperfections, the realisation led to a crushing sense of defeat and loss. Her reaction was to point out the faults to her boyfriend and challenge him on them. Understandably, he felt that only his faults were being identified. The outcome was a rather rapid deterioration in the relationship, which left Jenny staggering from the dizzying speed of decline, overcome by disappointment and disillusionment.

During their exploration, the coach introduced Jenny to what we call the rollercoaster model of dating: The relationship takes a steady but rather steep climb until it reaches the summit. From that position, the person feels on top of the world. However, before long and without warning, the relationship takes a precipitous downward turn. Unprepared for this fall, the blood rushes from the face, panic ensues, and in some cases the person is overcome with nausea. Under such circumstances, many people would be forgiven for 'wanting out'. The relationship – like the rollercoaster – seems wildly unpredictable, unsafe, and traumatic. Were it not for the restraining bar on rollercoasters, undoubtedly many would make their exit at that point. In relationships, there usually are no restraining bars, so a swift exit is often the reaction to the shock.

Another client, Jared, was prone to panic attacks, and would react extremely when he felt he was in the wrong relationship. He would wake up at night in a state of utter alarm, jumping several meters out of bed as if an assailant was about to stab him.

However, as with the rollercoaster, by then the worst is usually over and there will be fewer shocks and none so sudden and unexpected. There will continue to be some highs and some lows, a few bumps and sudden stops, but if the person manages to contain or overcome the instinct to panic at the first major crisis, then the prospects for the relationship may well be good. Once Jenny realised that this was happening and how it influenced her decision-making, she felt better able to react more calmly when the cycle reoccurred, and she would now reconsider before losing hope in a relationship.

This sense of alarm contributes significantly to some people's reluctance to commit to a relationship. While some people are just plain commitment-phobic (in all areas of their life), many who are comfortable making major business and professional commitments struggle to commit in a relationship. This suggests that the issue is not commitment per se but an unwillingness to 'settle for second best', as they often describe it.

Rachel is an attractive 38-year-old lawyer who had been unlucky in love. She explained that, 'Had I been interested in marrying a regular estate agent type, I'd have been married years ago', and that she was looking for something more suitable. Her coach suggested to her, 'Why don't we review what you are looking for? Maybe you should be going for something a bit different?'

Coaches need to help clients understand that it is not about accepting less than they want. Rather, it is about making sure they think carefully about what they truly need and look at their needs from different perspectives. When the realisation comes, people can find true happiness with a person they may have rejected or discounted for years, because their previous limiting attitude made that person seem unattractive as a partner.

Being in a relationship can also be met with some aspects of sorrow and loss, as the person realises that they have to give up on some elements of their independence and some of their dreams. They imagine that being in a relationship should be unmitigated bliss, and therefore become anguished by misgiving feelings: 'Relationships are supposed to be enjoyable. Why am I having such a hard time?' People may need help in understanding that initial disappointment need not be fatal to the relationship, and that the crushing feeling will often pass with little more than a reality check. Clients need help to respond to these inevitable disappointments in a sensible manner and not overreact. They need reassurance that, with patience and good sense, these feelings of disappointment can pass and give way to a more balanced appreciation of one another. Moreover, clients need to be supported in recognising that a perfect match is rare and not a realistic goal. In fact, a 'perfect match' is a myth; that some people may claim to have one is more a testament to their infatuation or accepting nature than the true levels of compatibility.

Yossi suggests to clients that 80% is probably the maximum perfection they could realistically expect, and that there will always be things they do not like and struggle to accept. He encourages them to consider their own perfection, and asks them to reflect on the fact that their future partner will need to learn to live with those imperfections. Clients sometimes need to be encouraged to reflect on the likelihood that some issues will simply fade into irrelevance as the relationship matures. The coach can help clients to determine which issues are truly significant and should be treated as critical threats to the relationship and which are likely to be overcome in time and with a bit of communication.

Avoidance and inflexibility

Some singles are avoidant, ambivalent, or even hostile to attachment. As noted in Chapter 4, attachment theory posits that patterns of attachment developed as a child impact significantly on our romantic relationships later in life (Feeney and Noller 1996). Adults have four attachment styles (Bartholomew and Horowitz 1991): secure, anxious–preoccupied (low confidence and high dependence in relationships), dismissive–avoidant (high independence and emotional self-sufficiency), and fearful–avoidant (desire and seek attachment but are afraid of rejection). Steele (2008: 71) suggested that many singles are 'attempting to avoid failure by avoiding commitment'. In fact, several studies of single women (Cole 1999; Lewis and Moon 1997) found that many have volatile emotions with regard to relationships: wanting intimate and emotional closeness but also valuing their personal and financial freedom.

People with an avoidant attachment style may sabotage their relationship efforts, often unconsciously. The coach can help the client to identify when and how this is happening. Once the client is aware that it is happening, it is already a great deal easier to address. Coaches can then work with the client on behaviour and attitude modification exercises to make their avoidance tactics less pronounced. In the case study that follows, this avoidant style is illustrated.

Dan, a 42-year-old software writer, had a history of entering into relationships and breaking off when things started to get 'too serious'. Now, he is in a relationship with Debbie, who everyone tells him is ideal and that walking away from her would irreparably damage his future chances, cementing his reputation as a heartbreaker. Dan, however, was experiencing his usual misgivings: 'There are some things about her that bother me. I can't go through with this'. Under enormous pressure not to break off the relationship, he spoke to an endless number of friends and relatives, even clergy, to help him decide what to do – all to no avail. By now, Debbie was ready to quit, having put up with Dan's prevarications for what seemed an eternity. Dan was helped to understand that he had an avoidance issue and that his misgivings about Debbie were based on an intense reluctance to commit. With assistance and support from the coach, Dan was able to establish that this was the right person for him and that the misgivings were more to do with his avoidance than Debbie's faults. It took him three attempts over one and a half hours, but Dan finally did propose!

The relationship coach can help clients to realise how they may be adopting unproductive behaviour patterns. While the coach does not seek to address the underlying psychological causes, he or she raises awareness of the attitudes and behaviours and prompts conscious decisions to change practical things that can enhance relationship success. Similarly, the coach can use various questioning techniques to encourage reflection and critical thinking and so encourage a range of new perspectives.

One of the more amusing, if perplexing, experiences Yossi had as a coach was when he received a panicky phone call from an upset young woman who seemed distraught by what her new boyfriend had told her:

'You're not going to believe what just happened – what he just said', vented the young woman to Yossi.

'Why, what did he say?'

'He said he loves me. That's disgusting.'

'What was offensive about that?' Yossi further enquired.

'What do you mean? It's like he wants to marry me or something. I'm not ready for this at all!'

Most people would consider it highly desirable to hear someone they are dating express their love. However, to people with avoidance issues, that can be read as 'I want to gobble you up. I want to consume you or suffocate you.' Rather than finding such expressions of affection flattering and endearing, some people find them to be threatening and alarming. Once people are aware of this, however, they will understand themselves better and can react more calmly.

Some single people date as 'singles' instead of acting like potential couples: they have difficulty being flexible or being accountable to another person. Some singles appear conflicted about how motivated they are to secure a committed relationship; their actions suggest they regard a relationship as nice but nonessential. The other person may experience this as half-hearted. However, the coach should understand that having constructed a whole life for themselves, a client may be reluctant to give it up. For a relationship to progress, individuals have to be willing to surrender a measure of their independence and accept that they are answerable to each other. Individuals in a dating situation have to practice compromise from an early point, which some people can find quite difficult.

Successful relationships require interdependence, which we define as the recognition by an individual that their thriving depends on their willingness and ability to develop and sustain a committed relationship with another person. This concept differs sharply from how this term is conceived by interdependence theory (Kelley and Thibaut 1978), based on transactional analysis (see Standford 2008), emphasising the self-serving conditions that motivated people to stay in a relationship (see Rusbult and Van Lange 2003 for a review). Our notion of interdependence asks both parties to focus on the needs of the other and become givers, on the understanding that only in so doing can a relationship truly thrive. It is closely related to Kegan's (1982) fifth level of the development – the 'interindividual self', where self-surrender and intimacy contribute to independent self-definition.

Interdependence is based on mutual dependence, meaning that both parties are equally needed. This creates a healthy balance in the relationship, whereby the parties are neither too close nor undifferentiated from one another. An interdependent relationship is not marked by high level of independence, nor excessive dependence. Instead, the couple maintain a degree of autonomy and self-sufficiency on the one hand, while also fostering a strong sense of closeness and intimacy (Johnson 2004). As Rusbult and Buunk (1993: 178) noted, 'Interdependence implies that partners in a close relationship influence one another's experiences and need each other to obtain valued outcomes such as instrumental support, affection, sexual fulfilment and emotional closeness'.

For people to be willing to surrender a degree of their independence, they need to be convinced that the relationship is of significant importance to them – that they will get something more valuable in return for what they are willing to give up. Simply urging a person to display greater flexibility will rarely result in any change, whereas an altered attitude towards dating and marriage will facilitate sustainable change. Willingness to accommodate another and make the necessary compromises to share one's life with another requires that both parties recognise the value of being with another person. Securing a life partner requires a willingness to give up the right to be detached. Entering into a confirmed sustained relationship is not synonymous with not being single. It is about losing the right to turn attachment and commitment on and off depending on the mood.

Martin was a successful 45-year-old professional who was dating someone twelve years his junior – a bright and impressive women. He was introverted and preferred after a typically long day at work to stay home to read, while his girlfriend wanted to go out at night. While Martin was keen for the relationship to succeed, his social inactiveness was causing a major strain on the relationship. In coaching, Martin was encouraged to explore what the concept of relationship meant to him, what it meant to his girlfriend and what qualities and practices strengthen or undermine effective relationships.

Many singles are busy professionals who are highly committed to their professional life and find it difficult to juggle their work demands with their desire for relationship success. Some singles, like Martin, are unaware of the extent to which they expect things to be on their own terms. Helping them to realise this and to think of ways to be more available or flexible would reduce some of the obstacles that some singles find in pursuing their relationships. Some singles have developed established personal and social patterns that they are reluctant to change. Many people expect that if the relationship is right, it will just fit. According to this thinking, there is no need to work on a relationship. Coaching can help to raise awareness about this mindset and nurture greater sensitivity to the perspective of the other person's needs in the relationship.

Miscommunication and poor conflict management

Sometimes seemingly trivial issues result in major relationship dramas. Miscommunications, conflicting expectations and the odd moment of foolishness quickly escalate into a relationship-threatening fracas. Sometimes played out in public or handled indiscreetly, these potentially manageable problems, normal in even the happiest of marriages, come to threaten the very survival of the relationship. The cause is that people are dating like singles, instead of like a potential couple.

Renee met Brad in England before relocating to the United States to try out a new job, so Brad suggested that he come over to spend a few days with her stateside. Having spent a couple of intense days together, Renee decided to invite over a few friends. Brad arrived to discover that there was company and flew into a rage: 'I've come all the way here to spend time with you and you invite friends over! You obviously don't want to spend time with me; I'm leaving for the airport!' Off he went to pack up and go. Renee was mortified. Distraught, she called her mother who proceeded to lecture her for 'always messing up'. She then turned to her best friend, who berated her for 'never being able to hold on to a man'. By the time she called her coach, she was an emotional wreck. A few minutes reviewing the situation was sufficient to reveal that this was a normal bump on the road to getting to know someone, and she needed to treat this as a learning opportunity. After some coaching, Renee called Brad and said the following, 'Brad, this may sound crazy, but I'm actually glad this has happened, as it has provided us with a valuable learning opportunity. You can see that I am more sociable and thought nothing of inviting over a few people, while I have discovered that this doesn't work for you. We should meet up and discuss it.'

Another client, Natalie, called her coach in distress. Her coaching sessions had been eye-opening for her and a relationship was progressing well with a man she never would have previously imagined to be compatible with her interests. However, Natalie's new partner had made a sexual advance towards her and she was quite upset. 'All he wants me for is one thing', she laments. 'I'm traditionally minded and do not consider it appropriate to have sex outside of a committed relationship', she explains. Adopting a solution-focused approach, her coach asks, 'Have you explained this to your boyfriend?' It turned out that she had not. Having switched from looking only at the problem towards finding a solution, it became quickly apparent that Natalie has simple options available to her to resolve the issue.

We sometimes get upset at another person, assuming it is obvious what we want. However, closer reflection often reveals that, without specifying, the other person had no way of knowing what our wishes were. People need to be encouraged to be open about their needs. Our happiness depends in large part on having needs met, and the only realistic way of achieving that is by letting our partners know what these needs are.

An issue that may arise in coaching is when to broach sensitive matters. Timing is vital, and clients may need to consider the most appropriate stage to raise it. Sometimes people rush to reveal all, before those they are dating have managed to establish the safety and intimacy required to handle delicate issues. By contrast, some people are so frightened to reveal things about themselves, lest they be judged, that they keep it to themselves far too long into the dating process, by which time the other feels deceived when it finally comes out.

Danielle, a 27-year-old teacher from a traditional background, had been previously married off by her parents at age 18. She was fearful that this would be held against her in future relationships, as she felt that when she mentioned it in her previous relationships her dates backed off. Now, she is with someone she really likes and is afraid to say something too soon, lest he also is frightened away. Here, the coach adopted a solutions-focused approach to help Danielle select the appropriate timing, but in particular the appropriate strategy for broaching the issue. Working out how to communicate sensitive topics can play an important role in nurturing a new relationship to maturity.

Of course, how we communicate around disagreements is critical to the health, even survival, of the relationship. Too often, people treat arguments as a pitched battle and fail to handle their disputes in a healthy and constructive manner. Research suggests that this behaviour can be fatal to a marriage; in a dating situation – where the commitment is often absent or weak – the damage is swifter and greater. Other people are desperate to avoid any conflict situation, and they treat a conflict as a major disaster, rather than viewing it as an opportunity for learning and growth.

Gottman's (1995) work on marital relationships showed that conflict itself is not harmful to the relationship. On the contrary, no conflict at all suggests a docile and feeble bond, where the parties do not trust the strength of the union to allow for a little 'creative tension'. However, Gottman's research strongly suggests that it is critical that conflict is handled appropriately. Gottman (1995: 28) wrote: 'If there is one lesson I have learned from my years of research is that a lasting marriage results from a couple's ability to resolve the conflicts that are inevitable in any relationship.' In particular, he advises that disagreements should be handled in a 'productive' manner, and that disagreeing couples should adopt 'repair mechanisms' to soothe their partner.

The coach's role thus is to help the client to recognise when communication is faltering, to explore strategies for improving interactions, and to learn how to view conflict as a constructive process that is both inevitable and healthy in relationships. Understanding the role of conflict will also help clients to identify the communication style they might look for in a partner.

A common issue in relationships is the way that people address their needs in a complaining or critical manner, rather than effectively conveying their wishes. Nonviolent (or compassionate) communication, developed by Rosenberg (2003), is an approach for people to communicate about their needs in a nonconfrontational manner by focusing on identifying and expressing their own and other people's needs. Rosenberg believes that most conflict arises from miscommunication about true human needs, which are often masked in demands or judgemental language. It encourages an empathetic approach that engages participants in communication to clarify their needs, their feelings, their perceptions, and their requests, and to seek the same of others. Doing so enables the discovery of strategies that allow both parties' needs to be met. Nonviolent communication is further discussed in the next chapter.

Summary

In this chapter, we explored various issues that single people frequently face when forming relationships. We presented a coaching model (GREAT) that, while being goal-directed is exploratory and developmental in nature to help to identify and address the issue(s) at play. Often, the coaching will be quite developmental, involving perspective transformation, which is then combined with cognitive behavioural or behavioural strategies to help clients to achieve relationship success.

Although we have covered numerous issues, we could not provide an exhaustive list. It should be noted that sometimes coaching may result in the client recognising the need to dissolve a relationships. Cynthia, a 52-year-old businesswoman, had five years earlier ended a twenty-year marriage and had been dating a successful but somewhat brash salesman. She loved his charisma and dynamism, but she kept continually breaking off the relationship due to his seeming lack of commitment. She found herself continually returning to the relationship after his protestations about how much he liked her and missed her, etc. Four years passed in this way, and now Cynthia was torn between feelings of anger at his self-centredness and hurtful behaviour on the one hand and her feeling of attraction and longing for him on the other.

Through coaching using the GREAT model, Cynthia was able to step back and recognise a pattern of behaviour in both herself and her on-off boyfriend. She came to recognise how she had allowed herself to be the victim of a partner who ignored her needs. It became clearer to her that her partner would repeatedly break trust and promises, and when challenged would play down the significance of the breach (Gunther 2010). As Cunningham et al. (2002) described, some people come to relationships as 'players' who reject commitment and have an ambivalent relationship orientation. Others, they explain, behave as 'predators' who have a habit of exploiting and then abandoning their partners. Now aware of the unhealthy nature of her relationship, Cynthia resolved to invest her efforts in seeking a more wholesome relationship and found the courage to draw a line under an ultimately frustrating and unfulfilling emotional helter-skelter.

Coaching can help people to enter dating with their eyes open and their minds engaged. Steele (2008) cautioned about how some people slide into what he terms 'mini-marriages', whereby the couple find the relationship fun and enjoyable enough not to want to end it, but yet insufficiently serious for it to become permanent. In some instances, these relationships result in marriage, but later struggle under their own instability. Coaching can encourage clients to give proper consideration to the qualities they require in a prospective partner. Ensuring that the fundamentals are thought through, rather than hastily acting as a couple, could help avoid the trauma of separation or a 'mini-divorce'.

Chapter 7

Coaching couples

Michael Neill (2013) explained how we are all born with a deep river of wisdom and well-being, but that over time the river gets iced over. Instead of going with the flow of the river, we continue our journey on what he called 'the treacherous ice roads of our psyche'. Neill suggests that coaches, as people who facilitate transformative conversations, can actually chip away at the 'ice' of our clients' long-held beliefs and assumptions while simultaneously 'presencing the river', tapping into the wisdom inside and drawing it up to the surface. In the ice-journey metaphor, Neill is very much describing the challenge that coaches face when working with couples on relationship issues: the well-spring that was the source of the relationship is often forgotten and the deep river of well-being that can flow from a close bond is ensnared in the pack-ice of rigid perceptions, habits, and expectations.

Regrettably, statistics show that, despite initial expectations, most long-term relationships falter in this way, with more than half coming to a complete end (Vernon 2013). The statistics also show that many long-term couples facing a break-up do seek professional help of some sort during the process. Sometimes, this involves couples intervention, at other times it may include family intervention or one or the other party seeking help as an individual. Generally, the help sought is counselling, although people turn to a variety of sources of support, including clergy, family, and friends.

There are many illustrations of the issues that couples face that could benefit from coaching. For example, a couple could disagree about whether or not to get married or whether or not to have a big wedding. It is not hard to see how refusal to get married or have a wedding could be interpreted by the other party as less than fulsome commitment, while the refusing partner can become enraged that merely declining an 'irrelevant ritual' should be sufficient to raise such doubts. Alternatively, if one partner wants children while the other does not, the partner who wants children may have to decide between the current partner and a potential child. The partner who does not want children may have to choose between refusing to be a parent and losing the relationship. These matters can become more sensitive and urgent if, say, a partner is already pregnant and one of them is insisting on an abortion and the other is resolutely opposed. Couples can also find themselves unable to resolve disagreements about where to live, whether to emigrate, gender roles, and so many similar issues.

When a couple presents for coaching, the coach should anticipate that they are coming with an expected outcome. The couple might expect the relationship to dissolve, for example, but they may want this to happen as amicably as possible, they may be uncertain about the relationship and want help deciding whether the relationship can be salvaged, or they may be hoping to rejuvenate the relationship and trying to work out how. The purpose of relationship coaching therefore is to help couples strengthen their relationship, repair a damaged one, or bring it to an orderly end if that is what, between them, they determine is the best option. Thus, we suggest, these illustrations fall into three main categories: remedial, restorative, developmental. However, although these seem very different, they all point to an initial task for the coaching to focus on. The coaching therefore begins with ascertaining the clients' goals for the relationship and exploring ways of attaining that goal. This might involve asking clients about what happiness means to them in that relationship and challenging them on what level of compromise they might be able to offer, emphasising to them that compromise is a gift they give to their relationship.

In this chapter, we suggest that coaching using a developmental, goal-focused approach can be helpful both as a remedial strategy and as a means of enhancing existing strong relationships. We introduce a coaching framework driven by the acronym COUPLE (Commitment, Openness, Understanding, Performance, Learning, Evolution). Using this framework, we explore how coaching can enhance couple relationships through encouraging an examination of values, beliefs, and assumptions and openness in communication. As a result, couples achieve a greater understanding of themselves, their partner, and their relationship.

After positioning the chapter within the existing literature base, we illustrate the COUPLE framework in action, providing short case studies of how coaching has helped couples to overcome problems and strengthen their relationships. We consider the role that coaching can play in supporting people in the face of marital crises or difficulties that may arise in a long-term romantic relationship. At the end of the chapter, we consider briefly the role of coaching in any decision to dissolve a relationship, as well as how receiving coaching may enable individuals to perceive a break-up in a more positive manner and move forward amicably.

The literature on coaching couples

There is very little written about coaching with couples. Miser and Miser (2008) have described coaching with expatriate couples, suggesting that 'coaching is a paradigm of possibility in which the coach is a collaborator with the couple in designing and creating the life the couple wants to achieve' (207). They explain that the ex-pat couple's life entails 'new levels of communication, problem-solving, negotiating roles and responsibilities, resolving conflict, planning and taking action together' (206) and suggest that their situation requires the couples to 'see the world from new perspectives, to be cognizant of the life they want, to be in alignment about their goals, to plan successfully together, and to learn from their experience' (206). We could argue that this sounds not dissimilar from what is happening to almost every relationship. Events put a strain on every couple – a new baby, moving house, illness, redundancy or job moves, elderly parents, disability, bereavement, etc. Life's challenges can, in a sense, make ex-pats of us all!

Bolstad (n.d.) is one of the few writers to focus on couples coaching. Drawing on Bandler's observations of Satir's work, he approaches working with couples from a neurolinguistic programming stance, suggesting that coaching couples involves transforming the way in which they communicate. He also extends Gottman's work to include a 'transforming communication' approach to helping couples to improve their communication.

Bolstad (n.d.) identified that when couples come to coaching, they are 'either experiencing serious, unpleasant, unresolved conflict or at least one partner feels lonely and has major unmet needs for love and closeness'. Often, he suggested, one of the partners may not be optimistic about the probability of creating what they need from their relationship. Indeed, he reported how '80% of divorced men and women said their relationship broke up because they gradually grew apart and lost a sense of closeness, or because they did not feel loved and appreciated'. Bolstad describes couples coaching as an emotionally positive experience, where the coach is 'an ally who helps identify and extend existing relationship strengths and supports clients in reaching for their own best dreams'.

Most of the empirical research concerned with helping couples with their relationships comes from the psychotherapy field, with Gottman's (1999, 2011) work probably being the most cited. Gottman's research supports the idea that, in happy relationships, each partner sees the other as a functional person and perceives disagreements as useful expressions of difference. He talked about the creation of a culture between partners and how it is this culture and the quality of the friendship between them that supports a successful relationship. Gottman's examples of conversations between happy and unhappy couples are revealing. He reported how happy couples use approximately 100 more words (or 30 seconds) of positive comments per day and concluded that this makes all the difference to the relationship. However, in more turbulent couple relationships, he noted, the partners see each other as flawed. In such cases, arguments are experienced as emotionally traumatic (1999: 19-21) and a negative culture develops. Gottman tends to use the power of these negative emotions as the starting point for the helping intervention, arguing for the 'crucial importance of emotional engagement and mutual soothing in the process of maintaining and healing a relationship' (Johnson and Lebow 2000: 24). By contrast, the approach to relationship coaching we advocate adopts as its starting point the creation of a shared vision that the couple wants to achieve, rather than exploration of the immediate problem.

Recently, in the field of positive psychology, Bao and Lyubomirsky (2013) explained how the process of 'hedonic adaptation' is responsible for the waning of passion in couple relationships, resulting in relationship boredom, which can prove toxic. They introduce a prevention model aimed at combating adaptation by introducing strategies to reduce or stop the hedonic adaptation. One such strategy is to increase the number of positive events and emotions that are experienced together. In the coaching model proposed in this chapter, we suggest that couples should set joint goals that bring them closer. Such goals would fulfil the requirement to maintain reasonable aspirations within the relationship (Bao and Lyubomirsky 2013).

Other psychological research has focused on strategies that can help with certain aspects of relationships, such as forgiveness. Browne's qualitative study in 2009 looked at the lived experience of 11 people over the age of 40 who had undergone forgiveness therapy to resolve a personal conflict. Findings suggested that the forgiveness process was a complex and difficult journey where participants were motivated eventually to 'let go of unforgiveness and find freedom from the stress caused by the transgression' (Browne 2009: ii). Browne explained how participants struggled with 'anger, rumination, and, in some cases, adverse health responses while employing a variety of means of coping as they meandered at their own pace towards forgiveness' (ii) and argued that the forgiveness process can alleviate distress. The concept of forgiveness seems useful in couples coaching, where acceptance of the faults of the partner are key to moving forward with the coaching task. Hill (2010) argued that, for estranged couples, forgiveness leads to a deep healing process and is 'one of the most critical processes for facilitating restored relational and emotional well-being' (178). He explained it as a process that involves 'the restoration of balance, the release of blame and reconciliation' (172). In accepting a situation and forgiving the parties involved (including sometimes ourselves), we protect ourselves from more hurt.

The COUPLE coaching framework

Drawing on relevant research and theories that we see as having value for coaching in a relationship context, such as those discussed in Chapter 5, we now introduce a coaching framework for working with couples. The framework has six elements, as shown in Figure 7.1 and described in the following sections.

Commitment

In their Couple Power model, Sheras and Koch-Sheras proposed that 'each partner comes to know and respect themselves more through their commitment to a joint couple vision supported by each of them' (2008: 112), so that they can be empowered by their relationship rather than feeling trapped in it. They also emphasised setting goals for the relationship, because otherwise 'the focus will likely remain on meeting the self-absorbed needs of the individual rather than commitment to the couple' (112). These authors argue that any stress on self-development of individual partners risks undermining a 'larger language of commitment'. When the helper begins by asking partners to describe the problem,

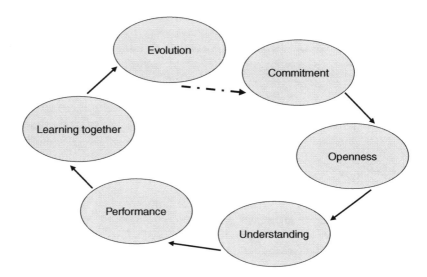

Figure 7.1 The COUPLE coaching framework

it is likely to reinforce individualistic needs and create 'more negativity in communication ... leaving little space for the couple to develop as an enduring or viable entity' (112). Gottman (2011) recommended reframing each partner's worst frustrations as dreams – but these are individual dreams. Sheras and Koch Sheras suggested starting by encouraging couples to set out joint dreams for the relationship, thereby gaining commitment to that relationship. The risk of Gottman's approach is that the partners become even more wedded to their individual dreams at the expense of the relationship and the partner.

Sheras and Koch-Sheras suggested that although it is vital to 'strike a balance between individualism and couplism such that each partner does not feel enmeshed or fused with the other' (2008: 112), the continued emphasis in society on the perceived needs of the individual are so ubiquitous that the needs of affiliation are neglected. They argued that 'a couple is not a place to 'get to'; it is a place to 'come from'. They advocated a paradigm shift towards a couple mentality because when the focus is on having our own needs met, it has adverse effects on our relationships. They further suggested that a couple should devise a 'couple proclamation' – a kind of mission statement or what we term a 'strap-line' – that generates and maintains an inspirational vision for their relationship, such as 'make joy a priority' or 'trust in our relationship together'. This also reinforces commitment to the relationship. Coaches can then encourage a cooperative project that supports the strap-line, such as organising regular theatre trips or dancing to 'make joy a priority'.

Compromise, which is often touted as the key to a successful relationship, could also be seen as a symptom of the individualist paradigm. It requires 'giving something up without necessarily getting what you want in return' (Sheras and Koch-Sheras 2008: 114). If we substitute cooperation instead of compromise, the disappointment inherent in compromise disappears and the commitment to the relationship is reinforced.

Many helpers begin their work with couples by suggesting that communication skills need to be improved, but Sheras and Koch-Sheras (2008) suggested that only once commitment and cooperation are established can clients be supported to develop their skills in this area: 'Getting clear about commitment to the couple can change how the partners think, feel and speak about their relationship' (2008: 110). These authors proposed that a couple should not be seen as two individuals with separate goals but as an entity in itself striving to reach both individual and common goals as a team' (110) and that the goals should be 'primarily designed to have the individuals operate inside of the framework of being a couple entity' (110). This concept was recognised by Shotter (2009: 26):

> [When] two or more forms of life 'rub together' … in their meetings, they always create a third or a collective form of life within which (a) they all sense themselves as participating, and which (b) has a life of its own, with its own voice, and its own way of 'pointing' towards the future.

Cox (2013: 53) suggests that coaching itself is one such 'co-construction': 'a production rather than a reproduction'. A couple can be viewed in much the same way: there is a dynamic at work that produces new, shared understandings that can move the partners forward.

Bolstad (n.d.) suggested that rather than specifying needs in 'away from' terms as Gottman does, a constructivist approach is preferable. Gottman (2011) asked couples to describe the story of their dilemma and to relive the positive aspects of their early relationship, but Bolstad argues that Gottman's research showed that merely 'resolving' individual conflicts does not ensure a good relationship. We would argue that coaches do not necessarily need to know what is wrong with a relationship in order to help to strengthen it; relationship coaching should not overly concentrate on what is perceived to be wrong in the relationship. We may not need to know and resolve the details of the couple's disagreements, just as we do not need to banish darkness before we can switch on a light. The coach can trust in a constructivist, goal-focused approach where new aspirations are discussed and described and the method of achievement is brought into focus. Seeing a solution, as discussed in Chapter 4, can usher in a resolution without the need for in-depth explorations.

Fritz (1984: 55) argued that the act of seeing a solution or vision of the future creates a structural tension – a gap between the vision and the reality. This tension can be resolved either by a change in the current reality – where, for example, a couple's relationship might begin to correspond more closely with the vision – or through a change in the vision, so that the result the couple thought they wanted is modified to match more closely what they have now. Setting up the picture of the current reality and the vision of the relationship that the couple want to create, we see five possible scenarios emerging:

1. Neither partner changes, so the discrepancy between the current reality and their separate visions continues.
2. Partner A changes to meet Partner B's vision of the relationship.
3. Partner B changes to meet Partner A's vision of the relationship.
4. Both partners change to meet their joint vision of the relationship.
5. The partners change their vision of the relationship to align with the current situation.

For the purposes of couples coaching, scenarios 4 and 5 are the most desirable outcomes.

To reiterate, Gottman's therapeutic work suggests that spouses should tell their own stories of their marital dilemmas (Johnson and Lebow 2000: 24). However, we contend that coaching is possible even without knowing all of the details. Using a goal-focused approach as described in Chapter 3, the coach can help the pair to construct a positive picture of their relationship (a realistic construction of an acceptable relationship), upon which may be based discussion of a joint goal or commitment. In doing this, there may be some disagreement between what is acceptable to each, but by strengthening the shared commitment to the relationship goal, the coach can help the couple to understand the place of individual needs within the context of the relationship.

Openness

A key feature of coaching with couples is the requirement to have both partners in the coaching room at the same time, discussing openly the potential of the relationship. Decisions regarding the future of a relationship cannot be made through coaching with one partner alone for a number of reasons, including the inability to take account of the partner's perspective. Leone (2013: 324–339) talked about the concept of the 'unseen spouse', where therapists hear a great deal about spouses or partners and naturally develop ideas and beliefs about that unseen other and about the causes of any relationship difficulties. Writing from a therapist's perspective, Leone cautions that there is a danger that therapists can

> lose touch with the fact that their impressions of an unseen spouse are constructions that have emerged from the transference/countertransference field, based on only partial or limited information – not veridical truths. They can then talk with the patient about his or her partner or relationship issues in ways that can ultimately do both patient and spouse a significant disservice and perhaps distract from the patient's own issues and analytic goals (324).

In our approach to couples coaching, we recommend that both partners are present. If one partner declines the offer of coaching, then coaching can still happen for the other partner, but it should not be defined as couples coaching. Bolstad (n.d.) confirmed that when just one partner wants to preserve the relationship and has hired the coach, the coach is working only on an individual client basis rather than being responsible to the relationship. Unless partners in the relationship share an agenda, there can be no couples coaching.

Furthermore, coaches should not be concerned that this is a dual encounter, but rather understand that the client in couples coaching is in fact the relationship, not the individual, so both parties need to be present to ensure openness. Also, because the agenda of the relationship is paramount, individual partners may need to be reminded from time to time that their personal agenda has to link with the relationship goals. So, in couples coaching, as Bolstad (n.d.) noted, there are three potential clients – the two individuals and the relationship, which acts as an entity itself. In our view, the relationship is the only client.

The focus on forgiveness that Browne highlighted also underscores being 'in a relationship first', rather than just being an individual. In fact, Kurtz and Ketcham (1992) argued that forgiveness becomes possible 'only when will is replaced by willingness; it results less from effort than from openness' (216). Couples can choose to forgive and so discover empathy and a shared human connection within their relationship. In a sense, they then override a selfishness that is particularly prevalent in western cultures.

Coaching a couple presents some interesting dynamics. It could be that one partner seems 'closer' to the coach than to the partner. This would indicate that there is work to be done on the joint relationship agenda. The partners and the coach may be equidistant from each other, which suggests that the coach is still prominent in the relationship. Ideally, at the end of the coaching assignment, the coach will be at a distance from the couple and the couple will be close.

Understanding

Once commitment and openness have been established, efforts to enhance understanding and communication between partners will have a more solid foundation. Bolstad's (n.d.) transforming communication skills model depends on initial checks on our understanding to see whether, at this moment, each partner actually owns his or her present internal state and whether the present state is the desired state. These checks identify whether there is a problem and who owns the problem. An example might be where one partner is unhappy and frustrated about something the other partner is doing or not doing. The partner would then own the problem by stating in an 'I message' the specifics of the situation in the general form: 'When you do (such and such), I feel unhappy because I am afraid/concerned (for your future/for our relationship/for some aspect of my well-being).'

In this sentence, by not suggesting a solution or attributing blame, the partner is being assertive rather than aggressive and merely stating how he or she feels. Therefore, there is nothing to argue with, but plenty for the other partner to think about. The problem-owning partner merely states the case and leaves it at that.

Gottman (1999) similarly stated that even conflict can become part of planned exploration of the couple's needs and dreams: rather than arguing, he suggested that they need not reach any conclusion, but should just listen to each other and share their responses without feeling the need to convince the other.

Bolstad (n.d.) further suggested that by alternating between the 'I message' and reflective listening, a two-step dance is created that transforms a couple's communications. The process can lead to one of three outcomes:

1.   The misunderstanding is resolved.
2.   A conflict of needs is identified, which can be tackled through a six-step win-win model of conflict resolution: identify the problem or issue; evaluate in terms of two sets of needs, rather than two conflicting solutions; brainstorm potential solutions that can meet both sets of needs; choose a solution to put into action; act; and evaluate the results.
3.   The conflict involves deeper beliefs and values.

Gottman (2011) found that more than two-thirds of relationship conflicts were in this third category, where basic beliefs and values were in conflict.

Miser (2008: 1) suggested that the foundations of any partnership are based upon sets of shared values that guide 'choices and actions in life together'. He explained how the values that a couple share and co-create could be seen as intrinsic to their 'coupleness' and are a vital part of a successful relationship: 'Some couples value mutual understanding, validation, openness, compromise, and friendship. Other couples value individuality, expressiveness and passion. Still other couples value harmony, common ground and autonomy' (Miser 2008: 1). This diversity of relationship patterns is important for coaches to understand and to help couples to recognise and work on during coaching.

For the coach, it may be that the conflicts of value will be most challenging to work with. Bolstad (n.d.) suggested joint tasks, such as the following:

•   Having a half-hour discussion about the conflict – without aiming to reach agreement, but more to understand the individual dreams connected to the value being expressed
•   Having partners each design an evening that meets one of their needs or values that is not currently met in the relationship and for them to share these evenings over the next week.

These tasks reinforce the kind of joint commitment suggested by Sheras and Koch-Sheras (2008). If couples can be encouraged to articulate their commitment to the relationship first, then discuss and understand how their individual values fit with that commitment, this may ameliorate or compensate for their values differences.

Gottman et al. (1998) studied the communication behaviours of happy and unhappy couples. For effective communication, people need to be able to truly hear what their partner is telling them. Poor relationships, the authors suggested, are characterised by inadequate listening and constant interrupting. In happy relationships, the partners seek clarification from one another, whereas in a troubled one they tend to make assumptions about what the other thinks and feels, often attributing negative thoughts and feelings without any evidence. The relationship coach can help to introduce the couple to the important principles of effective couple communication, some key ideas about which are briefly summarised here.

Even when acknowledging what their partner has said, poorly communicating couples will often respond to any complaint or criticism by countering with a complaint or criticism of their own, instead of listening to the partner. They rarely express their needs clearly. Rather, they will commonly launch into a barrage of complaints, such that it is unclear what is being asked for. In this way, a comparatively small matter is turned into a huge issue about the partner's overall competence, considerateness, or intelligence. Couples that communicate well do not change the subject to a counterattack, but deal with the source of the discontent (Miller et al. 2007). Effective communicators are able to make a specific request to a clear problem that can be met.

According to Gottman and Levenson (1992), troubled couples tend to express hostility when they communicate by responding to the partner's opinions or concerns with sarcasm and contempt, whereas successful couples talk in respectful tones. With happy couples, the partners see arguments as useful and manageable manifestations of their difference.

Another key dimension to mutual understanding is Chapman's (2010, 2009a, 2009b) suggestion that there are five main 'love languages' or ways of expressing and experiencing love: quality time, words of affirmation, gifts, acts of service, closeness and touch. We assume that others will express and experience love in the same way that we do, but people are different and it stands to reason that people will differ on this. Our partner may be trying hard to please us, but to us it does not feel that way because we have different needs that are not being met. In both cases, neither party understands what is going on, so the dissatisfaction and alienation continues apace. Consider the following examples of this type of miscommunication.

- Tricia felt let down that her fiancé Clive was indifferent about her. Clive was very indignant and hurt at being accused of indifference, as he had taken her on several exciting skiing and biking trips and thought he was doing a great job looking after her. After a bit of probing, it emerged that Clive was very poor at noticing, never mind mentioning, when Tricia made an effort to look good for him. To Tricia, never getting a compliment about her dress or hair was proof that he was not interested in her. All the trips and gifts were not doing the trick because that is not how Tricia experiences love.
- Sam is in a long-term relationship, and his partner Jennifer regularly complains that she does not feel loved. Sam is really offended, because he is

a nice guy and always compliments her and tells her nice things. It became clear in coaching that Jennifer wanted to be looked after, not complimented. What mattered to her was whether Sam would help around the house, and he was not doing that.

The problem in both instances is that Sam and Clive were not aware of the differences in 'love languages', nor were their partners. For some people, giving compliments can be quite difficult, but once Clive understood that this was the way to make Tricia happy, he was much more open to giving it a try. There is no reason to think that a couple will share the same love languages. The coach can guide the couple to discover how their partner most powerfully experiences love in order to ensure that they *feel* loved.

Gottman (1999: 330) talked about the importance of 'communicating empathy and understanding of the emotions, even if these emotions underlie misbehaviour'. According to Gottman and Silver, reflective listening is vital here. It involves restating the other person's own experience, opinions, and feelings in words that are similar to theirs. In fact, Gottman's research identified that reflective listening was the most powerful response offered by members of successful relationships (Gottman and Silver 1999: 87–89).

In Cox (2013: 66), reflective listening is aligned with paraphrasing and summarising, which are both forms of reassuring people that they are being listened to. Paraphrasing, like reflective listening, allows the listener to revise a sentence until it has truth value for both parties. It provides the opportunity for greater clarity, serving as a 'gift to the speaker while at the same time creating permission to move forward with more details' (Kee et al. 2010: 107). As a communication skill for couples, it is useful for helping partners to acknowledge other perspectives. This kind of active listening also suggests empathy because it demonstrates to the speaker that their perspective is beginning to be understood, which strengthens the relationship.

Such listening strategies, however, only work if a couple is not upset. Otherwise, as Gottman and Silver (1999: 11) pointed out, these strategies ask couples to perform 'Olympic-level emotional gymnastics when their relationship can barely work'. However, as Gottman and Silver found, couples who maintained happy marriages 'rarely do anything that even partly resembles active listening when they're upset' (Gottman and Silver 1999: 11). Still, while the absence of active listening sometimes is not critical for a happy marriage, it serves to enhance communication, which is especially valuable in a relationship under strain.

Gottman and Silver's (1999: 149) suggestion that couples need to make each other feel understood also involves expanding the way we perceive other people and genuinely taking their feelings and differences into account. Thus, at the heart of coaching with couples is work to expand meaning perspectives to enhance their capacity to understand the other. When the emphasis on individual needs is reduced, and a focus on the needs of the relationship brought to the fore, partners can begin to develop in new and meaningful ways.

Performance

When couples have confirmed their commitment to the relationship, established a new degree of openness, and have developed their understanding and trust through improved communication, they reach what we call the performance level. This is where they function together as a team as a result of the 'forming, storming, and norming' that occurs in the early part of the relationship. This performance level can be seen as similar to Tuckman's (1965) concept of 'performing', which was identified in small group development. If we think of a couple as a small group, then at this performance stage in their relationship, they have a level of intimacy and mutual synthesis that enables interdependence and performance. Just as a highly functional team, they are able to make decisions and solve problems effectively. When they do have a disagreement, they can work through it without damaging the relationship. At this stage, the couple is fully functional, with all the couple's energies channelled into the relationship.

Some couples may benefit from nonviolent communication (NVC) skills, as mentioned in the previous chapter. NVC is based on the notion that most conflict arises from miscommunication about real human needs, which in everyday inter-actions are often masked in demands or judgemental language (Rosenberg 2003). NVC advocates communication that conveys a need, feeling, perception, and request. It also encourages an empathetic approach because it recognises that the other person also has feelings and needs. This structure enables the discovery of strategies that allow the needs of both parties to be met. According to NVC, people need to express themselves in objective, neutral terms, using factual observations rather than judgmental language. Self-expression in NVC follows four basic steps:

1. Making a neutral observation: '*You were home late on Monday and Wednesday this week.*'
2. Expressing a feeling without any justification or interpretation: '*I feel quite worried when you are later than normal…*'
3. Expressing needs: '*…and I have a real need to know that you are safe.*'
4. Making a clear, feasible request: '*Would it be possible for you to text or phone me, just to say you'll be home at 9 or 10?*'

In response to this clarity of communication, partners should feel empathy with the speaker's feelings and needs and respond positively to the request. NVC can be a useful communication tool for getting short-term individual needs met, but in the context of relationship coaching it is underpinned by a consolidated commitment to a joint vision.

Learning together

Functioning together as a team, as described above, leads to the next stage of couple fulfilment: learning together. Batthyany-De La Lama et al. (2012: 285) pointed out that relationships are developmental, in that they 'grow and develop along a relationship life cycle that may run parallel to but does not always coincide with the individual partner's life cycle'. They proposed a 'soul mates model' of relationship development that adopts a positive psychology perspective. In this model, any problem in a relationship is considered as an opportunity to learn together, 'to seek out new resources and develop new strengths and skills that serve as springboards to a new developmental level'. The model is useful because it provides a seven-stage lifecycle of a couple's relationship: dating, commitment, intimacy, building a life, integrating the shadow, renewal, and completion; each stage has tasks to complete. At each stage of the model, problems are seen as developmental challenges to overcome in order to strengthen the relationship as a whole. For example, Batthyany-De La Lama et al. (2012: 288) suggested that 'integrating the shadow' involves the following:

- Reframing emotional stalemate and meaninglessness as a developmental crisis calling for inner work;
- Disentangling from distracting and counterproductive ideologies and unexamined cultural beliefs;
- Taking an existential stance, forgiving self, partner, others, and life at large;
- Addressing and treating psychological dysfunctions, seeking professional help where needed;
- Freeing energy and resources by letting go of physical, emotional, conceptual, and ideological baggage;
- Starting to focus on a cause greater than self and family to serve individually and jointly.

Coaches could use the soul mates model as a tool where both partners agree that they want to work together to develop as individuals, improve their relationship, and develop a joint commitment together.

In Chapter 2, we discussed the value of critical thinking to challenge and expand clients' views of the world. Cox (2013: 92) has also suggested that as we develop through relationships 'we are more tolerant as we begin to see ourselves through the eyes of others'. When coaching with couples, the benefits of this kind of perspective enhancement can be enormous, helping the couple to compare and contrast their experiences without blame or anger. Working within the safe environment of the coaching room, couples can be challenged on their assumptions, be encouraged to take different perspectives, and develop alternative ways of looking at things. Critical thinking can thus be used in two ways: to validate existing thinking or to transform thinking (Cox 2013). Validation is important at the start of the coaching to build trust in the process, but then the shift to transformation is important to enable mutual learning. The transformation is achieved by helping the couple to reflect on their experiences but then to think critically about how they perceive, think, and act as a couple, including integrating the shadow elements as suggested by Batthyany-De La Lama et al. (2012). During this process, they become aware of how social and environmental constraints impact their relationship and shape their responses and discover ways of being that result in evolution for their relationship. The coach's role is to create the space that will enable constructive conversation for the couple to examine together how they make meaning from their experience and from there go on to explore new possibilities.

Evolution

There are two ways in which the couple relationship can evolve as a result of ongoing commitment, understanding, and learning together. The first is to consolidate the performance relationship they have built up, strengthening the ways in which they cooperate and work together as a couple. The second is to evolve in the way that Batthyany-De La Lama et al. (2012) suggested in the final two stages of their model: to focus on renewal and completion. The renewal and completion stages involve couples in continued re-evaluation of their relationship, their philosophy of life, and their goals. The aim is to 'rebuild the interactive field with new awareness, content, love and care' (288), which entails considering all available resources and creating a new path for both individual and shared action. This new path should ideally involve leaving a legacy – perhaps serving a cause that is greater than self and family. This munificent action parallels Erikson's (1969) concept of 'care', which encompasses the generational need of the mature adult to give back something permanent to the world.

Case studies

Using the COUPLE framework as a guide, we now present case studies that demonstrate how some couple issues have been addressed using a coaching approach.

Case study: Kathy and Kim

Kathy and Kim have been together for eight years. They have come for coaching together because recently Kim has been coming home late from work and tensions are increasing. Kathy feels she is taking on more chores around the house because of Kim's increased overtime, and she feels he does not value their relationship. However, Kim is adamant that his extra time on this project at work will lead to a promotion and more money to support the home. Kathy says she's not worried about more money; she wants more time together.

Coaching recognises that the balance within the relationship is what is important:

> Problems in relationships occur when mates give few rewards to each other or make the costs of the relationship excessive. Problems also crop up when there is imbalance, when one spouse is reaping most of the rewards while the other is paying most of the costs.
>
> (Pines 1996: 57)

It has long been understood that relationships contain an element of 'exchange', whereby satisfaction is based on partners feeling that they are getting a sufficient return on their investment. In this case, Kathy felt as if she was paying most of the costs by not spending time with Kim, and that he was benefitting from the time spent on his career. Kim, however, felt that he was paying most of the costs by working to earn money that would allow him ultimately to spend time with Kathy. He actually felt that Kathy could be enjoying her time at home.

This is a typical scenario in many marriages. One partner appears to have a different set of goals. The role of coaching here was initially to provide a space for Kathy and Kim to explore their joint goals, and then to get commitment to the coaching task and ultimately to each other.

By describing how they would like to see their relationship evolving and then committing to joint high-level goals or 'abstract goals linked to values' (Ives and Cox 2012: 36), it was possible for Kathy and Kim to see how they wanted the same things (closeness, a nice home, time, and extra money so that they could be together for holidays and entertaining with family).

The emphasis on exploring goals for the relationship, rather than as individuals, was novel for Kathy and Kim. When the high-level goal was then broken down into project-level goals, Kathy was able to see that, in the short term, some push towards promotion for Kim was a useful option and an opportunity to help meet the relationship goal. It fit with the high-level goals upon which they had agreed. For Kim, a slight reduction on the number of evenings spent working late was made in order to create quality time for their relationship, but equally the project took priority in the short term so that longer-term goals could be achieved. A joint objective to begin to plan a major holiday together meant that a concrete project-level goal was also set for the relationship, contributing to unity. Such tangible targets ensure that couples have joint milestones and topics of conversation that contribute to keeping their commitment to each other alive.

Kathy and Kim also devised their strap-line, 'Continued Closeness', which acted as a quick reminder throughout the weeks that this was the essence of their relationship.

In the case study of Kathy and Kim, it is interesting to note that the coach encourages partners to focus on their joint rather than their individual needs. As Sheras and Koch-Sheras (2008: 111) explained, when couples are pushed to communicate their 'needs', it can sometimes promote 'a sense of entitlement for obtaining the kind of perfection they see in the media'. Rather than helping, expressions of need can only increase expectations of faultlessness. In coaching with couples, as explained earlier, individual needs are best visited in the context of the needs of the relationship. The coach may ask, 'If you have that particular need met right now, what impact will it have on your relationship goal?'

The coaching work with Kathy and Kim was still about balance, strengths, and optimisation. So, instead of needs, the coach asked Kathy and Kim to focus on identifying each other's strengths and adding them to the vision of the relationship. In this way, positive images were created that would drive the relationship goals forward. This positive psychology approach is useful in much coaching, but especially in work with couples. Kathy and Kim constructed their acceptable/ideal relationship on paper, mapping out the relationship as they wanted it to be. The joint enterprise was fun as they thought about metaphors for the relationship, images that could capture the strap line, and images to show the strengths each brings to the relationship. The use of active listening by the coach also role-modelled good communication practice and encouraged the partners to consider the other's perspective. To strengthen their communication, the coach may also have introduced the couple to methods of improved communication, such as NVC.

Whereas Kathy and Kim had a reasonably happy marriage, relationship coaching can also be helpful where the relationship is growing increasingly unsatisfactory to one or more parties but may not have completely deteriorated – where there is blame but perhaps not contempt. For the couple in our next case study, Karen and Martin, the tendency is to focus overwhelmingly on what is wrong in the marriage and extrapolate from that to the rest of the relationship.

Case Study: Karen and Martin

Karen and Martin met at university and married shortly after Karen received her master's degree in political science. Martin went into sales two years before, having received his bachelor's degree in history. Now seven years into their marriage, Karen feels she made a huge mistake. From her perspective, she and Martin are just too different. Worse, however, she feels that since their marriage, Martin has made no effort to bridge the gap. Even though they now have a child, Martin still 'hangs out' with his mates on Sundays, whereas Karen would want him in church and with the family. Martin is tired of being continuously urged to 'grow up' and made to feel inferior. So here we have a woman who feels she has an inconsiderate, boorish husband, and a man who feels he has a bossy and patronising wife.

Karen is better educated and the higher earner and, like Kathy in our previous case, was left to do the lion's share of the domestic work. Martin assumed the traditional male roles of gardening and washing the car; he considered it obvious that bathing the baby or doing the shopping was the wife's responsibility. This provoked Karen into lecturing Martin about how she is the main breadwinner and how his lazy attitude was entirely unjustified. Not surprisingly, this greatly antagonised Martin, who already was struggling with a sense of inferiority because of his wife's success. To protect his ego, Martin would find faults in Karen, in particular highlighting her weight gain since the baby arrived.

By the time they seek help, Karen is openly threatening to leave the marriage. Whereas before this crisis the couple was already growing apart, now a great wall seems to be dividing them. Martin wants to save the marriage but does not feel he can, and Karen wants to end it because she thinks it is not worth saving.

Sheras and Koch-Sheras (2008) highlighted how gender identity issues can play themselves out in relationships. When the man is not able to be, or prefers not to be, the main breadwinner, he can often feel displaced and discriminated against.

In the case of Martin and Karen, Martin was influenced to some extent by this thinking, although when this was highlighted he denied it. It was helpful for both Karen and Martin, though, to be aware of societal influences and expectations on their relationship.

Focused entirely on problems and wrapped up in negativity at the beginning of the coaching, Karen and Martin could not imagine any solution. The coach needed to shift the conversation from what was wrong to what was right, from what was disliked to what was preferred in its place. Using a solutions-focused orientation, the coach highlighted what was still working successfully in the marriage and began to build on that. Like the approach used with Kathy and Kim, the coach asked the couple to move away from obsessing about what each does not want in the relationship and instead to focus on what they each to wanted to see in the relationship. This approach recognised that some progress can be the beginning of the reversal from blame to hope, where even a small movement forward represents a vital change in direction.

As described in Chapter 5, solutions-focused coaching is a goal-focused approach that adopts a future-oriented position. However, as we argued in Ives and Cox (2012: 48–49), although the solutions approach is useful, it has to be supported by a rigorous goal-setting and action-planning process.

Using a solutions-focused approach with a couple such as Karen and Martin, the coach would do the following:

1. Ask for descriptions of the relationship outcome. For example, 'What has to be different as a result of the coaching?' 'When this problem is solved, what will you each be doing differently?' The coach may also ask scaling questions, such as, 'On a scale of 1–10, what is the likelihood of achieving that goal?'
2. In forming the description, the coach can ask about when the problem was not occurring: 'Describe a time when you noticed the problem was not there.' Some couples might say 'on holidays and weekends' or 'when people come over'.
3. Hypothetical questions can also be asked via the miracle question (Berg and de Shazer, 1993: 114). For example, 'If a miracle occurred overnight and suddenly you could both agree on what you wanted, what might that be? What will you notice that's different in the morning that will let you know the problem is solved?' After the miracle question, a coach might ask other follow-up questions, such as, 'What would your partner notice was different about you?' 'What would your partner do differently then?' 'What would it take to pretend that this miracle had happened?'

Delving deeper into the causes of the friction with Karen and Martin at this point in their relationship would only intensify and deepen the entrenchment. With emotions so raw, addressing the sore points that threaten the marriage is extremely dangerous. Therefore, coaching seeks to cordon off the most violent and destructive aspects of the tension and to focus on creating a positive future.

The COUPLE coaching approach to this situation would begin with a solution-focused methodology, as described above, asking the couple to imagine an ideal outcome for their relationship, however implausible it currently seems. Only once the commitment to the relationship is regained and a shared goal, however small, is agreed upon can the couple be introduced to tools, such as NVC, to smooth everyday communication.

It was a struggle for Karen to get Martin to meet with the coach, but eventually he agreed, if only for the sake of their child. After some initial contracting, where the dual, turn-taking nature of the coaching was explained and the open and creative nature of the initial session described, the subsequent dialogue began like this:

Coach [turning to Karen first]: If you could control the situation entirely, what would be a useful outcome?

Karen: A useful outcome was that we had a good marriage and were not in this mess – but that is not realistic.

Coach: Can you describe what a good marriage would look like? Can you draw it? [provides sheet of paper and coloured pens]

Karen: Well, our relationship wasn't always like this. We were quite in love in the beginning and had great times together. It wouldn't be possible to go back to that, because I guess I was being naïve. But we have a baby and we love her to bits [Karen draws two stick people, a heart and a baby] – so the ideal marriage includes us and her.

Coach [turning to Martin]: So Martin, what would need to happen to have that kind of relationship in the future? [Coach assumes here that Martin agrees with the parents and baby image.]

Martin: We've definitely grown apart. So we would need to grow together again somehow. Karen has developed into a continuous nag, so she'd have to stop that.

Coach [to both]: Would you say that Karen's nagging shows commitment to the relationship?

Martin: I suppose she sees it like that.

Coach: How would you draw that commitment in a positive way, Martin? [Martin draws a cloud; Karen adds a question mark.]

Coach [turning to Karen]: So Karen, what would need to happen to grow together in the relationship in the future?

Karen: I resent how Martin has given our relationship such a low priority recently. He doesn't show any commitment to the relationship when he is spending time with his mates instead of with the family.

Coach: So you believe Martin gives the relationship low priority? What would need to happen for him to give it higher priority? [Coach gives credence to Karen's views using active listening, but quickly shifts to a future focus.]

Karen: He would need to do things that show he is committed to the relationship – like helping around the house, not playing constantly on the computer.

Coach [to both]: What does he currently do that shows commitment? Can you draw those things?

Karen: To give him credit, Martin is a ball of fun, and he is great with the baby. He can be very loving and kind when he wants to be – often in very spontaneous ways. But we are not students anymore and his lack of responsibility drives me crazy. [Karen draws a clown face.]

Coach [to Martin]: What are the positive aspects of the cloud you have drawn? How does Karen show commitment?

Coach [to both]: Now that you have current commitment mapped out for the relationship, let's think about future commitment. What would you like to see in the relationship in the future?

Martin: I want to be a fun dad. We're still young and I don't mind Karen going to church but I'm not religious, so I don't go, but I could look after the baby. [Martin spontaneously offers a compromise.]

Karen [to Martin]: I want you to be fun, I used to love that about you, but I want to include some times when we are together – if you don't come to church and you're always at work or playing games, when will we be together?

This conversation continues with the couple offering some compromises and identifying new relationship activities that will bring them together. They conclude the coaching session by formulating the strapline: 'We're fun together.'

What we see in this dialogue is a coach who is helping the couple to move away from the intense feelings that focus on the past and are a barrier to resolving the issue, towards some small, practical future steps that might help bring them closer together. A joint relationship picture can continue to be created; hopefully from that, joint goals (however small) can emerge. This is a couple on the cusp of divorce and what is needed is to stabilise the situation and reduce the tension sufficiently that they can buy time and enable the more ingrained communication habits to be dealt with over time. Even if Martin is willing to make significant adjustments, this will not immediately erase the hurt and frustration felt by Karen. The emotional work required to rebuild the affection and commitment in the relationship will take a long time, but hopefully Karen and Martin will be able to give the relationship another chance.

Summary

Most people enter into relationships on the strength of heady feelings of attraction and cannot imagine ever not being madly in love with their partner (Vernon 2013). A consequence of this is that most couples do little to plan for the difficulties that can arise in a relationship, believing or assuming that they have no need to do so. However, the adage 'an ounce of prevention avoids a pound of cure' is true in many aspects of life, and coaching can provide a useful framework for couples to explore how to make their relationship stronger and better.

In this chapter, we introduced the COUPLE framework to guide coaching practice. This model is underpinned by current constructivist theories of relationship enhancement. Through the model and appropriate case studies, we explained how coaching can be used to strengthen and enhance dyadic relationships, encouraging openness in communication and leading to a greater understanding of the self and others.

Gottman (1999: 184) explained how in therapy the process of conflict resolution is based on the exploration of how to help the partner's dreams come true. We have suggested however, that in coaching, there is not only concern with the partner's dreams, but with the dream for the relationship, believing that through commitment to a relationship goal and the following of a mutual agenda, partners will strengthen their bond. Partners, at least for the duration of the coaching, have to agree to put their individual dreams on hold. The focus needs to be on how to make mutual dreams come true and hopefully to ensure that the partner's dreams are known and become part of that mutual plan.

Sometimes, although both parties are involved in the coaching, they have opposing aspirations with regards to the relationship, with only one party desiring its continuation. This is a difficult situation and one that may require referral to a counsellor or a shift to individual coaching. The role that coaching can play in helping to make the decision to rescue or dissolve the relationship is the same as in any other decision-making, scenario: If it is a joint decision to split up, a plan can be made for an effective dissolution, or, if partners are in total disagreement, individuals can be helped to examine the situation from different perspectives, to find ways of accepting and easing the transition, and to map out a course of practical action for themselves and other family members if necessary. Coaching can there-fore enable individuals to begin to perceive a break-up in a more positive manner and move forward amicably.

In the next chapter, we examine how coaching can support parents through the issues they face, recognising also the changes that parenting brings to their relationships.

Chapter 8

Coaching with parents

Some people argue that, in our postmodern era, parenting is a more complex and challenging task than ever before and that 'rapid social change has intensified pressure on the family' (Bamford et al. 2012: 134). Others adopt the view that it always been so, and that each generation thinks it has the most difficult task. Whichever the case, raising children today involves difficulties and struggles that leave many parents overwhelmed. The contemporary struggles faced by parents include issues compounded by changing family dynamics and long working hours (Berk 2006). However, these challenges are not limited to a single socio-economic stratum, as some populists imply: Whether rich or poor, parents or other caregivers will often feel the strain of raising children. Adults who are highly competent in their professional lives can be reduced to helplessness in the face of the challenges that parenting presents. In many situations, they feel out of their depth, convinced that nothing they do will work.

Speaking about parenting as a single construct is simplistic, however, because the role of the parent of an infant can be very different to the role of the parent of a teenager, and this is likewise very different from parenting a fully grown adult. In this chapter, we focus on coaching for two general parenting phases: early childhood (until around age 10) and adolescence (11 onwards). There are many differences between these two age groups. Whereas with a younger child parents may need to instruct, with an older child parents need to guide; whereas with a younger child the primarily role of the caregiver is to provide protection, for the older child the parent needs to offer progressive amounts of freedom; whereas with a younger child parents need to exercise authority, with an older child they need to negotiate authority; whereas with a younger child the role of the parent as the primary source of attachment is rarely challenged, with an older child parents can become increasingly replaced by peers as attachment figures. These and many other differences suggest that parenting is not a single homogeneous process. Mixed in are the cultures or backgrounds of the parents and of the society in which the children are raised. All of these factors play key roles in shaping the expectations of parents and their children and influence the relationships between them. Coaching in this context provides support for functioning families when the parents are honest enough to realise that what they are doing is not quite enough, their approach may not always be working, and it is time to look at alternative approaches.

Parents might battle with a range of issues on a daily basis, depending on the age of their children: sleepless nights, tantrums, eating the wrong foods, sibling rivalry, rudeness, helping with household chores, staying out late, truancy, etc. The list is very long, and coaching cannot solve the issues individually. Rather, coaching with parents is aspirational. It is for parents who believe that parenting should be positive and inspiring. Coaching also is for parents who think that parenting is too important to settle for second best and who are willing to see how working with a coach can help develop them as people and as parents, and so become better communicators and role models for their children.

Thus, there can be no one way to parent, and the role of the coach is not to tell parents what is wrong with their parenting or to tell them what they need to change. Rather, the coach helps parents to develop different ideas and perspectives by providing a space to reflect and examine their parenting practice. Specifically, the coach can help with the following:

- Identifying and clarifying goals and values as a parent
- Exploring new approaches to, and perspectives on, the parenting task
- Determining what action(s) might be required to achieve them

In this chapter we show how coaching can support parents in feeling more confident and competent. The coach can help them to gain clarity about their unique circumstances and then adapt their strategies and approach to suit the specific needs of the child and the situation. Mostly, parents do this on their own and with reasonable success. However, sometimes parents get stuck and would benefit greatly from the support and assistance of a knowledgeable and capable coach. Indeed, O'Brien and Mosco (2013: 93) pointed out how 'parenting styles are often not questioned until something goes awry' and that only then might parents look for help and 'discover they need to change how they are parenting'. They suggest that parents need help in order to be supportive to their children and so parent more positively. Using the relationship coaching model outlined in Chapter 5, the emphasis is therefore on supporting parents in gaining new perspectives on their interactions with their child/children.

It should be remembered, however, that a coach does not provide the answers to particular issues, but instead uses a coaching approach to help to generate ideas. Coaching does not tackle psychological issues, where, for example, the family may be already breaking down or is in crisis and in need of specialist help, but rather it is designed for the coach and the parent(s) to work together in order to deal with the challenges being presented in a functioning family. As discussed in Chapter 9 of this book, coaching is not a substitute for family therapy or counselling, which might focus more tightly on problems and problematic transactions within the family. However, coaching is one type of support that is stigma-free and positively oriented.

The chapter is divided into three main sections. First, we draw attention to five main assumptions that influence our discussion of coaching in the parenting context. Drawing on the available literature, we discuss the role of the coach before presenting a number of additional theories that can be useful to consider. Towards the end of the chapter, we present four case studies that illustrate how coaching can support parents through a variety of dilemmas with young children and adolescents.

Assumptions

The first assumption we make is that parents and children each have needs that should be respected. Effective parenting is not simply about better ways to manipulate children to do the things that adults want them to do. Behavioural techniques may sometimes allow us to get a child to do our bidding, but parenting must involve creating an environment that supports and nurtures the kinds of behaviours we value and would dearly like our children to value: parents need to socialise their children according to their own sets of cultural and community values. Children also have specific needs for attachment and individuation, and those needs differ according to age (Eagle 1995). It is important for parents to be aware of their children's need for a close and continuous caregiving relationship, which will provide good attachment. Also, parents themselves have needs, in particular to be recognised both as individuals and as a couple, where appropriate.

Our second assumption is that coaching can support parents in perceiving the home as an ecosphere: a family environment that comprises multiple elements that interact with one another, much like a weather system. However, as parents we need to remember that we do not have to control all the elements to make a positive or negative impact on the overall system – we just need to make small changes. In recent decades, family therapies based on systems thinking (Dallos and Draper 2010) have brought to the fore the way that small adjustments in the dynamics of the family can trigger broader impacts. The coach can therefore help parents to identify where changes could have the maximum impact and benefit.

Third, we believe that coaching should not just look at helping parents to address childrearing issues, but it should also support how the parents interact with one another. Whether the parents are living together in a happy union, whether the relationship is strained, or whether the parents are separated, the way that the parents interact with each other is a critical element in parenting. The coach can help parents to consider where their own parental exchanges are modelling unhelpful behaviour, and it can help them to find and rehearse alternative modes of communication so that their children will have a more constructive model to follow.

Parents can thus use their own interactions as an opportunity to demonstrate many of the important qualities that they wish their children to adopt: how to share, to respect each other's privacy, to keep each other's secrets, and so forth. The coach can encourage parents to view their own behaviour and communication with one another as a key platform for preparing their child for adulthood, as the patterns of communication between parents serve as the primary model of communication for the child. In their discussion of parents who were coaching their own children in a sports context, Littlefield and Larson-Casselton (2009: 190) also highlighted how 'what children learn about communication in the family setting will be reflected in their future communication with individuals outside of the family'.

Our fourth assumption is underpinned by Bandura's (1977) theory that human behaviour is learned through observing and modelling others. This, he said, is how ideas are formed and new behaviours adapted and used as a guide for actions in subsequent behaviour. Coaching can also be considered as a particularly intensive form of modelling, where the clients can emulate the coach's skills and communication style and implement these in their own setting. This kind of modelling is particularly appropriate for parents who want to change the communication patterns in their own families. Such modelling takes two forms: it may be implicit, where the coach's communication behaviours are reproduced in the family setting; or it may be used explicitly to role play potential conversations. An example is given later in this chapter in our case study with Claire.

Our fifth assumption is that both parents need to have a consistent approach and be supportive of each other in relation to their children's demands. These attributes can be developed through couples coaching techniques (described in the previous chapter). Thus, where there is more than one parent or caregiver in the family, we emphasise a 'co-parenting stance' (McHale and Fivaz-Depeursinge 2010).

The role of the coach

A review of the literature relating to coaching with parents reveals that coaching in this context is generally skills-focused rather than developmental and frequently focuses on parents with children who have some kind of disability. For example, Graham et al. (2009) proposed a process of occupational performance coaching (OPC), whereby parents are guided in solving problems related to achieving self-identified goals. OPC is particularly useful when parents have performance goals for children that cannot be negotiated with the child (i.e. because of cognitive limitations or motivational discrepancies), when goal achievement is highly dependent on the performance context, or when parents are seeking to develop their own skills in supporting their children's learning and performance. OPC is one example of the substantial range of support approaches available for improving outcomes for children with disability. OPC focuses specifically on parent-identified solutions to performance barriers: 'The therapist employs specific language, questioning and reflection cues to guide parents' self-discovery of solutions, and their implementation and evaluation within a problem-solving framework' (Graham et al. 2009: 16). OPC is designed to develop parents' problem-solving skills and help them to create more enabling environments for bringing up children.

Shanley and Niec's (2010) experimental study explained how the coaching techniques in their behavioural parent training were based on modelling skills.

They provided parents with phrases to repeat verbatim to their children and then praised their use of modelled phrases:

> Mothers received contingent praise each time they used any of the three positive parenting skills. When parents used the skills spontaneously, the coach decreased the frequency of modelling and if the parent decreased spontaneous use of the targeted skill, the coach increased modelling and contingent praise (284).

These elements of modelling are important aspects of behaviour-based parent coaching, but an important addition would need to be some form of discussion or debrief to encourage reflection on any attempts to achieve change.

McGoldrick and Carter (2001: 281) talked about how the goal of coaching is to 'help clients define themselves proactively in relationship to others in their families without emotionally cutting off or giving in'. Using family systems techniques, they explained that this is one of the hardest things to balance because parents do not want to distance themselves emotionally from their children, but neither do they necessarily want to give in and go against their beliefs about good parenting. In the systems model adopted by McGoldrick and Carter, parents can be encouraged to become observers and to examine their role and behaviour within the family. In effect, the coaching helps them to become researchers of the patterns that emerge within their day-to-day family life.

McGoldrick and Carter (2001) also confirmed that people within the family can only change themselves: 'a person's individual participation in any system is all he or she can change'; however, through bringing about change in oneself, 'other family members will be jarred out of their own unthinking responses' and will respond reciprocally (283). In two-person subsystems such as the parent–child relationship, 'the element of reciprocity of emotional functioning can be striking, as in … the involvement between the nagging parent and the dawdling child' (283). Any regular change in participation should result in consistent change in outcome, so if the parent ignores certain behaviours (if it is safe to do so) and provides distractions of some kind, different responses will come from the child. Using this approach, a coaching discussion might focus on patterns in a client's networks of relationships, rather than primarily on what McGoldrick and Carter called 'the individual's intrapsychic processes' (282). Indeed, many coaches already work like this. Coaches are not constrained by a specific therapeutic training and will employ approaches from across disciplines, wherever they seem appropriate, to support the client's unfolding agenda.

Bamford et al. (2012: 134) noted recently how coaching parents is different from other parenting interventions in that coaches are not coming from the position of a parenting expert to tell parents they are 'doing something wrong or that they must follow a certain script'. Instead, they described how a coaching approach focuses on using 'powerful questions to enable parents to understand themselves and their children better'. These authors also pointed out how coaching can reduce pressure on parents, improving the quality of their communication with their children, which can also impact on their effectiveness in other areas of their lives: 'Many of the skills that parents learn, such as active listening, positive communication, the impor-tance of praise and recognition, are skills that are transferable to the workplace' (134). Bamford et al. also highlighted the important benefits of better interaction with children, arguing that 'even small changes in parents' behaviour or speech patterns can have a significant impact on children's performance and motivation, self-esteem, and confidence' (134).

Haslett (2013) undertook a qualitative case study of the BabiesKnow project in the United Kingdom. She described BabiesKnow as a unique approach to helping parents as it is a developmental rather than a purely skills-based programme. According to Kitty Hagenbach, the founder (as quoted in in Haslett 2013: 4), the programme is 'rooted in helping parents to understand themselves better, their own feelings and emotions … developing emotional intelligence, for parents and children, from conception onwards'.

Haslett's (2013) findings confirm that while becoming a parent is a happy experience, it can be disruptive and disorienting. She found that new parents experienced some disorientation in relation to becoming a parent, and that this was accompanied by anxiety and the need for greater awareness of the issues parent-ing presents. However, during and following coaching, the young parents involved in the project developed in maturity: coaching provided a sense of perspective and the freedom to trust their own judgment. Haslett's respondents described how the coach helped them to develop new meaning perspectives: 'There seemed to be great value for the participants in not being told what to do, in not being given a set of rules or steps to follow but in just being heard by their coach' (38). As coaching progressed, respondents became more independent thinkers and had a range of perspectives. They relied less on expert advice, as through a challenging and empowering coaching process they had learned to apply their own critical judgement. One respondent explained how it lifted a huge weight off her shoulders. Parenting could therefore be viewed as a 'springboard' for individual development, especially when supported by a coach.

Haslett (2013: 43) likened coaching to having a 'focusing partner' (a term used by Gendlin 1962) – one who listens 'without judgement but seeks to clarify what is said as a means of facilitating a deeper understanding of experience'. She confirmed how listening was a vital aspect of coaching, giving the example of a mother who commented on how coaching impacted on her family: 'It was a direct result of my coaching where I learned to listen and she [her 3-year-old] has been listened to, so she thinks it is worth talking' (45).

Learning to listen to oneself and others was also seen as vital in development of the parent as a person. Haslett's (2013) respondents found their experience of being listened to during coaching was empowering and validating. Haslett further identified how listening in the coaching session can also serve as a model for listening in parent–child relationships, as one of her respondents noted:

She listened so non-judgementally … she really turned me around and pointed me back in the direction of myself. Through her listening of me I started to listen to myself. She never said, 'here are the steps, now take them'. More, 'you have all the information you need to guide you. Do you hear it? Listen to yourself ... listening to your baby' (2013: 45).

As well as drawing on the theories of developmental and goal-focused coaching that underpin the relationship coaching model, this chapter also highlights further theories that have relevance for coaching in this context. Allen (2013: 77) for instance, suggested that family life education is a model that can inform coaching in the family context and advocates a view of 'coach as expert', where the coach has valuable family process information and a background understanding of family relationships and psychology. The four additional theories and approaches discussed below represent our own selection of some of the most useful for coaches to consider when working with parents.

Parenting styles

Alegre's (2011) study found that children of parents who use a 'coaching style' of parenting are better behaved and have better physical health.

O'Brien and Mosco (2013) have discussed how different parenting styles impact different ages of children. For example, they suggested that 'proactive and responsive parenting, which 'tracks' the child during the day, allows adults to anticipate child needs, notice subtle cues such as tiredness, and ensure safety, including encounters with peers' (99). They explain how this helps toddlers in particular to cope with distress before it becomes too intense. They also suggest that 'authoritative' parenting, as a parenting style, 'maintains its effectiveness across the developmental journey and is particularly valuable during the adolescent stage in its more democratic nature' (102). Authoritative parents are warm and responsive and have 'high age-appropriate expectations and limits for their children and the provision of support to meet these' (92).

Darling and Steinberg (1993) discussed the development of Baumrind's seminal work on parenting style. They traced its development through to Maccoby and Martin's two-dimensional framework, involving a balance between responsiveness and demandingness (see Figure 8.1), and from there developed their own integrative model that differentiates 'parenting style' from 'parenting practice'. Darling and Steinberg (1993: 488) offered a model that defines parenting style as a 'constellation of attitudes towards the child that are communicated to the child'. They explained that style is 'a characteristic of the parent that alters the efficacy of the parent's socialisation efforts by moderating the effectiveness of particular practise and by changing the child's openness to socialisation' (488). They explained parenting practice as 'the mechanisms through which parents directly help their child attain their socialization goals' (493), which might include attending school events to show interest or helping a child understand the importance of hospitality. The dynamics between styles and practices are shown in Figure 8.1 – in particular, the moderating influences that parenting styles have on parenting practice.

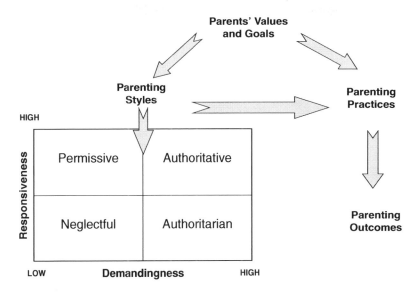

Figure 8.1 Styles and practices of parenting (adapted from Darling and Steinberg 1993:493)

Emotion coaching

The adolescent period is probably the most worrying and difficult time for parents because children in this age group struggle to regulate their own emotions as a result of hormonally induced increases in negative affect, such as anger (Larson and Sheeber 2008). Shortt et al. (2010: 3) explained how adolescence is a period of increased vulnerability because neural regulatory structures are still developing at the same time as the child is coping with increased emotionality and independence. They highlighted how adolescence increases the potential for 'externalising' behaviours such as through 'academic failure, school drop out, substance use, and delinquent peer affiliation' (2). To begin to address this problem, these authors studied the prevalence and effect of 'maternal emotion coaching', which they described as a 'socialisation process wherein parents provide guidance in understanding and coping with emotions' (2). Such guidance follows the work of Gottman et al. (1997) and includes parents showing respect for the child's emotional experience through offering comfort, helping them to understand the nature of emotions, advising on appropriate ways to express emotions, and discussing strategies for dealing with emotional situations.

Gottman et al. (1997) added that a child's emotional intelligence may be influenced by whether parental orientations tend towards emotion coaching or emotion dismissing. 'Emotion coaching' describes a way of talking about negative emotions with children in a differentiated manner. Parents who help their children with emotions – such as anger and sadness – are acting, in effect, like an emotion coach.

By contrast, parents with an 'emotion-dismissing' orientation view their child's anger or sadness as potentially harmful to the child, seeking to replace negative emotions for more positive ones, and encouraging the realisation that these negative emotions will not last and will soon pass. Gottman et al. (1997) found that emotion-dismissing parents were sensitive to their children's feelings, but their way of approaching anger, for example, was to ignore it as much as possible. These parents assume that the dismissing strategy will make the emotion go away. In their research, Gottman et al. found that emotion-dismissing parents described sadness as follows:

> [Sadness was] something to get over, ride out, but look beyond and not dwell on. They often used distractions when their child was sad to move the child along, and they even used comfort, but within specified time limits, as if they were impatient with the negative emotion itself. They preferred a happy child and often found these negative states in their child quite painful. They did not present an insightful description of their child's emotional experience and did not help the child with problem solving. They did not see the emotion as beneficial or as any kind of opportunity, either for intimacy or for teaching. Many dismissing families saw their child's anger (without misbehavior) as enough cause for punishment or a Time Out (1997: 51).

Havighurst et al. (2010) confirmed that emotionally unsupportive approaches impact negatively on a child's socioemotional functioning and can be linked to lower emotion regulation ability. Other studies suggest that mothers who used an emotion-coaching approach showed 'more validating and affectionate behaviour and less contemptuous and belligerent behaviour during the interactions' (Shortt et al. 2010: 8). Furthermore, this was found to have a positive effect on the kinds of externalising behaviours described above: children had less behavioural problems, better social skills, and fewer physical illnesses (Gottman et al. 1997).

Greenberg (2002: 60–63) described the principles of emotion coaching as follows:

- Increasing awareness of emotion, which involves facing the emotion and becoming aware of it, as well as naming the emotion in order to facilitate conceptual understanding. This awareness enables a child to trust their emotions and accept that it is okay to have them.
- Enhancing emotion regulation through distancing techniques, such as self-soothing through breathing and calming self-talk. Parents would show through their own responses how emotions are not avoided but are accepted and managed.
- Transforming a maladaptive emotion by replacing it with a more adaptive one in order to reduce intensity. For example, a child could be encouraged to replace hatred or disgust with a softer feeling of compassion, which generates understanding. This is not the same as dismissing or ignoring the emotion entirely; instead it acknowledges the emotion, but putting it into perspective helps the child to let go of his/her fixation with the object of the emotion.

Brackett et al. (2004) explained how emotional intelligence is connected with positive social relationships and emphasised the importance of understanding the contexts and situations where emotional abilities play a vital role. They pointed out how 'emotionally intelligent people can manage their emotions more effectively and, consequently, they should be able to cope better with life's challenges' (189).

Triangulating

Bowen (1978), writing from a family systems perspective, argued that tensions in relationships can be diminished through the introduction of a third party. According to Bowen, this kind of triangulating is natural and only becomes noticeable when it is dysfunctional. For example, a dysfunction may arise if parents avoid solving a significant adult relationship problem and instead argue about the behavioural problems of one of their children. The child is scapegoated as the issue, and the parents never deal with their own problem effectively because the tension is effectively 'outsourced' through the child. In this scenario, the child becomes a victim, while one parent takes on the role of persecutor, accusing the child, and the other becomes the rescuer, defending the child.

This triangulating phenomenon parallels what Karpman (1968) referred to as the drama triangle, where a person overidentifies with one point on the triangle – whether that is as a victim, persecutor, or rescuer. Most often, people see themselves as a victim and will try to find someone to rescue them from the perceived persecutor. Problems occur when people are not aware that drama triangles are being played out persistently and in many areas of their lives.

The role of the coach in helping parents to identify problematic triangles could include the following:

- Strengthening self-understanding through reflection and the examination of attitudes and beliefs about appropriate roles within family relations.
- Identifying triangles where they consistently operate as a rescuer, victim, or persecutor and looking at ways of becoming more resilient in situations where triangles are problematic for them.
- Becoming aware of co-dependent traits in themselves or members of their family: Habitual rescuers, for instance, generally have co-dependent belief systems and behaviours, whereas some people have long histories as 'victims' and encourage others to rescue them.

Individuation

In Chapter 4, we discussed attachment theory. This concept also has significance for coaching in a parenting context: it is important to establish healthy attachment patterns for children. However, attachment needs to be understood within a developmental framework. For example, as they mature through a process of separation-individuation, children become increasingly differentiated from relational attachments, such as the mother, and come to see themselves as separate and distinct from the familial context (Karpel 1976, Lapsley and Stey 2012). During childhood, changing demands for separateness and connectedness or intimacy necessitate an evolving attachment, involving ever-increasing autonomy. For children, this process involves a growing sense of empowerment and confidence that emerges from developing greater self-responsibility.

Attachment refers to the predisposition of human beings to make bonds with significant others. Individuation requires integration of unconscious and conscious forces, such as attachment, 'into a wholeness that represents the uniqueness of the individual' (Jung, as cited in Orenstein 2007: 28). Because these forces constantly impact behaviour, it is important to be aware of their existence in our daily lives and interactions with others. Children who are well individuated will have an acceptance of and compassion for themselves and others; they will be good natured, creative, and humorous. This development, in turn, impacts the intimacy that is required for children to develop successful relationships in the future. Intimacy develops from coming to know ourselves and from allowing ourselves to be known at a deep level. Whether people form successful intimate relationships as adults is influenced by how, as children, they learn the ability to strike an effective balance between close attachment and appropriate separation-individuation. Parenting that supports healthy separation and development of intimacy may mitigate the problems associated with over-attachment or attachment avoidance in adulthood.

According to Bowen (1978), a family's tolerance for an age-appropriate balance of separateness and connectedness is influenced by the level of differentiation. In well-differentiated families, individuality is expressed while remaining intimately connected to others. People who are poorly differentiated rely heavily on the acceptance of others; these 'acceptors' have weak individuality, constantly seek approval, and tend to adjust what they say and do to please others. Importantly, troublemakers and bullies can also be poorly differentiated, pretending to be individual by disputing the ideas of others or dogmatically asserting what they should do and pressuring them to conform. Such bullies actually rely on approval and acceptance as much as acceptors, but they push others to agree with them, rather than agreeing with others themselves. In poorly differentiated families, then, the boundaries are blurred, autonomy is seen as threatening, or there are rigid boundaries between family members because connection and intimacy are seen as a threat; family members are more emotionally reactive because each is seeking love and approval or attacking others for their lack of support and love.

It is also useful to note that human potential is always developed in context and that ideas about individuation differ according to different cultures. Parenting practices that promote the development of individuation are influenced by cultural norms. In the west, for instance, childrearing tends to cultivate a capacity for ambition, competitiveness, and autonomy and separation, whereas the ideas of sensitivity to others, dependence, interdependence, and the formation of a 'we-self' (Roland 1988) are more prevalent in eastern societies, such as Japan and India.

Byng-Hall (2008) argued that it is also important to help parents to examine how their own attachment strategies interact. Arguments between parents and children can be 'vicious circles' (141), which can in turn induce attachment reactions as both parents and children seek safety in their habitual responses. Byng-Hall advocated the use of a family tree exercise or genogram (see McGoldrick et al. 1999 for detailed explanations of how these can be used to encourage understanding of familial relationships in a therapy setting). Haslett (2013) suggested using a simpler 'Russian doll' exercise, where dolls of increasingly smaller size are nested inside one another and then revealed in turn to prompt stories about parental or other influences on thinking. Any strategy to facilitate discussion of family systems and relationships and so challenge assumptions and patterns can be useful for enabling insight and learning.

Case studies

Through some contextualised parenting problems, we now begin to show the features and processes that characterise coaching with parents of children of different ages. The first two case studies use examples of coaching with younger children, while the second two tackle mainly adolescent issues. Using these case studies, we hope to illustrate some of the highlighted theories and models in action.

Mealtime trauma

John and Mary's coaching goal was to understand why every attempt to persuade their two boys, aged 4 and 7 years, to sit at the dinner table at mealtimes and to eat their food turned into a running battle of tantrums and tears.

Using the goal-focused approach, the coach began by exploring what an acceptable outcome might be, if the coaching was successful. John and Mary agreed that they would like the boys to eat a reasonable amount – not necessarily a clean plate every time – and for them to sit at the table throughout the main course and preferably the whole meal. They also said that they wanted the boys to use a knife and fork properly and generally develop some polite table manners.

This kind of clarification is important. Some parents have a very clear sense of what they want their child to do and be, and are able to articulate this to themselves and to their children. However, many parents, like John and Mary, only know what they want from their child when the child does the very opposite of that. A parent may say, 'Stop eating with your hands, it's terribly impolite', but that parent may never have communicated properly the importance of using a knife and fork, nor explained consistently the importance of politeness at the table. So, here we have children who are being criticised for doing something that they only find out represents an issue when they receive criticism for failing. While the children may eventually get the message, this is not the most effective or reasonable method of achieving this goal.

For John and Mary's boys to accept new behaviours and internalise them, and for these to serve as a basis for the mature development into adolescence, they also need to learn the values that underpin these behaviours. Continuing with the example of politeness at the dining table, it is not enough that the children are actively taught about table manners; John and Mary also need to underpin these behaviours with the introduction of their overall value concept of politeness. This provides the context and meaning that support the detailed practices that are the habits of a polite person.

Therefore, when the boys were being taken to task for eating with their fingers or leaving the table, they were confused for two reasons. First, they may not ever have been taught how important it is to be polite, and second they may not properly know what 'polite' means. As adults, we often assume that our family values are obvious and that our children will either absorb them or immediately copy our behaviour and adopt our family culture, but this is not necessarily the case. When we combine this with the reality that many parents do not consistently practice even their own espoused behaviours, we see why they struggle to raise their children. Coaching can help parents to identify where gaps exist in their parenting repertoire and to plan a course of action to fill the gap.

Typically, parents use one of two methods to get their children to act appropriately when they are not being cooperative: carrot or stick – promise of reward or threat of punishment (see Calder 2007). Occasionally, some parents have resorted to violence (verbal or physical) or some other punishment or threat of punishment to achieve obedience. However, the majority of parents accept that this approach to parenting is inappropriate and therefore feel powerless to assert authority over their children. Sometimes, parents resort to continually rewarding every small measure of cooperation, which can result in selfish children who refuse to cooperate without a 'bribe'. However, as with John and Mary, there is a method to inspire expected behaviour from children without resorting to either carrot or stick, but rather by putting moral values at the heart of the family's and the child's choice-making. In this approach, parents help children to associate behaviours with values that are well understood and embraced by the entire family.

By 'values' we mean the immediate moral principles that guide a person's specific choices and actions, not high-level ideals such as understanding, wisdom, love, or enlightenment. Values are separate from states of being, such as happiness or sadness, and they are different from personality traits, such as being assertive or accepting. Values refer to the principles that guide everything that we think, say, and do; the moral virtues that influence the small steps by which we live our lives. Rather than acting on the basis of personal preference, children can make choices and act on the basis of moral and value considerations. While parents from different cultures and communities have varying priorities and values, O'Brien and Mosco (2013: 102–103) noted that 'the majority of parents in any population endorse the importance of supportive parenting behaviours'.

Research being conducted by Ives and colleagues suggests that a five-part approach to imparting values and good behaviour to children can be effective. Their approach is based on the notion that character-building in young children needs to combine ideas and action. On the basis of this approach, we introduce a

VALUES model that involves the following six elements – generally to be communicated in this order:

- **Vision** – Introducing an idea, such as 'showing hospitality', and explaining to children what it is. Parents should share with children the idea of treating guests as important and ensuring they feel welcome.
- **Authority** – Providing a story or individual role model (current or historic, real or mythical) as an 'authority' that the child can relate to that personifies and typifies the concepts being taught. Many children's books can be found that tackle behavioural-, moral-, and values-based issues.
- **Life** – Relating the concept to real life, to concrete behaviours (the more specific, the better) to ensure they are relevant to the life of child. In this case, hospitality could begin at the child's own birthday party.
- **Utterance** – Using a short slogan or catchphrase to reinforce the concept, such as 'We love having guests'.
- **Epithet** – Giving the concept a name to which all can refer (e.g. hospitality).
- **Sustain** – Ensuring the value is reinforced frequently.

Using this VALUES model, parents can encourage and role-model mutually understood and continually reinforced social and cultural values to foster positive behaviours in their children. For example, children who are brought up to understand the value of hospitality – reinforced by celebrating this as an honour, by storytelling, and with positive messages – may then respond with more cooperation when asked to clean the house as visitors are about to arrive. A child who may otherwise be strongly reluctant to help clean up could drive parents to use aggressive tactics or to promise a reward in a desperate attempt to achieve compliance. However, if the child is socialised to accept the value of hospitality, he or she may be willing to comply as the concept of hospitality is deeply ingrained as the right thing to do.

The VALUES model can be used to encourage any new value or behaviour, especially at a young age. John and Mary could be encouraged to use this model by using the catchphrase 'Let's have dinner together' and the children's book *Eat your Dinner* (Miller 2008) to reinforce the value of table manners. Another example might be to improve personal hygiene, where the book *Georgie Grub* (Willis and Chamberlain 2012) could be introduced as a negative role-model.

Several caveats in relation to this approach are worth mentioning. For example, the VALUES model is not a panacea for all situations and issues. There is still bound to be a measure of negotiation and discussion between parents and children when introducing new ideas – as is indeed proper and healthy. If there is no other choice, the 'carrot or stick' options are still available, but we believe it should in most cases be possible to reach an understanding with the child based on mutually respected values.

We also suggest that parenting cannot operate in a vacuum; parents themselves need to internalise and abide by the values they hope will inspire their children. Values-based parenting begins with the parents' own behaviour and attitudes, because when values are modelled by parents, children will learn by example. For example, a parent who wants to encourage a child to treat learning as important should create a culture of learning in the home. Parents who show they value books and continue to learn demonstrate to their children that learning and developing as people is a lifelong process and relevant to reality. The coach can help parents to identify where their own lifestyle may be adjusted to be more conducive to role-modelling their goals as parents.

Coaching is above all about achieving alignment between a person's values and lifestyle, between their goals and their actions. The field of parenting is no different. Parents who would like to see their children motivated to study need to consider their own attitude towards hard work. If they are watching television while the kitchen remains a mess, for example, they may need to consider how this affects efforts to encourage the children to stop electronic gaming in favour of doing homework.

Access stress

When she first came to coaching, Claire was a single mother with two girls, aged 7 and 10 years. She had been divorced from the girls' father for nine months. She came to coaching with the goal of improving the girls' behaviour, particularly following visits to see their father. After the girls had been with their father on access days, they seemed to be even more cheeky and rude on returning home. For example, whenever Claire asked them about their day out with dad or what they had been doing at school, they both either shrugged and said, 'Nothing much', or they were deliberately rude, brushing her aside with retorts, such as 'What's it to you?'

The coach started by asking Claire what kind of relationship she would see as preferable for her and the girls. Claire said that she recognised their unhappiness about the divorce and wanted to be their friend, to be close to them, and for them to share their hopes and fears with her. Coaching can successfully incorporate role-modelling a communication style, so the coach in this situation decided to model how Claire could encourage the girls (perhaps individually rather than together) to open up and share their feelings, as it was evident that they were in some pain following the divorce. The following dialogue models how Claire could help the girls to talk about their loss. This dialogue follows the Nonviolent Communication (NVC; Rosenberg 2003) model outlined in Chapter 7. NVC is useful in situations where children seem perturbed by issues arising from school – maybe around achievement or bullying – as well as in more personal situations, such as the loss of a parent or following a divorce. The dialogue that follows shows the coach modelling the NVC process:

Coach: Claire, when you come to coaching and you are upset because the girls have been rude to you again, I feel quite powerless. I'd like to help you to think about how you can open up a conversation with them that will enable them to share their hopes and fears. Would you be open to that?

Claire: I'd love that to happen.

Coach: You know your girls, so would it be better to talk to them on a one-to-one basis?

Claire: Yes, I think I'd start with Jackie. She's the eldest.

Coach: Following the NVC model that we talked about earlier, what would you say to Jackie next time she makes you uncomfortable?

Claire: I'll say something like, 'Jackie, when you tell me to mind my own business, I feel sad. Because you're my little girl and I love you, I'd really like to share in some of the things you've done today. Is there one thing you would be able to share?'

Coach: That sounds fine – there's no judgement in there.

Claire: Then to Jess, I'll say something similar, but slightly different. I want it to sound genuine, but I guess that will come with practice.

Claire was able to use the NVC approach to make changes to the way she encouraged the girls to share their experiences, not just of access days but also of school and social events. Gradually making just some small changes was able to have a greater impact on the ecosphere of the home. The key element of NVC is its nonjudgemental approach, so it has particular synergies with an authoritative parenting style and with coaching – particularly emotion coaching, which concentrates on the recognition and management of feelings.

The emotion coaching principles discussed earlier might also be used as steps for helping children and adolescents to cope with their emotional experiences. If Claire found that the girls were regularly feeling anger, especially as they become teenagers, then she could adopt these principles to augment the NVC approach.

A teenager accuses parents of favouritism

In the case study that follows, we see how Peter and Penny were struggling with their eldest daughter, Suzy, who was 16 years old. Peter and Penny had three children – all girls and all teenagers. They came to coaching because Suzy was causing a lot of anxiety: she had violent mood swings, stayed out late, and was rude to both parents and her sisters. Peter and Penny explained that they had always thought of themselves as consistent in the way they have brought up the three girls. However, Suzy was accusing her father of having favourites and discriminating against her unfairly because she is the eldest. She very much saw herself as the victim and tried on several occasions to invite Penny to take the rescuer role. However, Penny wisely decided not to take sides but to seek coaching instead.

Bachkirova (2011: 107) argued that the stories we tell ourselves (our self-narratives) may become impediments to change. This happens, she argued, if the stories 'do not correspond to any real mini-self'. The implication of such narratives in a relationship context is that other people may perceive us as inconsistent; we think we are responding in a particular way, but in reality we are not. In Mezirow's (1991) transformative learning theory, our meaning perspectives or habits of mind can also function as impediments to change, unless we recognise their often limiting effects.

Relationship coaching can help people with contradictory self-perceptions to become aware of when their actions are in conflict with their self-narratives and so align their actions with their thoughts and words. In this case, Peter and Penny's assurances that they are always consistent may be accurate, or they might be an illustration of the limiting effects of fixed perspectives. Therefore, in the coaching that followed, it was useful to encourage some reflection on day-to-day events. The coach used the 'content, process, premise' model of critical reflection described by Mezirow (1990: 6). In their reflection, both Peter and Penny were asked to recall a problematic event where they thought they were being fair and yet Suzy felt she was being discriminated against. They then described the content (the facts about the problem) before reflecting on the process they followed in trying to solve the problem and finally exploring the premises or presuppositions that shed light on why it was a problem in the first place. Mezirow explained how 'reflective interpretation is the process of correcting distortions in our reasoning and attitudes' (1990: 7). It was certainly helpful for our couple to examine their interpretations of events and, in this case, to acknowledge where there had been some unfairness in the expectations placed upon Suzy.

Following a series of coaching sessions, both Penny and Peter apologised to the girls for appearing to be inconsistent and asked for forgiveness. As mentioned in Chapter 7, forgiveness is an important aspect of healthy families; it is closely related to empathy and requires emotional intelligence, so opportunities to achieve real forgiveness are beneficial in the family context (Karremans and Van Lange 2008).

Stepfamily values

In this case study, we see how a coaching session helped a stepfamily to consolidate their family values and boundaries. Cate and Colin had been married for two years when they came for coaching. They each had two early-teenage children from their previous marriages. They had managed to buy a big-enough house so that the children could each have their own bedroom. Thinking that this would go a good way to prevent potential arguments, they have been surprised that they are still struggling to keep the peace in the household. They came to coaching to find out how they could encourage the family to cohere and to avoid the arguments that occurred between them and the children as they tried to set boundaries. This turned out to be quite difficult for the couple as they both had different expectations for their own children and expected the other children to comply. Colin liked a lot of order and routine with regard to bedtimes, mealtimes etc., whereas Cate was more easygoing, allowing her children to take separate meals if they wanted to and to negotiate bedtimes. It seemed as if they both had different parenting styles, as highlighted in Figure 8.1. Each parent stood firm in relation to their own ideals and, as a consequence, the children railed against the inequity between them.

The coaching began by asking Cate and Colin to each describe their preferred family culture. To help to bring them into some alignment, the couple was asked to draw the family and to illustrate their values. The coach then suggested that the couple share their high-level goals to try to identify some common values. By talking through what their joint values and expectations were and sketching them out on paper, they could begin to see how coherent boundaries could be introduced. The couple realised that they needed to speak and act as one in front of the children and formulated some actions. Once their conflicting styles had been highlighted, Cate and Colin could decide how they needed to show solidarity. They could work out a plan so that the children would know the boundaries and recognise that those boundaries were fair for all.

The outcome for Cate and Colin was almost immediately discernible. They themselves felt closer and the children noticed the difference, accepting that they could not drive a wedge between the parents.

Summary

In this chapter, we explored a number of theories, approaches, and assumptions that underpin coaching with parents and included some discussion of child development needs and parenting styles. We considered how parents need to create a home environment that supports their values and yet meets children's needs for attachment and independence, according to age. We also acknowledged how the family is a system where small changes can have bigger impacts, thus reassuring parents that they are not necessarily impotent in any given situation. They can, in many circumstances, change a situation through modelling the kinds of behaviours they value, but most often they will need to communicate those values through adopting an authoritative, emotion-coaching style with their children and ensuring this style pervades their parenting practice. We also suggested that parents need to be role models. In a sense, parents need to be the change they want to see in their children

In the literature, we found that much coaching with parents follows a behavioural approach, but more recently a developmental coaching philosophy is being adopted. Haslett's (2013) work, in particular, shows how coaching can provide a sense of perspective and gives permission for parents to trust their own judgment.

In our case studies, we illustrated some common problems facing parents of different ages. We explored ways in which a coach can help parents to reflect and think critically about the issues they face, providing a sounding board to help them to gain perspective on their parenting tasks.

Allen (2013) argued that there is a need for debate around the theory underpinning coaching in the family context, as well as further empirical research. She said that 'so little is written on this topic that first steps must include identifying theoretical foundations, understanding current practices, and creating a national dialogue to create this field of study' (78). We would second this, and we hope that our chapter has contributed to highlighting some issues within the field.

Chapter 9

Professional and ethical issues

A number of professional and ethical dilemmas present themselves in connection with relationship coaching. However, because coaching is a relatively young profession, the norms and conventions of the discipline are far from established. The coaching profession as a whole is unregulated, and no licence is necessary to practice, which means that coaches have to develop their own individual professional responsibility. In addition, there is no standardised training for coaches, which may have implications for ethical understanding and behaviour.

That said, there are professional membership bodies that provide coaching codes of practice for their affiliates. In recent years, great strides have been made to professionalise the practice of coaching in order to protect both coaches and their clients from unethical behaviour. Indeed, Brennan and Wildflower (2014: 431) explained how being held accountable for ethical conduct 'builds public confidence for practitioners'. They argued that accountability provides more surety than mere reliance on to the coach's wish to 'do no harm' and involves working 'conscientiously towards positive results for the client' (434).

Grant and Cavanagh (2014) also advocated a 'more ethically-grounded approach to the use of life coaching' (307). They reported an increasing interest in using life coaching with 'at-risk or vulnerable populations' and recognised the need for professional accountability. The authors suggested, for example, that the public is at risk 'when life coaches who are untrained in mental health interventions attempt to treat psychological problems such as depression [and] do not recognise or take into account the nature of the vulnerabilities of people with mental health problems' (306).

In this chapter, in order to raise awareness of issues facing relationship coaches, we first discuss the codes of ethical practice advocated by three of the main professional associations that coaches can align themselves with. Then we highlight a range of areas where relationship coaching can require complex ethical considerations. We suggest that forewarned is forearmed. When coaches reflect on exemplars outside of the real-life coaching situation, it enables them to better judge the appropriate professional response to an actual situation. Our goal here is to address a sample of realistic issues that could be faced by a relationship coach.

Ethical codes of practice

All coaching organisations have clear ethics policies and all reputable coach train-ing institutions would include ethics in their coach development. Brennan and Wildflower (2014) noted how these ethical codes have been developed from other professions, such as law, psychology, and psychotherapy, and that they broadly cover similar issues and concur on how to approach them. Building on Rubenstein (2006), these authors identified seven of the most common ethical issues: contract-ing, confidentiality, misrepresentation, conflict of interest, dual and multiple relation-ships, competence, and self-management. These also align with de Jong's (2006: 208) six key aspects of ethical practice for coaching, as follows:

- *Beneficence* – Always seeking a client's best interest
- *Nonmalfeasance* – 'Doing no harm'
- *Fidelity* – Being true to our commitments and obligations to others
- *Promoting autonomy* – Encouraging the client to be independent
- *Justice* – Being fair and impartial
- *Self-care and respect* – Paying attention to our own self-development and self-knowledge

Additionally, Law introduced the 'six Rs' (2010: 186–187), which cover simi-lar aspects of ethical concern: rights, respect, recognition, relationship, represen-tation, and responsibility. Law explained how the purpose of ethical codes is to ensure client safety and protection and manage boundaries and conflict. He described ethical coaching as a 'preventative practice' (198), stressing how 'managing the multiple boundaries, relationships and conflicts is particularly important in coaching. It requires coaches to have ethical attitudes, knowledge and skills in handling their coaching relationship' (189).

One of the major international professional membership associations for coach-ing is the International Coaching Federation (ICF). Their standards of ethical conduct are divided into four sections (as shown in Table 9.1). The ICF explained:

ICF Professional Coaches aspire to conduct themselves in a manner that reflects positively upon the coaching profession; are respectful of different approaches to coaching; and recognize that they are also bound by applicable laws and regulations (2008).

Similarly, the European Mentoring and Coaching Council (EMCC), in the preamble to their code of ethics, described the following:

The coach/mentor will acknowledge the dignity of all humanity. They will conduct themselves in a way which respects diversity and promotes equal opportunities. It is the primary responsibility of the coach/mentor to provide the best possible service to the client and to act in such a way as to cause no

Table 9.1 Ethical responsibilities of three professional membership coaching bodies

International Coaching Federation	European Mentoring and Coaching Council	Association for Coaching
Professional conduct at large	Competence	Fitness to practice
Professional conduct with clients	Context	Contracting
Confidentiality/privacy	Boundary management	Statutory and legal duties
Conflicts of interest	Integrity	Maintaining good practice
	Professionalism	

harm to any client or sponsor. The coach/mentor is committed to functioning from a position of dignity, autonomy and personal responsibility (2008: 2).

The EMCC is a popular professional organisation in Europe. Their ethical code includes five themes (shown in Table 9.1).

Also shown in Table 9.1 are the essential elements identified by the UK-based Association for Coaching (AC). The AC said that it expects all of its coaches and coaching supervisors to adhere to the principles of competent and ethical practice. Like the EMCC with its emphasis on coach competence, the AC (2014) identified 'fitness to practise' as an important ethical consideration.

It is important to note that these ethical codes do not purport to present moral arguments. Instead, they emphasise the responsibility and capability of individual coaches in arriving at their own conclusions through judging the application of principles that are relevant in particular cases. In the following section, we discuss examples of where coaches might need to exercise such judgement. There are rarely simple right-or-wrong answers; coaches need to consider what seems ethical at the time, guided by their relevant code of practice.

Ethical considerations

Having outlined the importance of various guides to ethical practice, we want to stress again that the implementation of ethical practice is heavily influenced by the individual values of the coach. Familiarity with ethical guidelines does not replace the professional and moral judgement of the coach. Moreover, the specific situational context will need to shape the coach's response to moral dilemmas.

In this section, we aim to raise awareness of some of the real ethical difficulties that can arise during relationship coaching. To enable a discussion of competence, we have chosen to group the example under the five ethical responsibilities identified by the EMCC, as shown in Table 9.1.

Competence

The stress on their capability as a coach should be foremost in coaches' minds as they contract with their client(s). Issues arise in particular when coaches are tempted to exaggerate their capabilities or experience for commercial gain or even to make a client feel better. During contracting, the coach needs to be honest with the client and to recognise that coaching is not the answer to all relationship challenges. Some relationship issues will very likely be outside of the coach's competence. Some problems, for example, may be the consequence of deep-seated emotional or other psychological distress that coaching is not designed to address. If a client displays signs of serious depression, self-harming thoughts, or delusions, these are alarm bells that must be heeded and immediate referral considered. For this reason, Cavanagh (2005) and Garvey et al. (2009) judged it essential that the coach is psychologically aware. Cavanagh and Buckley (2014) further emphasised that understanding when not to coach is a vital skill. It is our view that all coach training should include exploration of these complex considerations.

We would also add that, in relationship coaching, it is important that the coach has an understanding of relationship issues in order to be able to identify referral cases. The relationship coach needs to ensure that every client – whether a single person looking for a romantic attachment, a couple seeking to save their relationship, or a parent keen to gain insights into raising a teenager – has an opportunity to explore expectations at the outset. This is also where coach competence can be judged. A coaching assignment could break down later if, for example, a parent assumes that the coach can offer a set of solutions, or if one partner in a couple expects the coach to be able to turnaround his abusive partner. Where there is serious abuse, a referral needs to be made to appropriate treatment and/or support, rather than pretending that the couple can get help from the coach on this issue.

A coach therefore needs to know and to abide by his or her own limits. For example, if it is clear that the client has difficulties with sexual intimacy or has violent tendencies, these issues should only be approached by a coach with proper training. Most likely, a coach would refer the client to an appropriately trained sex therapist for intimacy issues or a counsellor who can advise on targeted support for perpetrators of domestic violence. One of the most serious mistakes a coach can make is getting involved in matters for which he or she is not professionally qualified. Peltier (2001: 225) compared coaching to therapy in this regard: 'No ethical psychotherapist would attempt to treat every patient who calls for an appointment.'

Gottman (1999) set out two scenarios where he declined to take on clients for couples coaching: one where one partner is violent and another where there is an ongoing extramarital affair. Gottman explained why these issues are not coachable: In the first scenario, it may not be realistic to expect a client whose life may be in danger to participate openly in the coaching relationship; secondly, the presence of physical violence necessitates a system of safety mechanisms that most likely will not be possible for the coach to provide. Gottman's research also showed that, in these situations, shame can result in the abused partner covering up his or her real feelings in the conjoint coaching sessions. There is also a recognised difficultly when working with just one party in a relationship. If there is an ongoing extramarital affair, for instance, then the coaching session will be unable to include all the pertinent people. Gottman suggested that it is not possible to discuss relationship dynamics when part of that relationship is missing. It is interesting to consider whether the issue of inclusion has the same potency for coaching with parents where the child or children will not be present: equally, they have no voice. However, in our view, some form of individual coaching could be suitable to help an abusive or unfaithful partner to recognise the vital need to take ownership of the problem and make plans to seek help.

It should also be noted here that ethical principles are considered to be *prima facie*. This legal term was described by Zygmond and Boorhem (1989) as implying that an ethical principle must be upheld, unless it is in conflict with other ethical principles; for example, if a client discloses his intention to harm himself or others, 'the ethical principle, *nonmaleficence*, takes precedence over the principle of autonomy and fidelity (that is, the right to privacy)' (269). In such cases, helpers need to judge the likelihood that the client will follow through with the threat. If clients are dangerous to themselves or others, then, as Zygmond and Boorhem suggested, the helper needs to 'uphold the principle of nonmaleficence even if it infringes upon a client's right to autonomy or fidelity' (269). In the relationship coaching setting, the best course of action here would be immediate referral to an appropriate counsellor or clinic.

Context

The second EMCC responsibility highlighted foregrounds *context* as an important requirement for coaching, by which the professional ensures that a physical environment is advantageous for coaching. While other coaching codes do not specifically highlight this issue, they all regard coaching as a learning opportunity; thus, coaching should be conducted in an environment that is conducive to learning.

In relationship coaching, it is likely to be the case that the client's own home is not the right environment. Some coaches do meet successfully in cafés or hotel lobbies, but coaches need to consider whether this is also the right setting for the learning experience of the client, for confidentiality, and for the professionalism of the coach. It is also useful to remember that physical barriers can be created by a room that is very noisy or too cold or too hot. The room needs to be comfortable, private, and located somewhere where the client(s) can feel comfortable.

Usually, a neutral setting is best for relationship coaching, but it does not necessarily need to be indoors. Often, an outdoor setting can be reviving and promote clear thinking, so a walk in the park or a garden bench can work – again, so long as it is private.

Integrity

All professional bodies recognise integrity and confidentiality as key ethical concerns. For example, the ICF highlights upholding strict levels of confidentiality for client information, including drawing up an agreement or contract before releasing information to another, unless required by law, and having a clear agreement about how coaching information will be exchanged. In addition, it is clearly inappropriate for a coach to disclose information that could result in a client being identified. The relationship between the coach and client is built on trust, and this should not be compromised.

While it is fundamental that the coaching alliance is bound by normal concepts of confidentiality, the coaching literature is replete with discussion about the real-world difficulties that are sometimes posed (e.g. Williams and Anderson 2005; Law 2010). When coaching a couple, for instance, trust would be in jeopardy if the coach responded outside the coaching sessions to a partner's pleas for advice on what to do about the spouse's ongoing misdemeanours. Contracting should clarify that the couple brings a joint agenda. The coach could encourage the perturbed partner to try and gain agreement for the issue to be explored together at the next session.

As discussed in Chapter 7, there is often little to be gained by exploring relationship issues with only one partner present. However, there are some issues that pertain to a single partner and that can be addressed on an individual basis. For example, if one party is struggling with the other's aggression, the victimised party may need help coping with the stress while the essential issue is being addressed. Another example would be where one partner is considering filing for divorce but wants to think it through carefully before taking the decision; this is a perfectly legitimate matter for coaching on an individual basis.

Problems also arise when the ability to maintain confidentiality is compromised by issues arising from the coaching itself. For example, the choice of life partner that single clients make is not the business of the coach, but it becomes far trickier when the client has a seriously problematic past or present and is concealing it from those he or she dates. For example, if the client has a serious criminal past, has committed child abuse, or has been a victim of significant child abuse, not disclosing such information to a potential life partner can be ruinous. Coaching someone to be successful in forming a relationship based on deceit is also morally problematic for the coach. The matter can get worse when a significant part of the client's plan is to ensure their dating partner does not find out about the issue in question. We are not suggesting that this is a black-and-white situation or that there is a clear right-and-wrong answer, but these are some of the most difficult problems a relationship coach can face.

It is also possible for a coach to be faced with a client who is seeking to achieve a goal that is entirely inappropriate. For example, a coach may find it hard to work with the client who is seeking help to get back together with an abusive partner. On the one hand, the client's agenda has to be respected, but the coach may also believe that he or she has a moral obligation to speak the truth. Here again, this is not a clear-cut situation, but the coach needs to carefully consider how appropriate it is to be coaching this client when the agenda compromises the coach's own moral, value-based concerns.

Similarly, we might consider what a coach should do if he or she suspects that a female client with small children is dating a suspected paedophile. Sexual predation is by no means the only risk that adults can pose to children or that people can pose to others more generally, but this is an extreme example of how the coach can come into possession of information of a potential risk situation.

It is also important to consider whether the coach has moral obligations towards the children in a parenting context. When coaching parents, it may become apparent that a young teenager has been having underage sex or has been in possession of drugs. Depending on the severity of the situation, coaches would need to consider whether they alert relevant authorities or maintain total confidentiality. There are moral and legal issues for coaches to consider before making an ethical decision. We recommend that when faced with serious moral dilemmas, coaches consult a respected colleague or supervisor to ensure that the matter is considered from all angles.

Relationship coaching may seem innocuous, and perhaps it may not be expected that criminal matters will arise. However, in the close and trusting relationship that coaching provides, sometimes details of serious criminality can arise. The coach is not a law enforcement official, and it is not obvious that every illegal act that comes to the coach's attention must be reported. Still, where a clear and present danger is posed to innocent people, it is hard to see how the coach could turn a blind eye to the harm others will suffer. The European Mentoring and Coaching Council (2008: 3) is explicit on this point: The coach should 'act within applicable law and not encourage, assist or collude with others engaged in conduct which is dishonest, unlawful, unprofessional or discriminatory'. The EMCC also suggests that coaches only disclose information where it is explicitly agreed with the client, unless they believe they have 'convincing evidence of serious danger to the client or others if the information is withheld' (3).

One way for coaches to protect themselves against unlawful revelations and also against professional litigation is to have a written contract. This enables a discussion of the coach's code of practice, an explicit conversation about expectations, and an opportunity to explain any necessary contextual constraints and limitations. It is an important way of protecting both coach and client.

Boundary management

The EMCC also identifies boundary management as key. As the AC specifically pointed out to its members:

> A client may need levels of psychological support you are not competent to provide. If so, the Client should be referred to an appropriate source of care, such as the Client's [general practitioner], a counsellor, psychotherapist, or another appropriate service or agency (2014).

We have already stressed the importance of referral in relationship cases where coaching is not the most appropriate intervention. Coaching is not a substitute for counselling or other kinds of support such as family therapy. Counselling involves a more in-depth and typically longer relationship between the helper and the client, with the agenda focusing on deeper, mainly psychological concerns.

As well as referral issues, other boundary questions can arise. For example, if a coach receives payment for referral to a dating agency or singles events (or perhaps even a wedding planner), this could represent a conflict of interest, whereby the coach is biased towards a particular supplier that may not be in the best interest of the client. It is pretty clear that such interests need to be disclosed to the client if relevant. Moreover, failure to do so could lead to a massive loss of faith in the coach and lead to potentially significant reputational damage.

The coach also has an ethical obligation to maintain a professional relationship with the client and not allow the client to become too friendly or familiar. In relationship contexts, where clients might be lonely or emotionally upset, situations could occur where a client attempts to form an attachment with the coach. In such circumstances, the ethical response is to refer the client to another coach.

Conversely, relationship coaches are privy to privileged information about clients' relationship preferences and concerns. This puts them in a uniquely powerful position should they wish to advance their own romantic aspirations with a client. However, it is hard to imagine how a coach can continue coaching a client for whom he or she harbours a romantic interest. Indeed, most people would agree that it is inevitable that the coaching relationship needs to come to an end if there is a strong romantic interest, whether reciprocated or not. Interestingly, de Jong (2006) argued that the coach should consider a four- to eight-week cooling-off period between the termination of the coaching and actively pursuing the romantic interest. This is in contrast to guidance from the EMCC and others; the European Mentoring and Coaching Council advised that a coach should not exploit the client in any manner, 'including, but not limited to, financial, sexual or those matters within the professional relationship' and directed that coaches understand that their responsibilities persist beyond the termination of the coaching relationship and should include 'the avoidance of any exploitation of the former relationship' (2008: 3). Law (2010) has also suggested that a coach's ethical responsibilities continue beyond the period of the coaching.

Professionalism

All three professional bodies discussed in this chapter identify a range of concerns under the general banner of professionalism (see Table 9.1). In this section, we highlight some issues that may arise, particularly during relationship coaching.

Numerous coaching texts acknowledge the risk of clients continuing to be coached despite making little or no progress (e.g. Brennan and Wildflower 2014; Whitworth et al. 2007). It may be argued that if the client, who is a grown adult, desires to persist with coaching sessions, there is nothing illegitimate in providing the client with this service. Yet, a coach has a unique responsibility, given the caring nature of the profession, to ensure the bond created via coaching empowers the client rather than fosters dependency. Thus, few coaches would disagree that if the coaching is truly achieving nothing, then a continuation of the service would suggest that an unhealthy dynamic has set in, which the coach should not be facilitating. Thus, the European Mentoring and Coaching Council explicitly said, 'The coach/mentor will ensure that the duration of the coach/mentoring contract is only as long as is necessary for the client/sponsor' (3).

Another important issue to draw attention to is where clients with serious health, psychological, or interpersonal issues try and hide their situation. They may have learned from experience that when they date and the partner learns of their condition, the relationship is typically swiftly ended. The client is, of course, free to do as he or she wishes. However, the matter becomes an ethical one for the coach when the coaching is being directed specifically towards looking to manage this challenge. On the one hand, it is right and proper for the coach to side with the client and look to advance his or her interests rather than take an impartial stand. On the other hand, when the coach is being asked to help the client figure out ways of masking or concealing these issues, it becomes tricky indeed.

The matter becomes even more complicated when there is good reason to believe that the condition could have a massive impact on any current or future partner. For example, if the client is HIV-positive, we might expect that this is something that would need to be declared at the outset, given its significance to the relationship. However, what if the client wishes to conceal the diagnosis until much later on in the relationship? How would the client's partner feel after several months of dating to learn of this? Or, if the client suffers from extreme bouts of manic depression, is it acceptable to go along with a plan to conceal this by inventing a story, such as having to go away from home for work purposes, often at short notice? Some may argue that, from an action-planning point of view, this is a very poor strategy anyway because the client is bound to get caught. However, coaches will need to ask themselves when they stop having an ethical responsibility to the client if this is in direct conflict with their moral and ethical responsibility to society.

Similar moral- and value-based issues arise from cultural and religious sensitivities. While most of us tend to think of ourselves as broadly respectful of diverse cultures and religious traditions, we often fail to realise how dismissive we can sometimes be of such concerns. Those who are not strongly religious, or for whom cultural ties are not a dominant feature of their lives, may not realise how they can casually marginalise such concerns. As an example, and at great risk of being accused of stereotyping, we consider a woman from the Asian subcontinent who is contemplating breaking up with her partner on the grounds that he has what she considers to be outmoded and patronising attitudes towards women. Many coaches would instinctively sympathise with her position, but to do so without any critical thinking would mean to fail to note that what we consider normal in one culture is not necessarily acceptable in another. If this client plans to find another partner within her own community, then this is by no means a straightforward agenda. Coaches have an obligation to check that their value system is not taking prominence, resulting in them overlooking the culture and values of the client and his or her context.

Following on from the previous point, we think it is vital that a relationship coach is sensitive to issues of culture. Many will consider it uncontroversial for people of diverse religious and cultural backgrounds to marry each other – and may even celebrate this multicultural union. However, coaching is not about the coach, but the client. If a client comes from a background that has a major issue with marrying outside one's own group, this could become a major source of friction, even rupture, in the client's family. It is not the role of the coach to take a side on this matter, but it is the role of the coach not to play the matter down – even if he or she has little concept of the strength of feeling of possible consequences. There have been cases where family members have been disowned or removed from a will, resulting in massive strain on any subsequent marriage. A conscientious coach will know how to help the client consider the wisest choice under the circumstances.

The foregoing sample of issues is, we believe, sufficient to illustrate that relationship coaching is not only affected by numerous ethical considerations but moreover poses unique challenges. The aim has not been to pronounce on any of these topics but to generate thought and sensitivity to them. What this demonstrates is that coaching is a complicated business, and ongoing coach learning and development are valuable to prepare coaches to handle these issues and make appropriate ethical decisions. Indeed, Passmore and Mortimer (2011) confirmed that ethical codes can only ever be guidelines for action. They presented a useful 'action model' for ethical decision-making, which begins with an awareness of personal beliefs and values as well as ethical codes that might be available via coaching bodies. This awareness is combined with different types of reflective activity, such as supervision and personal reflection, to arrive at what they call 'ethical options', which can then be checked back against values and ethical codes and organisational contracts, if applicable, before deciding on the appropriate ethical action.

The issues discussed in this chapter are just a few examples of the kind of professional judgements that the coach is likely to face in the course of relationship coaching. For the more knotty problems, it would seem obvious that the coach should seek collegial advice from a coaching supervisor. In the last decade or so, coaching supervision has been introduced as a way of providing continuing professional development for coaches (Garvey et al. 2009; Bachkirova et al. 2012), and we would always recommend that relationship coaches ensure they have an appropriate coach-supervisor who can provide an opportunity for interactive reflection on their work in order to become better practitioners. The professional complexities of relationship coaching are such that a coach needs this kind of formal support mechanism to deal with more challenging situations.

Summary

In this chapter, we have examined the current codes of practice of a number of international professional membership organisations for coaching. We also highlighted typical issues that relationship coaches might face, including some of the moral decisions that they might encounter as part of their practice. These moral issues require careful consideration in light of ethical practice, but also in relation to the coach's own value system.

Some authors believe that coaches need to be a 'moral compass' (Law 2010). Law suggested that this also means taking 'personal responsibility for clients' unethical behaviour' (191). We consider such responsibility to be an enormous undertaking. We have already talked a great deal about values in this book, and one way to ensure coaches and clients are aware of their values is through joint discussion. If the client continues with unethical behaviour following discussion and awareness-raising, as long as it is within the law, we suggest that the coach's only responsibility is to himself or herself and whether it is then possible to continue coaching under such circumstances. The coach needs to consider, for example, whether in a parenting context the client is doing something patently wrong, such as abusing a child in some way, or whether he or she is just adopting a different parenting style or set of parenting values. From there, the coach would need to decide to report to the authorities, respect autonomy, or end the coaching, after raising the client's awareness to the fact that others may see their approach as wrong.

The need for significant awareness of ethical issues is vital in all coaching – but probably even more so in a relationship coaching context, where sensitive emotional issues are involved. Good coach training will encourage membership of a coaching body and therefore the use of an appropriate ethical code to guide practice together with ongoing supervision. In addition, all reputable coach training would stress the need for ethical contracting and boundary setting at the start of a coaching assignment, where the essential rules of engagement are set out so that the coach and the client can explore their assumptions of coaching.

Chapter 10

Conclusion

We started this book by highlighting the fact that many people who could benefit from coaching either do not know it exists or they are not sure what human concerns it might usefully address. Help with relationships is one area that seemed to us to be insufficiently recognised amongst the repertoire of help that coaching can provide, and we believe it is too important to be left unexamined. In this book, we have therefore sought to raise awareness of how coaches might adapt coaching to relationship contexts.

To this effect, the book combines a guide to some of the issues relationships face and to how a relationship coaching framework might be used to enhance the key personal relationships that are so central to people's happiness and well-being. Indeed, we have seen how, rather than choosing between muddling through on their own or going for counselling or therapy, coaching offers single people, couples, and parents a viable alternative that enhances their lives in significant ways.

To explain the relationship coaching framework, we began in Chapter 2 with an exposition of a range of developmental theories, such as life course development and transformative learning, whereby people are deemed to mature through a process of taking a wider or longer-term perspective on their problems. We highlighted how adults' thinking and emotions pass through developmental stages that relate to the way they think about themselves and their relationship with others, and how this is connected to the way they make meaning of events in their lives. We also presented case studies illustrating the role of the coach in facilitating growth and development in relationship contexts.

We then examined how clients' goals are important for self-regulation. We suggested that even though relationship coaching is principally about client development, it is helpful to recognise that relationship success is typical a highly valued goal. The relationship coach helps clients to clarify and set goals and plan effective action to achieve their aims. Achievement of goals also requires motivation, which is important for keeping on track with necessary change.

In Chapter 4, we highlighted some useful psychological theories and approaches that inform coaching in relationship contexts. Then, in Chapter 5, we brought the theories together into a framework, suggesting that the integration of this particular mix of different approaches was particularly suited for supporting people with relationship issues. The three context-related chapters that followed provided examples of the kinds of relationship issues that people commonly face and included many case studies of how coaching had helped them.

The framework for relationship coaching that we have proposed can be seen as an example of integrative coaching in action; it uses a 'multifaceted methodology' (Grant 2006: 187) to help people to tackle their relationship dilemmas. However, although we have made specific suggestions for the theoretical foundations of the framework, it can also be adapted and augmented according to a particular coach's strengths and client's requirements. For example, some coaches may want to include a narrative or positive psychology approach or even a neurolinguistic programming element, depending on their training and their perception of the client's needs (see Cox et al. 2014 for a full discussion of coaching approaches). Similarly, a range of techniques and tools can be used within the framework.

What is unique about relationship coaching?

In the course of this book, we have highlighted several ways in which our approach to relationship coaching may be different from other helping approaches. Relationship coaching foregrounds the client's agenda, in which the aim is not to 'fix' the client in order to return them to some 'norm'; coaches do not want to make the client better or more functional and they do not generally work to one particular theory or model, although they need a good understanding of many. Instead, they wait to see which way the client needs to go. Techniques such as listening and asking questions that are used in coaching are also used in couples counselling and in mediation, for example, but in a coaching framework particular weight is given to the client's agenda. This emphasis is not limited to a focus on the issue the client brings, which becomes the focus of the intervention, but governs the whole trajectory of the coaching assignment: what the client brings each time is the 'life force' of each coaching session. Coaching is a way of being with clients that involves moment-to-moment and concentrated engagement with the client's thinking and only then, almost intuitively, drawing on appropriate approaches or techniques. It is this that makes coaching so powerful (Cox 2013).

We have also highlighted how relationship coaching is forward focused, facilitating a future orientation. While other forms of helping also seek to support clients on a journey toward a more fulfilling and successful future, coaching leverages the goal or the intended future state as a key force for motivating and guiding progress. This injects coaching with a strong sense of purpose and direction.

Across this book, we have sought to convey how relationship coaching is first and foremost development oriented. Underpinning this focus on development is the understanding that people's choices in and reaction to relationships are largely attitudinal, shaped by our perspectives on ourselves, others, and the interactions between. Coaches do not tell clients how to think, but they do encourage them to widen their mental horizons and challenge their assumptions. Thus, coaching is a twin-track journey: towards an outcome or goal and towards a new state of perception or maturity – and often these goals are one and the same.

Understanding relationship contexts

Coaches practice in a variety of environments and settings. It is acknowledged that these contexts bring their own historical, cultural, social, and physical constraints and their own challenges for the coach (Bachkirova et al. 2014). Thus, the techniques used in coaching, such as listening, questioning, and challenge, cannot be independent of context. They have to be underpinned by a certain amount of contextual knowledge. As Cox (2003: 13) explained, their very application depends upon the 'amount of background or contextual knowledge the coach ... has, as well as the context within which he or she is working and through which all action is framed'. Cox (2003: 20) also pointed out how it is not enough to remain at a superficial or meta level of challenge when working with clients, because this may place the credibility of the coach in jeopardy:

> The contextual imperative implies that coaches ... need the relevant experience and understanding to help them comprehend the situations they will encounter, to provide them with the wisdom to enable them to use the personal capacities and process skills of coaching or mentoring and to provide credibility for themselves, their clients and the profession. It is incumbent upon educators and trainers to recognise the imperative that context places on the enhancement of professional practice.

Similarly, Svensson confirmed that professional knowledge and skill 'depend strongly on the individual and the context' (1990: 62). Allen's (2013: 77) view is that the coach needs to be an expert, with necessary process information and a background understanding of the client's context. Moreover, Drake (2011: 149) argued that coaches require what he termed 'foundational knowledge', which includes 'knowledge of coaching in general' while extending to 'the requirements of specific applications'. Drawing upon Ryle (1963) and Jarvis (1992), Drake suggested that the knowledge types a masterful coach requires are 'knowledge how', 'knowledge that', and 'knowledge why'. However, Drake argued that the role of knowledge is not merely to decrease uncertainty about how to achieve particular outcomes, but it also involves the ability to manage uncertainties.

We would go further still and argue that some domains of practice, such as relationship coaching, are highly involved, requiring the coach to have a solid grasp of the field to be an effective coach. A sound foundation in the understanding of relationship issues will not only help to 'create an effective working alliance', as Drake (2011: 149) argued, but it is also critical for providing a useful coaching experience. For example, if a client's relationship history is governed by profound avoidance of relationships, all plans to pursue relationships will be pointless unless this issue is in some way addressed. Greater knowledge and understanding about relationships will enhance the coach's capabilities, in particular when helping clients to go beyond the issues that may be holding them back through expanding horizons and gaining new perspectives. Thus, part of the coach's commitment to the client to should be a commitment to expanding his or her own knowledge.

To that end, here are some suggestions for additional reading as starting points to supplement existing coaching knowledge:

Additional reading list

Handbook of relationship initiation. Sprecher, S., Wenzel, A., and Harvey, J. (Eds.). 2008. New York: Psychology Press.

For an extensive range of studies on the early stages in relationships, this book is invaluable. It covers all key contemporary theories of relationships, both in theory and in practice. Topics include such basic topics as seeking information about romantic partners as well as the role of self-disclosure in formation of relationships, and more contemporary issues, such as speed dating and finding a mate through the internet.

Adult attachment: Theory, research, and clinical implications. Rholes, W. S., and Simpson, J. A. (Eds.). 2004. New York: Guilford Press.

This is a comprehensive collection of authoritative chapters covering both the theoretical and practical implications of attachment theory. Understanding why people struggle to become attached or conversely seem to become overattached is critical to the work of coaching in the adult relationship context.

Conscious dating: Finding the love of your life and the life that you love. Steele, D. 2008. Campbell, CA: RCN Press.

In this book, an experienced relationship coach shares his ideas and approach to coaching single people or those in the early stages of their relationship. His book adopts a cognitive behavioural approach and presents ten principles of successful dating, such as being 'the chooser' and a 'successful single'.

Creating connection: A relational-cultural approach with couples. Jordon, J. V., and Carlson, J. (Eds.). 2013. New York: Routledge.

This book adopts a relational-cultural approach to examine and help us to understand a number of complex relationship issues, such as step-parenting, mixed-race couples, and divorce. At the heart of this book is the idea that development is not about helping the client to become detached, independent, and self-sufficient, but rather it is about encouraging connection that leads to well-being.

Positive relationships: Evidence-based practice across the world. Roffey, S. 2013. London: Springer.

This book takes a positive psychology approach to relationship issues. There are chapters on well-being and resilience in young people, positive couple relationships, and positive parent–child relationships. Chapter 4 focuses on how parents can support their children to develop the skills and understanding to enable them to achieve positive relationships.

Parenting from the inside out. Siegel, D.J. 2004. London: Penguin.

A useful book that considers how self-understanding contributes to the parenting role. Not a 'how to' book, but more of a 'how we' book.

Further research

The coaching literature has long recognised the potential of the coach as practitioner-researcher. In daily contact with real-life clients and coaching situations, the practicing coach is uniquely positioned to further knowledge and understanding of coaching through testing new ideas and techniques. Fillery-Travis and Cox (2014) called for research into coaching that is at once rigorous in its design and practical in its application. They argued that 'there is a strong need within the discipline for coherent, well-managed programmes of research that can add to the body of academic knowledge' (445). Their chapter presents several innovative research methodologies suited to the particular challenges of coaching research.

Practitioners undertaking research in the field have often adopted an action research approach. Action research involves the *intent* to affect social change, to study an actual intervention instigated by the researcher (Eden and Huxham 1996). It draws together action (change, improvement) with research (understanding, knowledge), allowing both to be achieved simultaneously. Numerous approaches to action research are available, but in general, the research framework will consist of the following main stages:

- *Diagnose* – Gather data about the context and identify a need.
- *Plan action* – Formulate and secure agreement for the intervention.
- *Take action* – Introduce and monitor the change.
- *Evaluate* – Analyse results.

As mentioned at the start of this book, coaching in general is a comparatively new profession. Research into coaching is even more recent, while research into relationship coaching has hardly begun. Coaches already involved in relationship coaching or who are considering becoming involved can help to drive this field forward through contributing vitally important research, ensuring that it is in keeping with the now widely accepted evidence-based coaching agenda (Cox and Ledgerwood 2003). For example, Yossi conducted research amongst young professionals from across Europe and found that there was a close parallel between the age of the respondent and how well they rated their relationship success on the one hand, and how much they gained from relationship education and how likely they considered themselves to take up relationship coaching on the other hand. Further research could explore whether, in fact, these factors are linked and in which ways. Implications of this research would be manifold, including whether relationship coaching is more suited for those of a particular age or experience of relationships.

As another example, in Chapter 7 we suggest that couples' coaching requires both parties to participate. We also acknowledge that sometimes one party is reluctant to do so; in such cases, coaching can help to work towards creating the conditions for both parties to join the coaching sessions. Research would be highly valuable to assess how best to manage this anomaly of couples coaching while only one party is currently willing to participate.

The components of relationship coaching are not new. However, as this book has attempted to show, coaching can be given new purpose through a particular theoretical and practical synthesis and a specific contextual perspective. The result is an approach to improving relationships where the whole is greater than the sum of its parts.

References

Achtziger, A., and Gollwitzer, P. M. (2008). Motivation and volition during the course of action. In J. Heckhausen and H. Heckhausen (Eds), *Motivation and action* (pp. 272–295). London: Cambridge University Press.

Addis, M. E., and Mahalik, J. R. (2003). Men, masculinity and the contexts of help seeking. *American Psychologist*, 58, 5–14.

Alexander, G. (2006). Behavioural coaching: The GROW model. In J. Passmore (Ed.), *Excellence in Coaching* (pp. 83–93). London: Kogan Page.

Alexander, G., and Renshaw, B. (2005). *Supercoaching*. London: Random House.

Allan, J., and Whybrow, A. (2007). Gestalt coaching. In S. Palmer and A. Whybrow (Eds), *Handbook of coaching psychology: A guide for practitioners* (pp. 133–159). London: Routledge.

Allen, K. (2013). A framework for family life coaching. *International Coaching Psychology Review*, 8(1), 72–79.

Anderson, H., and Goolishian, H. (1992). The client is the expert: A not-knowing approach to therapy. In S. McNamee and K. Bergen (Eds), *Therapy as social construction*. Newbury Park, CA: Sage.

Arriaga, X. B., and Rusbult, C. E. (1998). Standing in my partner's shoes: Partner perspective taking and reaction to accommodative dilemmas. *Personality and Social Psychology Bulletin*, 24, 927–948.

Association for Coaching. (2014). *AC code of ethics and good practice*. Available at http://uk.associationforcoaching.com/pages/about/code-ethics-good-practice (accessed 2 February 2014).

Auerbach, J. E. (2006). Cognitive coaching. In D. Stober and A. M. Grant (Eds), *Evidence-based coaching handbook* (pp. 103–128). New York: Wiley.

Bachkirova, T. (2007). Role of coaching psychology in defining boundaries between counselling and coaching. In S. Palmer and A. Whybrow (Eds), *Handbook of coaching psychology* (pp. 351–366). London: Routledge.

Bachkirova, T. (2011). *Developmental coaching: Working with the self*. Maidenhead, UK: Open University Press.

Bachkirova, T., and Cox, E. (2007). A cognitive-developmental approach for coach develop ment. In S. Palmer and A. Whybrow (Eds), *Handbook of coaching psychology: A guide for practitioners*, 325–350, Hove: Routledge.

Bachkirova, T., Jackson, P., and Clutterbuck, D. (2012). *Coaching and mentoring supervision: Theory and practice*. Maidenhead, UK: Open University Press.

Bachkirova, T., Cox, E., and Clutterbuck, D. (2014). Introduction. In E. Cox, T. Bachkirova, and D. Clutterbuck (Eds), *The complete handbook of coaching* (pp. 1–18), London: Sage.

Baldwin, M. W. (1992). Relational schemas and the processing of social information. Psychological Bulletin, 112, 461–484.

Baldwin, M. W., and Fehr, B. (1995). On the instability of attachment style ratings. *Personal Relationships*, 2, 247–261.

Baldwin, M. W. (1997). Relational schemas as a source of if-then self-inference procedures. Review of General Psychology, 1, 326–335.

Baldwin, M. W., Keelan, J. P. R., Fehr, B., Enns, V., and Koh-Rangarajoo, E. (1996). Social-cognitive conceptualization of attachment working models: Availability and accessibility effects. *Journal of Personality and Social Psychology*, 71(1), 94–109.

Bamford, A., Mackew, N., and Golawski, A. (2012). Coaching for parents: Empowering parents to create positive relationship with their children. In C. van Nieuwerburgh (Ed.), *Coaching in Education*. London: Karnac.

Bandura, A. (1977). Self-efficacy: Toward a unifying theory of behavioral change. Psychological review, 84(2), 191.

Bandura, A. (1986). *Social foundations of thought and action: A social cognitive model*. Englewood Cliffs, NJ: Prentice-Hall.

Bandura, A. (1991). Social cognitive theory of self-regulation. *Organizational Behavior and Human Decision Processes*, 50, 248–287.

Bandura, A. (2001). Social cognitive theory: An agentic perspective. *Annual Review of Psychology*, 52, 1–26.

Bandura, A., and Cervone, D. (1983). Self-evaluative and self-efficacy mechanisms governing the motivational effects of goal systems. *Journal of Personality and Social Psychology*, 45(5), 1017–1028.

Bao, K. J., and Lyubomirsky, S. (2013). Making it last: Combating hedonic adaptation in romantic relationships. *The Journal of Positive Psychology*, 8(3), 196–206.

Bartholomew, K., and Horowitz, L. M. (1991). Attachment styles among young adults: A test of a four-category model. *Journal of Personal and Social Psychology*, 61(2), 226–244.

Batthyany-De La Lama, L., De La Lama, L., and Wittgenstein, A. (2012). The soul mates model: A seven-stage model for couple's long-term relationship development and flourishing. *The Family Journal*, 20, 283–291.

Baumeister, R. F., and Leary, M. R. (1995). The need to belong: Desire for interpersonal attachments as a fundamental human motivation. *Psychological Bulletin*, 117, 497–529.

Beck, A. T. (1976). *Cognitive therapy and the emotional disorders*. New York: International Universities Press.

Berg, I. K., and Szabo, P. (2005). *Brief coaching for lasting solutions*. New York: W. W. Norton.

Berger, J. G. (2006). Adult development theory and executive coaching practice. In D. Stober and A. M. Grant (Eds), *Evidence-based coaching handbook* (pp. 77–102). New York: Wiley.

Berk, L. (2006). *Child development*. London: Pearson/Allyn and Bacon.

Blumenfeld, P. C., Pintrich, P. R., Meece, J., and Wessels, K. (1982). The formation and role of self-perceptions of ability in elementary classrooms. *The Elementary School Journal*, 82, 401–420.

Bolstad, R. (n.d.). *Couples coaching: A 21st century NLP approach to working with couples*. Available at http://www.transformations.net.nz/trancescript/couples.html (accessed 16 December 2013).

Bordin, E. (1979). The generalizability of the psychoanalytic concept of the working alliance. *Psychotherapy: Theory, Research and Practice*, 16, 252–260.

Bowen, M. (1978). *Family therapy in clinical practice*. New York: Jason Aronson.

Bowlby, J. (1951). *Maternal care and mental health*. Geneva, Switzerland: World Health Organization.

Bowlby, J. (1958). The nature of the child's tie to his mother. *International Journal of Psycho-Analysis*, 39, 350–373.

Bowlby, J. (1969). *Attachment and loss, Vol. 1: Attachment*. New York: Basic Books.

Bowlby, J. (1973). *Attachment and loss: Vol. 2. Separation: Anxiety and anger*. New York: Basic Books.

Bowlby, J. (1988). *A secure base: Parent-child attachment and healthy human development*. New York: Basic Books.

Boyce, L. A., Jackson, R. J., and Neal, L. J. (2010). Building successful leadership coaching relationships: Examining impact of matching criteria in a leadership coaching program. *Journal of Management Development*, 29(10), 914–931.

Brackett, M. A., Lopes, P. N., Ivcevic, Z., Mayer, J. D., and Salovey, P. (2004). Integrating emotion and cognition: The role of emotional intelligence. In D. Y. Dai and D. Sternberg (Eds), *Motivation, emotion and cognition* (pp. 175–194). Mahwah, NJ: Lawrence Erlbaum.

Bramson, R. (1984). *Coping with difficult people*. New York: Ballantine Books.

Bredow, C. A., Cate, R. M., and Huston, T. L. (2008). Have we met before? A conceptual model of first romantic encounters. In S. Sprecher, A. Wenzel, and J. Harvey (Eds), *Handbook of relationship initiation*. New York: Psychology Press.

Bredow, C. A., Huston, T. L. and Glenn, N. D. (2011). Market value, quality of the pool of potential mates, and singles' confidence about marrying. *Personal Relationships*, 18(1), 39–57.

Brennan, D., and Wildflower, L. (2014). Ethics in coaching. In E. Cox, T. Bachkirova, and D. Clutterbuck (Eds), *The complete handbook of coaching* (pp. 430–444). London: Sage.

Bresser, F., and Wilson, C. (2006). What is coaching? In J. Passmore (Ed.), *Excellence in coaching: The industry guide* (pp. 9–15). London, England: Kogan Page.

Bresser, F., and Wilson, C. (2010). What is coaching? Excellence in coaching: The industry guide, 9–26. London, UK: Kogan Page.

Bretherton, I., and Munholland, K. A. (1999). Internal working models in attachment relationships: A construct revisited. In J. Cassidy and P. R. Shaver (Eds), *Handbook of attachment: Theory, research and clinical applications* (pp. 89–114). New York: Guilford Press.

Bridges, W. (1991). *Managing Transitions Making the Most of Change. Reading*, MA: Addison-Wesley.

Bridges, W. (2001). *The way of transition: Embracing life's most difficult moments*. Cambridge, MA: Perseus.

Brockbank, A. (2008). Is the coaching fit for purpose? A typology of coaching and learning approaches. *Coaching: An International Journal of Theory, Research and Practice*, 1(2), 132–144.

Brockbank, A., and McGill, I. (2006). *Facilitating reflective learning through mentoring and coaching*. London: Kogan Page.

Brown, S. P., Jones, E., and Leigh, T. W. (2005). The attenuating effect of role overload in relationships linking self-efficacy and goal level to work performance. *Journal of Applied Psychology*, 90(5), 972–979.

Browne, P. E. (2009). *Forgiveness as a counseling intervention*. PhD Dissertation, Capella University. Available at http://media.proquest.com/media/pq/classic/doc/1711359521/fmt/ai/rep/NPDF?_s=HOGthK4LRx9pM9UWugymRL%2F84Bk%3D (accessed 17 February 2014).

Browne, P.E. (2009). *Forgiveness therapy: A qualitative study of the forgiveness experience of people who have undergone forgiveness as a counseling intervention*. PhD dissertation, Capella University. Available at http://media.proquest.com/media/pq/classic/doc/1711359521/fmt/ai/rep/NPDF?_s=qh7UOLUzf27o7EigcZKcKDDEitg%3D (accessed 9 December 2014).

Burns, D. (1990). *The feeling good handbook*. New York: Penguin Group.

Busch, H., and Hofer, J. (2012). Self-regulation and milestones of adult development: Intimacy and generativity. *Developmental Psychology*, 48(1), 282–293.

Butler, A. C., Chapman, J. E., Forman, E. M., and Beck, A.T. (2006). The empirical status of cognitive-behavioral therapy: A review of meta-analyses. *Clinical Psychology Review*, 26, 17–31.

Byng-Hall, J. (2008). The crucial roles of attachment in family therapy. *Journal of Family Therapy*, 30, 129–146.

Cagen, S. (2004). *Quirkyalone: A manifesto for uncompromising romantics*. San Francisco, CA: HarperCollins.

Calder, M. C. (Ed.) (2007). *The carrot or the stick? Towards effective practice with involuntary clients in safeguarding children work*. Dorset, UK: Russell House Publishing.

Cantor, N., and Kihlstrom, J. F. (1987). *Personality and social intelligence*. Englewood Cliffs, NJ: Prentice-Hall.

Carnelley, K. B., and Janoff-Bulman, R. (1992). Optimism about love relationships: General vs. specific lessons from one's personal experiences. *Journal of Social and Personal Relationships*, 9, 5–20.

Carver, C. S. (2007). Self-regulation of action and affect. In R. F. Baumeister and K. D. Vohs (Eds), *Handbook of self-regulation* (pp. 13–39). New York: Guilford.

Carver, C. S., and Scheier, M. F. (1998). *On the self-regulation of behaviour*. New York: Cambridge University.

Cavanagh, M. (2005). Mental-health issues and challenging clients in executive coaching. In M. Cavanagh, A. M. Grant, and T. Kemp (Eds), *Evidence-based coaching, Vol. 1: Theory, research and practice from the behavioural sciences* (pp. 21–36). Bowen Hills, Queensland, Australia: Australian Academic Press.

Cavanagh, M. (2006). Coaching from a systemic perspective: A complex adaptive approach. In D. Stober and A. M. Grant (Eds), *Evidence-based coaching handbook: Putting best practices to work for your clients* (pp. 313–354). Hoboken, NJ: Wiley.

Cavanagh, M. and Buckley, A. (2014). Coaching and mental health. In E. Cox, T. Bachkirova and D. Clutterbuck (Eds), *The complete handbook of coaching* (pp. 405–417). London: Sage.

Cavanagh, M., and Grant, A. M. (2014). Solution focused coaching. In E. Cox, T. Bachkirova, and D. Clutterbuck (Eds), *The complete handbook of coaching* (2nd ed., pp. 51–64). London: Sage.

Chapman, G. (2009a). *The five love languages: Singles edition*. Chicago, IL: Northfield Publishing.

Chapman, G. (2009b). *Love is a verb: Stories of what happens when love comes alive*. Bloomington, MI: Bethany House.

Chapman, G. (2010). *The five love languages: The secret to love that lasts*. Chicago, IL: Northfield Publishing.

Chase, A., and Wolfe, P. (1989). Off to a good start in peer coaching. *Educational Leadership*, 46(8), 37.

Collins, N. L., and Read, S. J. (1990). Adult attachment, working models, and relationship quality in dating couples. *Journal of Personality and Social Psychology*, 58, 644–663.

Collins, S. D., and O'Rourke, J. S. (Eds) (2008). *Managing conflict and workplace relationships* (2nd ed.). Mason, OH: South-Western Cengage.

Cox, E. (2003). The contextual imperative: Implications for coaching and mentoring. *International Journal of Evidence Based Coaching and Mentoring*, 1(1), 9–22.

Cox, E. (2006). An adult learning approach to coaching. In D. Stober, and A. M. Grant (Eds), *Evidence Based Coaching Handbook*, 193–217. New York: Wiley.

Cox, E. (2010). Last things first. In S. Palmer and A. McDowall (Eds), *The coaching relationship: Putting people first* (pp. 159–181). London: Routledge.

Cox, E. (2012a). Individual and organisational trust in a reciprocal peer coaching context. *Mentoring and Tutoring*, 20(3), 427–443.

Cox, E. (2012b). Managing emotions at work: An action research study of how coaching and group work affect retail support workers' performance and motivation. *International Journal of Evidence Based Coaching and Mentoring*, 10(2), 34–51.

Cox, E. (2013). *Coaching understood: A pragmatic inquiry into the coaching process*. London: Sage.

Cox, E., and Ledgerwood, G. (2003). Editorial: The new profession. *International Journal of Evidence Based Coaching and Mentoring*, 1(1).

Cox, E., and Jackson, P. (2014). Developmental coaching. In E. Cox, T. Bachkirova, and D. Clutterbuck (Eds), *The complete handbook of coaching* (pp. 215–227). London: Sage.

Creasey, G., and Jarvis, P. (2009). *Attachment and marriage. Handbook of research on adult learning and development*, 269–304. London: Routledge.

Critchley, K. (2010). *Coaching Skills Training Course. Business and Life Coaching Techniques for Improving performance using NLP and Goal Setting*. Lancashire, UK: Universe of Learning.

Cupach, W. R., and Spitzberg, B. H. (Eds) (2011). *The dark side of close relationships – II*. New York: Routledge.

Cunningham, M. R., Barbee, A. P., and Philhower, C. L. (2002). Dimensions of facial physical attractiveness: The intersection of biology and culture. In G. Rhodes and L. A. Zebrowitz (Eds), *Facial attractiveness: Evolutionary, cognitive, and social perspectives* (pp. 193–238). Westport, CT: Ablex.

Dallos, R., and Draper, R. (2010). *An introduction to family therapy*. Maidenhead, UK: Open University Press.

Daloz, L. (2012). *Mentor: Guiding the journey of adult learners*. New York: John Wiley.

Darling, B. and Steinberg, L. (1993). Parenting style as context: An integrative model. *Psychological Bulletin*, 113(3), 487–496.

Davila, J., and Sargent, E. (2003). The meaning of life (events) predicts changes in attachment security. *Personality and Social Psychology Bulletin*, 29, 1383–1395.

Davila, J., and Cobb, R. J. (2004). Predictors of change in attachment security during adulthood. In W. S. Rholes and J. A. Simpson (Eds), *Adult attachment: Theory, research, and clinical implications* (pp. 133–156). New York: Guilford Press.

de Haan, E. (2008). *Relational coaching: Journeys towards mastering one-to-one learning*. Chichester, UK: John Wiley.

de Haan, E., Duckworth, A., Birch, D., and Jones, C. (2013). Executive coaching outcome research: The contribution of common factors such as relationship, personality match, and self-efficacy. *Consulting Psychology Journal: Practice and Research*, 65(1), 40–57.

de Jong, A. (2006). Coaching ethics. In J. Passmore (Ed.), *Excellence in coaching: The industry guide* (pp. 204–214). London: Sage.

de Shazer, S. (2005). *More than miracles: The state of the art of solution-focused therapy.* Binghamton, NY: Hawthorn Press.

de Shazer, S., Berg, I. K., Lipchik, E., Nunnally, E., Molar, A., Gingerich, W. C., and Weiner-Davis, M. (1986). Brief therapy: Focused solution development. *Family Process*, 25, 207–221.

Deci, E. L., and Ryan, R. M. (2002). *Handbook of self determination research* (pp. 87–100). Rochester, NY: University of Rochester Press.

Delahaye, B., and Becker, K. (2006). Unlearning: A revised view of contemporary learning theories? In *Proceedings of Lifelong Learning Conference*. Available at http://eprints. qut.edu.au/6532/1/6532.pdf (accessed 22 March 2014).

Dembkowski, S., and Eldridge, F. (2003). Beyond GROW: A new coaching model. *The International Journal of Mentoring And Coaching*, 1(1).

Dembkowski, S., and Eldridge, F. (2008). Achieving tangible results: The development of a coaching model. In D. Drake, D. Brennan, and K. Gortz (Eds), *The philosophy and practice of coaching: Insights and issues for a new era* (pp. 195–211). London: Wiley.

Dembkowski, S., Eldridge, F., and Hunter, I. (2006). *The seven steps of executive coaching.* Oxford, UK: Thorogood.

Dion, K. K., and Dion, K. L. (1975). Self-esteem and romantic love. *Journal of personality*, 43(1), 39–57.

Dion, K., Berscheid, E., and Walster, E. (1972). What is beautiful is good. *Journal of Personality and Social Psychology*, 24(3), 285.

Dobson, D. J. G., and Dobson, K. S. (2009). *Evidence-based practice of cognitive-behavioral therapy.* New York, NY: Guilford Press.

Downey, M. (1999). *Effective coaching.* London: Orion Business Books.

Drake, D. B. (2008). Thrice upon a time: Narrative structure and psychology as a platform for coaching. In D. B. Drake, D. Brennan, and K. Gortz (Eds), *The philosophy and practice of coaching: Insights and issues for a new era* (pp. 55–71). London: Wiley.

Drake, D. B. (2011). What do coaches need to know? Using the Mastery Window to assess and develop expertise. *Coaching: An International Journal of Theory, Research and Practice*, 4(2), 138–155.

Drake, D. B. (2014). Narrative coaching. In E. Cox, T. Bachkirova, and D. Clutterbuck (Eds), *The complete handbook of coaching* (pp. 117–130). London: Sage.

Dryden, W., and Branch, R. (2008). *The fundamentals of rational emotive behaviour therapy: A training handbook* (2nd ed.). Chichester, UK: Wiley.

Dunbar, R. I. (2009). The social brain hypothesis and its implications for social evolution. *Annual Journal of Human Biology*, 36, 562–572.

Du Toit, A. (2006). The management of change in local government using a coaching approach. *The International Journal of Mentoring and Coaching*, 4(2), 45–57.

Eagle, M. (1995). The developmental perspectives of attachment and psychoanalytic theory. In S. Goldberg, R. Muir, and J. Kerr (Eds), *Attachment theory: Social, developmental, and clinical theory* (pp. 123–150). Hillsdale, NJ: Analytic Press.

Eden, C., and Huxham, C. (1996). Action research for the study of organizations. In S. Clegg, C. Hardy, and W. Nord (Eds), *The handbook of organisation studies*. Beverly Hills, CA: Sage.

Elliot, A. J., and Harackiewicz, J. M. (1996). Approach and avoidance achievement goals and intrinsic motivation: A mediational analysis. *Journal of Personality and Social Psychology*, 70, 461–475.

Ellis, A. (1958). Rational psychotherapy. *The Journal of General Psychology*, 59, 35–49.

Ellis, A. (1985). Expanding the ABC's concept of rational-emotive therapy. In M. Mahoney and A. Freeman (Eds), *Cognition and psychotherapy* (pp. 313–323). New York: Plenum.

Emmons, R. A. (1986). Personal strivings: An approach to personality and subjective wellbeing. *Journal of Personality and Social Psychology*, 51, 1058–1086.

Erikson, E. H. (1959). *Identity and the life cycle*. New York: Norton.

Erikson, E. H. (1969). *Ghandi's truth*. Magnolia, MA: Peter Smith.

European Mentoring and Coaching Council. (2008). *Code of ethics*. Available at http://www.emccouncil.org/src/ultimo/models/Download/4.pdf (accessed 2 February 2014).

Feeney, J., and Noller, P. (1996). *Adult attachment*. London: Sage.

Feeney, J. A., Noller, P., and Callan, V. J. (1994). Attachment style, communication and satisfaction in the early years of marriage. In K. Bartholomew and D. Perlman (Eds), *Advances in personal relationships: Attachment processes in adulthood* (Vol. 5, pp. 269–308). London: Jessica Kingsley.

Figley, C. R. (1979). Tactical self-presentation and interpersonal attraction. In M. Cook and G. Wilson (Eds), *Love and attraction*. pp. 91–99. Oxford: Pergamon Press.

Fitzgerald, C., and Berger, J. G. (Eds). (2002). *Executive coaching*. Nicholas Brealey Publishing.

Fritz, R. (1984). *The path of least resistance*. Salem, MA: Stillpoint Publishing.

Fillery-Travis, A., and Lane, D. (2006). Does coaching work or are we asking the wrong questions? *International Coaching Psychology Review*, 1(1), 23–36.

Fillery-Travis, A., and Cox, E. (2014). Researching Coaching. In E. Cox, T. Bachkirova, and D. Clutterbuck, (Eds), *The complete handbook of coaching* (pp. 445–459). London: Sage.

Flaherty, J. (2005). *Coaching: Evoking excellence in others*. Oxford, UK: Elsevier.

Ford, M. (1992). *Motivating humans: Goals, emotions, and personal agency beliefs*. Newbury Park, CA: Sage.

Foucault, M. (1988). Technologies of the Self. In L. H. Martin, H. Gutman and P. Hutton (Eds), *Technologies of the Self: A Seminar with Michel Foucault* (pp. 16–49). Amherst: The University of Massachusetts Press.

Fredrickson, B. L., and Losada, M. (2005). Positive affect and the complex dynamics of human flourishing. *American Psychologist*, 60(7), 678–686.

Garvey, B., Stokes, P., and Megginson, D. (2009). *Coaching and mentoring: Theory and practice*. London: Sage.

Gendlin, E. T. (1962). *Experiencing and the creation of meaning*. New York: Free Press.

Gendlin, E. T. (1969). Focusing. *Psychotherapy*, 6, 4–15.

Goffman, E. (1959). The Presentation of Self in Everyday Life New York: Doubleday Anchor.

Goleman, D. (1998). *Working with emotional intelligence*. New York: Bantam Books.

Gollwitzer, P. M. (1996). The volitional benefits of planning. In P. M. Gollwitzer and J. A. Bargh (Eds), *The psychology of action: Linking cognition and motivation to behaviour* (pp. 287–312). New York: Guilford.

Gollwitzer, P. M., and Brandstaetter, V. (1997). Implementation intentions and effective goal pursuit. Journal of Personality and Social Psychology, 73, 186–199.

Gollwitzer, P. M., and Schaal, B. (1998). Metacognition in action: The importance of implementation intentions. *Personality and Social Psychology Review*, 2(2), 124–136.

Gollwitzer, P. M., Fujita, K., and Oettingen, G. (2007). Planning and the implementation of goals. In R. F. Baumeister and K. D. Vohs (Eds), *Handbook of self-regulation* (pp. 211–228). New York: Guilford.

Goodman, R. (2002). Coaching senior executives for effective business leadership. In C. Fitzgerald and J. Berger (Eds), *Executive Coaching: Practices and Perspectives* (pp. 135–156). Palo Alto: Davies-Black.

González-Prendes, A., and Resko, S. M. (2012). Cognitive-behavioral theory. In S. Ringel and J. R. Brandell (Eds). *Trauma: Contemporary directions in theory, practice, and research* (pp. 14–40). Thousand Oaks, CA: Sage.

Gottman, J. M. (1995). *Why some marriages succeed and fail: and how to make yours last.* New York: Fireside.

Gottman, J. M. (1999). *The marriage clinic.* New York: Norton.

Gottman, J. M. (2011). *The science of trust: Emotional attunement for couples*, New York: Norton.

Gottman, J. M., and Levenson, R. W. (1992). Marital processes predictive of later dissolution: Behavior, physiology, and health. *Journal of Personality and Social Psychology*, 63(2), 22–233.

Gottman, J. M., and Silver, N. (1999). *The seven principles for making marriage work.* New York: Crown Publishing.

Gottman, J. M., Katz, L. F., and Hooven, C. (1997). *Meta-emotion: How families communicate emotionally.* Mahwah, NJ: Erlbaum.

Gottman, J. M., Coan, J., Carrere, S., and Swanson, C. (1998). Predicting marital happiness and stability from newlywed interactions. *Journal of Marriage and the Family*, 60(1), 5–22.

Graesser, A. C.; Person, N. K., and Magliano, J. P. (1995). Collaborative dialogue patterns in naturalistic one-to-one tutoring. *Applied Cognitive Psychology*, 9(6), 495–522.

Graham, F., Rodger, S., and Ziviani, J. (2009). Coaching parents to enable children's participation: An approach to working with parents and their children. *Australian Occupational Therapy Journal*, 56(1), 16–23.

Grant, A. M. (2003). The impact of life coaching on goal attainment, metacognition and mental health. *Social Behavior and Personality: An International Journal*, 31(3): 253–264.

Grant, A. M. (2006). An integrative goal-focused approach to executive coaching. In D. Stober and A. M. Grant (Eds), *Evidence-based coaching handbook* (pp. 153–192). New York: Wiley.

Grant, A. M. (2007). Enhancing coaching skills and emotional intelligence through training'. *Industrial and Commercial Training*, 39(5), 257–266.

Grant, A. M., and Cavanagh, M. (2014). Life coaching. In E. Cox, T. Bachkirova, and D. Clutterbuck (Eds), *The complete handbook of coaching* (pp. 298–312). London: Sage.

Grant, A., Green, L. S., and Rynsaardt, J. (2010). Developmental coaching for high school teachers: Executive coaching goes to school. *Consulting Psychology Journal: Practice and Research*, 62(3), 151–168.

Gray, D. E. (2006). Executive coaching – Towards a dynamic alliance of psychotherapy and transformative learning processes. *Management Learning*, 37(4), 475–497.

Green, L., Oades, L., and Grant, A. (2006). Cognitive-behavioral, solution-focused life coaching: Enhancing goal striving, well-being and hope. *The Journal of Positive Psychology*, 1(3), 142–149.

Greenberg, L. S. (2002). *Emotion-focused therapy*. Washington, DC: American Psychological Association.

Greenberg, L. S. (2004). Emotion-focused therapy. *Clinical Psychology and Psychotherapy*, 11(1), 3–16.

Greenberg, L. S. (2010). Emotion-focused therapy: A clinical synthesis. *The Journal of Lifelong Learning in Psychiatry*, 3(1), 32–42.

Greenberg, L. S., and Goldman, R. (2008). *Emotion-focused couples therapy: The dynamics of emotion, love and power*. Washington, DC: American Psychological Association.

Greene, J., and Grant, A. M. (2003). *Solution-focused coaching: A manager's guide to getting the best from people*. London: Pearson Education.

Greenleaf, R. K. (1996). *On becoming a servant leader*. San Francisco, CA: Jossey-Bass.

Grimley, B. (2014). The NLP approach to coaching. In E. Cox, T. Bachkirova, and D. Clutterbuck (Eds), *The complete handbook of coaching* (pp. 185–198). London: Sage.

Grolnick, W. S., and Ryan, R. M. (1989). Parent styles associated with children's self regulation and competence in schools. *Journal of Educational Psychology*, 81, 143–154.

Gunther, R. (2010). Relationship saboteurs. Oakland, CA: New Harbinger Publications.

Haines, S. G. (1998). *The manager's pocket guide to systems of thinking and learning*. Amherst, MA: HRD Press.

Harris, T. (1976). *I'm OK – You're OK*. New York: Avon Books.

Hart, E. W. (2003). *Developing a coaching culture*. Center for Creative Leadership. Available at http://citeseerx.ist.psu.edu/viewdoc/download?doi=10.1.1.197.234andrep=rep1andtype=pdf (accessed 22 March 2014).

Haslett, S. G. (2013). *How do parents experience coaching? A case study of 'BabiesKnow.'* Unpublished MA dissertation, Oxford Brookes University, Oxford, UK.

Hatfield, E., and Rapson, R. L. (2002). Passionate love and sexual desire: Cross-cultural and historical perspectives. In A. Vangelisti, H. T. Reis, and M. A. Fitzpatrick (Eds), *Stability and change in relationships* (pp. 306–324). Cambridge, UK: Cambridge University Press.

Havighurst, S. S., Wilson, K. R., Harley, A. E., and Prior, M. R. (2010). Tuning in to kids: An emotion-focused parenting program – Initial findings from a community trial. *Journal of Community Psychology*, 37(8), 1008–1023.

Hawkins, P., and Schwenk, G. (2010). The interpersonal relationship in the training and supervision of coaches. In S. Palmer and A. McDowall (Eds), *Putting people first: Understanding interpersonal relationships in coaching* (pp. 203–221). London: Routledge.

Hawkins, P., and Smith, N. (2010). Transformational coaching, In E. Cox, T. Bachkirova, and D. Clutterbuck (Eds), *The complete handbook of coaching* (pp. 231–244). London: Sage.

Hawkins, P. and Smith, N. (2014). Transformational Coaching. In E. Cox, T. Bachkirova and D. Clutterbuck (Eds), *The complete handbook of coaching*, (pp. 228–243). London: Sage.

Hazan, C., and Shaver, P. R. (1987). Romantic love conceptualized as an attachment process. *Journal of Personality and Social Psychology*, 52(3), 511–524.

Hazan, C., and Shaver, P. R. (1994). Attachment as an organizational framework for research on close relationships. *Psychological Inquiry*, 5, 1–22.

Heckhausen, H., and Gollwitzer, P. M. (1987). Thought contents and cognitive functioning in motivational and volitional states of mind. *Motivation and Emotion*, 11, 101–120.

Hedberg, B. (1981). How Organizations Learn and Unlearn. In P. Nystrom and W. H. Starbuck (Eds), *Handbook of Organizational Design (Vol. 1)*. London: Cambridge University Press.

Higgins, E. T. (1987). Self-discrepancy: a theory relating self and affect. *Psychological review*, 94(3), 319.

Hill, E. W. (210). Discovering forgiveness through empathy: Implications for couple and family therapy. *Journal of Family Therapy*, 32, 169–185.

Hindy, C. G., and Schwarz, J. C. (1985). Lovesickness in dating relationships: An attachment perspective. Paper presented at the 93rd Annual Convention of the American Psychological Association, Los Angeles, CA.

Hollenbeck, J. R., Brief, A. P., Whitener, E. M., and Pauli, K. E. (1988). An empirical note on the interaction of personality and aptitude in personnel selection. *Journal of Management*, 14, 441–451.

Hudson, F. M. (1999). *The handbook of coaching*. San Francisco: Jossey-Bass.

Hunt, J., and Weintraub, J. (2007). *The coaching organization: A strategy for developing leaders*. Thousand Oaks, CA: Sage.

International Coach Federation. (2014). *Code of ethics*. Available at http://www.coachfederation.org/about/landing.cfm?ItemNumber=854andnavItemNumber=634 (accessed 2 February 2014).

Ives, Y. (2008). What is 'coaching'? An exploration of conflicting paradigms. *International Journal of Evidence Based Coaching and Mentoring*, 6(2), 100–113.

Ives, Y. (2010). *Goal-Focused coaching*. Unpublished PhD dissertation, Oxford Brookes University, Oxford, UK.

Ives, Y. (2011). What is relationship coaching? *International Journal of Evidence Based Coaching and Mentoring*, 10(2), 88–99.

Ives, Y. (2012). *Interdependence: The key value in dating*. Available at http://taginstitute.org/wp-content/uploads/2011/12/Inderdependece-value-in-forming-lasting-relationships-Final2.pdf (accessed 31 March 2014).

Ives, Y., and Cox, E. (2012). *Goal-focused coaching: Theory and practice*. New York: Routledge.

Jackson, P. Z. and McKergow, M. (2008). *The solutions focus: Making coaching and change simple*. London: Nicholas Brealey.

Jacobs, M. (2004). *Psychodynamic counselling in action*. Thousand Oaks, CA: Sage Publications.

Jacques, E. (1965). Death and the mid-life crisis. *International Journal of Psychoanalysis*, 46, 502–514.

James, W. (1999). The self. In R. F. Baumeister (Ed.), *The self in social psychology. Key readings in social psychology* (pp. 69–77). New York: Psychology Press.

Jarvis, P. (1992). Learning practical knowledge. *New Directions for Adult and Continuing Education*, 55, 89–94.

Johnson, S. M. (2004). *The practice of emotionally focused marital therapy. Creating connections* (2nd ed.). New York: Brunner/Mazel.

Johnson, S. M., and Lebow, J. (2000). The coming of age of couple therapy: A decade review. *Journal of Marital and Family Therapy*, 26(1), 9–24, 23–38.

Jones, G., and Spooner, K. (2006). Coaching high achievers. *Consulting Psychology Journal: Practice and Research*, 58(1), 40–50.

Jung, C. G. (1953). *Two essays on analytical psychology*. Trans. R. F. C. Hull. The Collected Works of C. G. Jung (Vol. 7). New York: Pantheon Books.

Kanfer, R., and Ackerman, P. L. (1989). Motivation and cognitive abilities: An integrative/aptitude treatment interaction approach to skill acquisition. *Journal of Applied Psychology*, 74, 657–690.

Kaplan and Manuck (1994). Antiatherogenic effects of β-adrenergic blocking agents: Theoretical, experimental, and epidemiologic considerations. *American Heart Journal*, 128(6) Part 2, 1316–1328.

Karpel, M. (1976). Individuation: From fusion to dialogue. *Family Process*, 15, 65–82.

Karpman, S. (1968). Fairy tales and script drama analysis. *Transactional Analysis Bulletin*, 7(26): 39–43.

Karremans, J. C., and Van Lange, P. A. (2008). Forgiveness in personal relationships: Its malleability and powerful consequences. *European Review of Social Psychology*, 19(1), 202–241.

Katz, E. M., and Holmes, L. (2006). *Why you're still single*. New York: Penguin.

Kauffman, C. (2004). *Pivot point coaching*. Annual Meeting of the International Coaching Federation, Quebec, Canada.

Kauffman, C. (2006). Positive psychology: The science at the heart of coaching. In D. Stober, and A. M. Grant (Eds), *Evidence-based coaching handbook* (pp. 219–254). New York: Wiley and Sons.

Kee, K. M., Anderson, K. A., Dearing, V. S., Harris, E., and Shuster, F. (Eds). (2010). *Results coaching: The new essential for school leaders*. Corwin Press.

Kegan, R. (1982). *The evolving self: Problem and process in human development*. London: Harvard University Press.

Kegan, R. (1994). *In over our heads*, London: Harvard University Press.

Kegan, R. and Lahey, L. L. (2001). *Seven languages for transformation*. San Francisco, CA: Jossey-Bass.

Kegan, R., and Lahey, L. L. (2009). *Immunity to change: How to overcome it and unlock potential in yourself and your organization*. Cambridge, MA: Harvard Business Press.

Kelley, H. H., and Thibaut, J. W. (1978). *Interpersonal relations: A theory of interdependence* (p. 341). New York: Wiley.

Kemp, T. (2006). An adventure-based framework for coaching. In D. Stober and A. M. Grant (Eds), *Evidence-based coaching handbook* (pp. 277–312). New York: Wiley.

Kemp, T. (2008). Self-management and the coaching relationship: Exploring coaching impact beyond models and methods. *International Coaching Psychology Review*, 3(1), 32–42.

Kerr, M., and Bowen, M. (1988). *Family evaluation*. New York: Norton.

Khan, S., and Quaddus, M. A. (2004). Group decision support using fuzzy cognitive maps for causal reasoning. *Group Decision and Negotiation*, 13, 463–480.

Kilburg, R. (1997). Coaching and executive character: Core problems and basic approaches, *Consulting Psychology Journal: Practice and Research*, 53(4), 251–267.

King, P., and Eaton, J. (1999). Coaching for results. *Industrial and Commercial Training*, 31(4), 145–151.

Kirschenbaum, H., and Henderson, V. L. (1989). *Carl Rogers: Dialogues*. Boston, MA: Houghton Mifflin.

Klein, H. J., Wesson, M. J., Hollenbeck, J. R., and Alge, B. J. (1999). Goal commitment and the goal-setting process: Conceptual clarification and empirical synthesis. *Journal of Applied Psychology*, 84(6), 885–896.

Klinger, E. (1975). Consequences of commitment to and disengagement from incentives. *Psychological Review*, 82, 1–25.

Knowles, M., Holton, E. F. III, and Swanson, R. A. (2005). *The adult learner: The definitive classic in adult education and human resource development* (6th ed.). Burlington, MA: Elsevier.

Koller, A. (1981). *An unknown woman: A journey to self discovery*. New York: Henry Rinehart and Winston.

Kombarakaran, F. A., Yang, J. A., Baker, M., and Fernandes, P. B. (2008). Executive coaching: It works! *Consulting Psychology Journal: Practice and Research*, 60(1), 78–90.

Kurtz, E., and Ketcham, K. (1992). *The spirituality of imperfection: Story telling and the search for meaning*. Nashville, TN, Abingdon.

Langlois, J. H., Kalakanis, L., Rubenstein, A. J., Larson, A., Hallam, M., and Smoot, M. (2000). Maxims or myths of beauty? A meta-analytic and theoretical review. *Psychological bulletin*, 126(3), 390.

Lapsley, D., and Stey, P. (2012). *Dysfunctional individuation in early and late adolescence*. Paper presented at the 14th Biennial Meeting of the Society for Research on Adolescence, Vancouver, March 10.

Larson, R. W., and Sheeber, L. B. (2008). The daily emotional experience of adolescents: Are adolescents more emotional, why, and how is that related to depression? In N. B. Allen and L. B. Sheeber (Eds), *Adolescent emotional development and the emergence of depressive disorders* (pp. 11–32). Cambridge, UK: Cambridge University Press.

Laske, O. (2006). From coach training to coach education: Teaching coaching within a comprehensively evidence based framework. *International Journal of Evidence Based Coaching and Mentoring*, 4(1), 45–57.

Latham, G. P. (2007). *Work motivation: History, theory, research, and practice*. London: Sage.

Law, H. (2010). Coaching relationships and ethical practice. In S. Palmer and A. McDowall (Eds), *The coaching relationship: Putting people first* (pp. 182–202). Hove, UK: Routledge.

Lee, G. (2014). The psychodynamic approach to coaching, In E. Cox, T. Bachkirova, and D. Clutterbuck (Eds), *The complete handbook of coaching* (2nd ed., pp. 21–33). London: Sage.

Leone, C. (2013). The unseen spouse: Pitfalls and possibilities for the individual therapist. *Psychoanalytic Dialogues*, 23(3), 324–339.

Levinson, D. (1978). *The seasons of a man's life*. New York: Ballantine Books.

Linnerbrink, E. A., and Pintrich, P. R. (2002). Achievement goal theory and affect: An asymmetrical bidirectional model. *Educational Psychologist*, 37, 69–78.

Little, B. R. (1993). Personal projects and the distributed self: Aspects of a conative psychology. In J. M. Suls (Ed.), *The self in social perspective: Psychological perspectives on the self* (Vol. 4, pp. 137–185). Hillsdale, NJ: Erlbaum.

Littlefield, R. S., and Larson-Casselton, C. (2009). Coaching your own child: An exploration of dominance and affiliation in parent–child communication in the public sphere. In T. J. Socha and G. H. Stamp (Eds), *Parents and children communicating with society* (pp. 189–206). London: Routledge.

Locke, E. A. (1996). Motivation through conscious goal setting. *Applied and Preventative Psychology*, 5, 117–124.

Locke, E. A., and Latham, G. P. (1990). *A theory of goal setting and task performance.* Englewood Cliffs, NJ: Prentice-Hall.

Locke, E. A., and Latham, G. P. (2002). Building a practically useful theory of goal setting and task motivation: A 35-year odyssey. *American Psychologist*, 57, 507–717.

London, M., Smither, J. W., and Adsit, D. J. (1997). Accountability: The Achilles' heel of multisource feedback. *Group and Organization Management*, 22(2), 149–161.

Love, J. (2004). NLP and coaching, *Selection and Development Review*, 20(4), 6–8.

Lowman, R. L. (2007). Coaching and consulting in multicultural contexts: Integrating themes and issues. *Consulting Psychology Journal: Practice and Research*, 59(4), 296–303.

Luebbe, D. M. (2005). *The three-way mirror of executive coaching. Dissertation Abstracts International: Section B: The Sciences and Engineering*, 66(3-B), 1771.

Luft, J., and Ingham, H. (1950). The Johari window, a graphic model of interpersonal awareness. *Proceedings of the western training laboratory in group development.* Los Angeles: UCLA.

Manderlink, G., and Harackiewicz, J. M. (1984). Proximal versus distal goal setting and intrinsic motivation. *Journal of Personality and Social Psychology*, 47, 918–928.

Macdonald, A. (2011). *Solution focused therapy: Theory, research and practice.* London: Sage.

Mashek, D. J., and Sherman, M. (2004). Desiring less closeness with intimate others. In D. J. Mashek and A. Aron (Eds), *Handbook of closeness and intimacy* (pp. 343–356). Mahwah, NJ: Erlbaum.

Maslow, A. (1998). Some basic propositions of a growth and self-actualization psychology. *Towards a Psychology of Being*, 2, 189–214.

Mason, B. (1993). Towards positions of safe uncertainty. *Human Systems*, 4, 189–200.

McDowall, A., and Millward, L. (2009). Feeding back, feeding forward and setting goals. In S. Palmer and A. McDowall (Eds), *The coaching relationship: Putting people first* (pp. 55–78). Hove, UK: Routledge.

McGoldrick, M., and Carter, B. (2001). Advances in coaching: Family therapy with one person. *Journal of Marital and Family Therapy*, 27(3), 281–300.

McGoldrick, M., Gerson, R., and Shellenberger, S. (1999). *Genograms: Assessment and intervention* (2nd ed.). New York: W.W. Norton.

McHale, J. P., and Fivaz-Depeursinge, E. (2010). Principles of effective co-parenting and its assessment in infancy and early childhood. In S. Tyano, M. Keren, M. Herrman, and J. Cox (Eds), *Parenthood and mental health* (pp. 357–373). Chichester, UK: John Wiley.

McLeod, A. I. (2003). *Performance coaching: The handbook for mangers, HR professionals and coaches.* Carmarthen, UK: Crown House.

McLeod, A. I. (2004). Performance coaching and mentoring in organisations. *Resource Magazine*, 1(1), 28–31.

McLeod, A. I. (2010). *The four pillars and coaching, Acuity 1.* Hemel Hempstead, UK: The Association of NLP. Available at http://angusmcleod.com/wp-content/uploads/2012/07/Four-pillars-and-coaching.pdf (accessed 22 March 2014).

McMahon, G. and Archer, A. (2010). *101 Coaching strategies and techniques: Essential coaching skills and knowledge.* London: Routledge.

Mezirow, J. (1990). How Critical Reflection Triggers Transformative Learning. In J. Mezirow and Associates (Eds), *Fostering Critical Reflection in Adulthood.* San Francisco: Jossey-Bass.

Mezirow, J. (1990). *Fostering critical reflection in adulthood.* San Francisco, CA: Jossey-Bass.

Mezirow, J. (1991). *Transformative dimensions of adult learning.* San Francisco: Jossey-Bass.

Mezirow, J. (2000). Learning to think like an adult: Core concepts of adult learning theory. In J. Mezirow (Ed.), *Learning as transformation: Critical perspectives on a theory in progress.* San Francisco, CA: Jossey-Bass.

Miller, R. B., and Brickman, S. J. (2004). A model of future oriented motivation and self-regulation. *Educational Psychology Review*, 16, 9–33.

Miller, R. S., Perlman, D., and Brehm, S. S. (2007). *Intimate relationships* (4th ed.). New York: McGraw Hill.

Miller, W. R., and Rollnick, S. (2002). *Motivational interviewing: Preparing people for change*. New York: Guilford.

Miller, V. (2008). *Eat your Dinner*, London: Walker.

Mischel, W., and Ayduk, O. (2007). Willpower in a cognitive-affective processing system. In R. F. Baumeister and K. D. Vohs (Eds), *Handbook of Self-Regulation* (pp. 99–129). New York: Guilford Press.

Miser, A. L. (2008). *Connecting with your 'couple-ness.'* Available at http://www.elysianenterprises.net/wp-content/uploads/2011/09/Connecting-with-your-Couple-ness.pdf (accessed 18 February 2014).

Miser, A. L., and Miser, M. F. (2008). Couples coaching for expatriate couples. In M. Moral and G. Abbott (Eds), *The Routledge companion to international business coaching* (pp. 203–217). Abingdon, UK: Routledge.

Moen, F., and Skaalvik, E. (2009). Coaching and the effects on performance psychology. *International Journal of Evidence-Based Coaching and Mentoring*, 7(2), 31–49.

Mone, M. A., and Shalley, C. E. (1995). Effects of task complexity and goal specificity on change in strategy and performance over time. *Human Performance*, 8(4), 243–262.

Munch, J., and Swasy, J. (1983). A conceptual view of questions and questioning in marketing communications. In R. Bagozzi and A. Tybout (Eds), *Advances in consumer research 10* (pp. 209–214). Ann Arbor, MI: Association for Consumer Research.

Myers, D. G., and Diener, E. (1995). Who is happy? *Psychological Science*, 6, 10–19.

Nace, E. P. (2010). The history of alcoholics anonymous and the experience of patients. In M. Galanter and H. D. Kleber (Eds), *Psychotherapy for the treatment of substance abuse* (pp. 351–374). Washington, DC: American Psychiatric Publishing.

Nakamura, J., and Csikszentmihalyi, M. (2002). The concept of flow. In C. Snyder and S. Lopez (Eds), *Handbook of positive psychology*. Oxford, UK: Oxford University Press.

Natale, S. M. and Diamante, T. (2005). The five stages of executive coaching: Better process makes better practice. *Journal of Business Ethics*, 59, 361–374.

Neill, M. (2013). *Michael Neill's weekly coaching tip #888 – An honest day's work*. Available at http://www.supercoach.com (accessed 18 February 2014).

Nelson-Jones, R. (2006). *Human relationship skills: Coaching and self-coaching*. London: Routledge.

Newman, R. S. (1998). Adaptive help-seeking: A role of social interaction in self-regulated learning. In S. A. Karabenick (Ed.), *Strategic help-seeking: Implications for learning and teaching* (pp. 13–37). Mahwah, NJ: Erlbaum.

Nichols, M. P., and Schwartz, R. C. (1995). *Family therapy*. Boston, MA: Allyn and Bacon.

Nicholson, P., Bayne, R., and Owen, J. (2006). *Applied psychology for social workers* (3rd ed.). Basingstoke, UK: Palgrave.

Nuttin, J. (1984). *Motivation, planning, and action: A relational theory of behavior dynamics*. Hillsdale, NJ: Erlbaum.

O'Brien, K., and Mosco, J. (2013). Positive parent–child relationships. In S. Roffey (Ed.), *Positive Relationships* (pp. 91–107). London: Springer.

O'Broin, A., and Palmer, S. (2009). Co-creating an optimal coaching alliance: A cognitive behavioural coaching perspective. *International Coaching Psychology Review*, 4(2), 184–194.

O'Connell, B. (1998). *Solution-focused therapy.* London: Sage.

O'Connell, B. and Palmer, S. (2007). Solution-focused coaching. In S. Palmer and A. Whybrow (Eds). *Handbook of coaching psychology: A guide for practitioners*, 278–292, Hove: Routledge.

O'Neill, M. B. (2000). *Executive coaching with backbone and heart: A systems approach to emerging leaders with their challenges.* San Francisco, CA: Jossey-Bass.

Oppenheimer, V. K. (1988). A theory of marriage timing. *American Journal of Sociology*, 94, 563–591.

Orenstein, R. L. (2007). *Multidimensional executive coaching.* New York: Springer.

Palmer, S. (2002). Cognitive and organisational models of stress that are suitable for use within workplace stress management/prevention coaching, training and counselling settings. *The Rational Emotive Behaviour Therapist*, 10(1): 15–21.

Palmer, S., and Szymanska, K. (2007). Cognitive behavioural coaching: An integrated approach. In S. Palmer and A. Whybrow (Eds), *Handbook of coaching psychology* (pp. 86–117). London: Routledge.

Palmer, S., and Panchal, S. (Eds) (2011). *Developmental coaching: Life transitions and generational perspectives* (pp. 161–182). Hove, UK: Routledge.

Parsloe, E. and Wray, M. (2000). *Coaching and Mentoring.* London: Kogan Page.

Passmore, J. (2005). The heart of coaching: A coaching model for managers. *The Coaching Psychologist*, 1(2), 6–9.

Passmore, J. (2007). An integrative model for executive coaching. *Consulting Psychology Journal: Practice and Research*, 59(1), 68–78.

Passmore, J., and Whybrow, A. (2007). Motivational interviewing: A specific approach for coaching psychologists. In S. Palmer and A. Whybrow (Eds), *Handbook of coaching psychology: A guide for practitioners* (pp. 160–173). London: Routledge.

Passmore, J., and Mortimer, L. (2011). Ethics in coaching, In G. Herenz-Broome and L. A. Boyce (Eds), *Advancing executive coaching.* San Francisco, CA: Jossey-Bass.

Peltier, B. (2009). *The psychology of executive coaching: Theory and application* (2nd ed.). New York: Brunner-Routledge.

Peltier, B. (2001). *The psychology of executive coaching: Theory and application* (1st ed.). New York: Brunner-Routledge.

Pemberton, C. (2006). *Coaching to solutions: A manager's toolkit for performance delivery.* Oxford, UK: Butterworth-Heinemann.

Peterson, D. B. (2006). People are complex and the world is messy: A behavior-based approach to executive coaching. In D. Stober and A. M. Grant (Eds), *Evidence-based coaching handbook* (pp. 51–76). New York: Wiley.

Peterson, D. B., and Hicks, M. D. (1996). *Leader as coach: Strategies for coaching and developing others.* Minneapolis, MN: Personnel Decisions International.

Piaget, J. (1962). *The Language and Thought of the Child*, London: Routledge & Kegan Paul. [*Le Langage et la pensée chez l'enfant* (1923)]

Pines, A. M. (1996). *Couple burnout: Causes and cures.* London: Routledge.

Pintrich, P. R., and Schunk, D. H. (1996). *Motivation in education: Theory, research, and application.* Englewood Cliffs, NJ: Prentice-Hall.

Pintrich, P. R., and Schunk, D. H. (2003). *Motivation in education: Theory, research, and application* (2nd ed.). Upper Saddle River, NJ: Merrill.

Popovic, N., and Jinks, D. (2014). *Personal consultancy: A model for integrating counselling and coaching.* Hove, UK: Routledge.

Purnell, C. (2004). *Attachment theory and attachment-based therapy.* London: Karnac Books.

Rahim, M. A. (1983). A measure of styles of handling interpersonal conflict. *Academy of Management Journal*, 26(2), 368–376.

Reeves, D. B., and Allison, E. (2009). *Renewal coaching*. San Francisco, CA: Jossey-Bass.

Roland, A. (1988). *In search of self in India and Japan*. Princeton, NJ: Princeton University Press.

Rogers, C. R. (1951). *Client-centered therapy: Its current practice, implications and theory*. London: Constable.

Rogers, C. R. (1959). A theory of therapy, personality, and interpersonal relationships as developed in the client-centered framework. In S. Koch (Ed.), *Psychology: A study of a science: Formulations of the person and the social context* (Vol. 3, pp. 184–256). New York: McGraw-Hill.

Rogers, J. (2008). *Coaching skills: A handbook*. New York: Open University Press.

Rosen, C. (2008). New technologies and our feelings: Romance on the Internet. In L. G. Whitaker (Ed.), *Getting started in sociology* (pp. 147–156). New York: McGraw Hill.

Rosenberg, M. (2003). *Nonviolent communication: A language of life* (2nd ed.). Encinitas, CA: Puddle Dancer Press.

Rowan, J. (1986). Holistic listening. *Journal of Humanistic Psychology*, 26(1), 83–102.

Rowan, J. (2014). The transpersonal approach to coaching. In E. Cox, T. Bachkirova and D. Clutterbuck (Eds).*The complete handbook of coaching* (pp. 145–156). London: Sage.

Rubenstein, D. (2006). *Cracking the code: Unveiling the mystery – Beta test and walk away with the new ICF ethics education program*. Paper presented at the International Coach Federation Annual Conference, St. Louis, Missouri.

Rubin, R. S. (2002). Will the real SMART goals please stand up? *The Industrial-Organizational Psychologist*, 39(4), 26–27.

Rusbult, C. E., and Buunk, B. P. (1993). Commitment processes in close relationships: An interdependence analysis. *Journal of Social and Personal Relationships*, 10, 175–204.

Rusbult, C. E., and Van Lange, P. A. (2003). Interdependence, interaction, and relationships. *Annual Review of Psychology*, 54(1), 351–375.

Ryan, R. M., and Deci, E. L. (2000). Self-determination theory and the facilitation of intrinsic motivation, social development, and well-being. *American Psychologist*, 55, 68–78.

Ryan, R. M., and Deci, E. L. (2003). On assimilating identities to the self: A self-determination theory perspective on internalization and integrity within cultures. In M. R. Leary and J. P. Tangney (Eds), *Handbook of self and identity* (pp. 253–272). New York: Guilford.

Ryle, G. (1963). *The concept of mind*. London: Penguin.

Santrock, J. W. (2008). *Life-span development*. New York: McGraw-Hill.

Scamardo, M., and Harnden, S. (2007). A manager coaching group model: Applying leadership knowledge. *Journal of Workplace Behavioral Health*, 22(2), 127–143.

Schwarzer, R., and Leppin, A. (1992). Social support and mental health: A conceptual and empirical overview. In L. Montada, S.-H. Filipp, and M. J. Lerner (Eds), *Life crises and experiences of loss in adulthood* (pp. 435–458). Hillsdale, NJ: Erlbaum.

Seijts, G. H., and Latham, G. P. (2001). The effect of distal learning, outcome, and proximal goals on a moderately complex task. *Journal of Organizational Behavior*, 22, 291–302.

Shanley, J. R., and Niec, L. N. (2010). Coaching parents to change: The impact of in vivo feedback on parents' acquisition of skills, *Journal of Clinical Child and Adolescent Psychology*, 39(2), 282–287.

Sharma, B., and Cook-Greuter, S. (2010). *Polarities and ego development: Polarity thinking in ego development theory and developmental coaching*. Available at http://integraltheory   conference.org/sites/default/files/itc-2010-papers/Cook-Greuter%20&%20Sharma_ITC%202010.pdf (accessed 22 March 2014).

Sheras, P. L., and Koch-Sheras, P. R. (2008). Commitment first, communication later: Dealing with barriers to effective couples therapy. *Journal of Contemporary Psychotherapy*, 38, 109–117.

Shortt, J. W., Stoolmiller, M., Smith-Shine, J. N., Eddy, J. M., and Sheeber, L. (2010). Maternal emotion coaching, adolescent anger regulation, and siblings' externalizing symptoms. *Journal of Child Psychology and Psychiatry*, 51(7), 799–808.

Shotter, J. (2009). Listening in a Way that Recognizes/Realizes the World of 'the Other'. The International Journal of Listening, 23(1), 21–43.

Simpson, J. A. (1990). The influence of attachment styles on romantic relationships. *Journal of Personality and Social Psychology*, 59, 971–980.

Sintonen, M. (2004). Reasoning to hypotheses: Where do questions come? *Foundations of science*, 9(3), 249–266.

Skiffington, S., and Zeus, P. (2008). *Behavioral coaching: How to build sustainable personal and organizational strength*, Sydney, Australia: McGraw-Hill Australia.

Spence, G. B. (2007a). GAS powered coaching: Goal attainment scaling and its use in coaching research and practice. *Coaching Psychology Review*, 2, 155–167.

Spence, G. B. (2007b). Further development of evidence-based coaching: Lessons from the rise and fall of the human potential movement. *Australian Psychologist*, 42(4), 255–265.

Sperling, M. B. (1985). Discriminant measures for desperate love. *Journal of Personality Assessment*, 49(3), 324–328.

Stacey, R. D. (2000). *Strategic management and organisational dynamics: The challenge of complexity*. Essex, UK: Pearson.

Starr, J. (2007). *The coaching manual: The definitive guide to the process, principles and skills of personal coaching*. Upper Saddle River, NJ: Prentice Hall.

Steele, D. (2007). *Conscious Dating: Finding the Love of Your Life and That You Love*. Relationship Coaching Institute.

Stelter, R. (2009). Coaching as a reflective space in a society of growing diversity – Towards a narrative, postmodern paradigm. *International Coaching Psychology Review*, 4(2), 207–217.

Stern, L. R. (2004). Executive coaching: A working definition. *Consulting Psychology Journal: Practice and Research*, 56(3), 154–162.

Stober, D. (2006). Coaching from the humanistic perspective. In D. Stober and A. M. Grant (Eds), *Evidence-based coaching handbook* (pp. 17–50). New York: Wiley and Sons.

Sugarman, L. (1986). *Life-span development*. London: Methuen.

Summerfield, J. (2006). Do we coach or do we counsel? Thoughts on the 'emotional life' of a coaching session. *The Coaching Psychologist*, 2(1), 24–27.

Svensson, L. (1990). Knowledge as a professional resource: Case studies of architects and psychologists at work. In R. Torstendahl and M. Burrage (Eds), *The Formation of Professions*. London: Sage.

Szabo, P. and Meier, D. (2009). *Coaching Plain & Simple: Solution-focused Brief Coaching Essentials*. New York, NY: W. W. Norton & Co.

Taylor, K. (1999). Development as separation and connection: Finding a balance. In M. C. Clark and R. E. Caffarela (Eds), *An update on adult development theory: New ways of thinking about the life course*. San Francisco, CA: Jossey-Bass.

Taylor, K., Marienau, C., and Fiddler, M. (2000). Developing adult learners: Strategies for teachers and trainers. San Francisco, CA: Jossey-Bass.

Tennov, D. (1979). *Love and limerence: The experience of being in love*. New York: Stein and Day.

Tomm, K. (1988). Interventive interviewing: Part III. Intending to ask lineal, circular, strategic or reflexive questions. *Family Process*, 26, 167–183.

Treboux, D., Crowell, J. A., and Waters, E. (2004). When 'new' meets 'old': Configurations of adult attachment representations and their implications for marital functioning. *Developmental Psychology*, 40(2), 295.

Tuckman, B. (1965). Developmental sequence in small groups. *Psychological Bulletin*, 63(6), 384–399.

Vallacher, R. R., and Kauffman, J. (1996). Dynamics of action identification: Volatility and structure in the representation of behavior. In P. M. Gollwitzer and J. A. Bargh (Eds), *The psychology of action: Linking motivation and cognition to behaviour* (pp. 260–282). New York: Guilford Press.

Vernon, A. (2013). I will always love you: Dispelling marital myths through applications of rational-emotive behaviour therapy. *Journal of Rational-Emotive Cognitive-Behavior Therapy*, 31, 57–66.

Visser, C. F., and Schlundt Bodien, G. (2009). Supporting clients' solution building process by subtly eliciting positive behaviour descriptions and expectations of beneficial change. *InterAction*, 1(2), 9–25.

Wade, J. (1996). *Changes of mind: A holonomic theory of the evolution of consciousness.* Albany, NY: SUNY Press.

Wasik, B. (1984). *Teaching parents effective problem-solving: A handbook for professionals.* Unpublished manuscript. Chapel Hill, NC: University of North Carolina.

Wasylyshyn, K. M. (2003). Executive coaching: An outcome study. *Consulting Psychology Journal: Practice and Research*, 55(Spring), 94–106.

Weldon, R., and Yun, S. (2000). The effects of proximal and distal goals on goal level, strategy development, and group performance. *Journal of Applied Behavioural Science*, 36(3), 336–344.

Whitmore, J. (2003). *Coaching for performance.* London: Nicholas Brealey.

Whitmore, J. (2009). Will coaching rise to the challenge? *The OCM Coach and Mentor Journal*, 2009.

Whitworth, L., Kimsey-House, H., and Sandhal, P. (2007). *Co-active coaching: New skills for coaching people toward success in work and life.* Palo Alto, CA: Davies-Black.

Wilber, K. (2001). *No boundary: Eastern and western approaches to personal growth.* Boston, MA: Shambhala.

Williams, H., Edgerton, N., and Palmer, S. (2014). Cognitive behavioural coaching. In E. Cox, T. Bachkirova, and D. Clutterbuck (Eds), *The complete handbook of coaching* (2nd ed., pp. 34–50). London: Sage.

Williams, P., and Anderson, S. K. (2005). *Law and ethics in coaching.* Hoboken, NJ: Wiley.

Williams, S. (2002). Psychotherapeutic ends and endings. *British Journal of Psychotherapy*, 13, 337–350.

Willis, J. and Chamberlain, M. (2012). *The Tale of Georgie Grub.* London: Anderson.

Zamfir, C. M. (2011). NLP techniques integration in negotiation. *Ovidius University Annals, Economic Sciences Series*, 5(2), 1337–1342.

Zimmerman, B. J. (2000). Attaining self-regulation: A social cognitive perspective. In M. Boekaerts, P. R. Pintrich, and M. Zeidner (Eds), *Handbook of self-regulation* (pp. 13–39). San Diego, CA: Academic Press.

Zygmond, M., and Boorhem, M. S. (1989). Ethical decision making in family therapy. *Family Process*, 28, 269–280.

Index

Made in the USA
Las Vegas, NV
19 May 2023

72256514R00105